BEAUTIFUL CRESCENT

A History of New Orleans

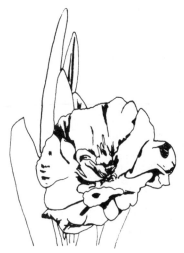

Oleander,
The City Flower

Seal of the City
of New Orleans

The City Flag

The oleander was brought from Cuba by the Spanish after the fires of 1788 and 1794 had devastated plant life in New Orleans. It was adopted as the city flower June, 1923. The seal, adopted in 1805 and redesigned in 1852, shows a pair of Indians, the region's first inhabitants; recumbent Father Mississippi; and an alligator from the swamplands. The flag was accepted by Mayor Martin Behrman on February 9, 1918.

BEAUTIFUL CRESCENT

A History of New Orleans

by
Joan B. Garvey
and
Mary Lou Widmer

GARMER PRESS, INC.
NEW ORLEANS, LOUISIANA

First Edition 1982
Second Edition 1984
Third Edition 1988
Fourth Edition 1989
Fifth Edition 1991
Sixth Edition 1992
Seventh Edition 1994

Eighth Edition 1997

Published by
Garmer Press
981 Navarre Ave.
New Orleans, Louisiana 70124

Library of Congress Number 111-123
ISBN #0-9612960-0-3

Rose Printing Company
Tallahassee, Florida

To Walter and Al,
with love

Foreword

BEAUTIFUL CRESCENT is a good short basic history of New Orleans—and more. We use it as a textbook in training Friends of the Cabildo volunteers. It's a foundation, a springboard, an appetizer—just enough factual political history, just enough "people" history to tantalize and whet our appetites to delve into the books in the Bibliography. The wonderful lists of governors, mayors, noted personalities, and the chronology make *Beautiful Crescent* an indispensable tool for tour guides—and indeed fun for everyone else who loves New Orleans.

Jane Molony
Training Committee
Friends of the Cabildo

Preface

History is a story, and as a story, differs with the story-teller. The story-teller's point of view becomes the attitude with which the history is related. For this reason, the following chronology is *a* history of New Orleans, not *the* history of New Orleans.

We maintain that there is no definitive history, only stories told with more or less documentation. Opinions cannot be documented, nor importance decided, except through a personal approach. Our approach is a "people approach." We have tried to view the city through the people who came here, some to stay, some to make their mark and then move on. We hope to share with you our view of the development of New Orleans in this narrative.

Joan B. Garvey
Mary Lou Widmer

. . . so very difficult a matter is it to trace and find out the truth of anything in history.

PLUTARCH

Where Is New Orleans?

"I never could find out exactly where New Orleans is. I have looked for it on the map without much enlightenment. It is dropped down there somewhere in the marshes of the Mississippi and the bayous and lakes. It is below the one and tangled up among the others, or it might some day float out to the Gulf and disappear. How the Mississippi gets out I never could discover. When it first comes in sight of the town, it is running east; at Carrollton, it abruptly turns its rapid, broad, yellow flood and runs south, turns presently eastward, circles a great portion of the city, then makes a bold push for the north in order to avoid Algiers and reach the foot of Canal Street, and encountering then the heart of the town, it sheers off again along the old French Quarter and Jackson Square due east, and goes no one knows where."

From *Harper's New Monthly Magazine*
(New York: Harper and Brothers)
"Sui Generis," by Charles Dudley Warner
(1887)

Acknowledgments

We would like to thank Dr. Joseph G. Tregle, Jr. Professor Emeritus, History Department, University of New Orleans, for reading our manuscript for accuracy. We also feel greatly indebted to the late Leonard V. Huber for making his extraordinary picture collection available to us. Many thanks to photographer Joseph P. Rodriguez and to Peggy Culligan of the Board of Commissioners, Port of New Orleans, for the beautiful pictures provided; Lawrence Bodet, retired Chief engineer of the New Orleans Levee Board for information on the Wartime Lakefront; Clinton Fairleigh at the New Orleans Levee Board for perusing through old maps; and Jane Molony of Friends of the Cabildo, for her Foreword.

We thank Coralie Davis and the Louisiana Collection at the Earl K. Long Library at UNO; Pamela D. Arceneaux, Dr. Patricia Schmidt, and Stanton Frazer at the Historic New Orleans Collection; and Collin B. Hamer at the New Orleans Public Library for help in researching our text and illustrations. Thanks to Evelyn and Eileen Garvey for current photographs of New Orleans; to Darius Kalil, the artist who sketched the symbols of New Orleans shown on our opening pages, and Carla Widmer, for her assistance in this effort.

In advance, we thank our many school-teacher and tour-guide friends, who have so generously offered to help us promote our history of New Orleans. But most of all, we thank our husbands for support and understanding during the many years of our preoccupation with this engrossing project.

The Authors

TABLE OF CONTENTS

New Orleans from the Lower Cotton Press, 1852.

CHAPTER I

The Part the River Played

Before there could be a city, there had to be a *place* for a city, but for millions of years, there was no land where New Orleans stands today. The entire state of Louisiana was part of a huge body of water, an extension of the sea into the continent. The Mississippi River did not exist until a million years ago (a brief period in geologic terms), when it began to meander southward unobtrusively.

During the Ice Age, 25,000 years ago, sheets of ice covered the North American continent but did not come within 500 miles of the site of New Orleans. The Ice Age wiped out a number of other drainage systems in the Midwest and rerouted drainage toward the Mississippi, enlarging the river considerably. Embedded in the ice were tons of debris, and during the period, there were violent windstorms that deposited silt in the Mississippi Basin. Then, when the ice melted, the water flowed rapidly, taking its debris with it and causing the Mississippi to extend its delta, filling in its southern end.

As the delta filled, the sea retreated, leaving Lake Pontchartrain behind, a child of the Gulf, separated from its parent about 5,000 years ago. Between the lake and the river, a stretch of swamp land emerged, which would in time become the site of the city of New Orleans.

Of all the geologic factors that shaped the site of the city, the river played the leading role. Its serpentine course and erratic behavior in the last several thousand years determined the exact location and dimensions of the city, the arteries of transportation and communication, and even, in time, the patterns of colonization and styles of architecture. The colonists who would later settle on the crescent of marshland would be forced to develop a lifestyle that could be supported by their water-locked environment. It is the story of these people that will be told here.

The process of shaping and molding is not complete, even today. The city is still sinking at a rate of about three inches per century. There are places in the delta where sugar cane fields, planted in the 18th century, are now under water. Yet, there would have been no city at all, no site for a city, and no delta, except for the Ice Age and its aftermath.

The bedrock, or sand strata, that lies on the floor of the saucer beneath New Orleans is of pre-glacial material, dating back to the Pleistocene era, a million or so years ago. It consists of clay, silt, and silty sand. North of Lake Pontchartrain, this Pleistocene material is at the surface, forming a bluff paralleling the lakeshore. The Pleistocene has eroded into low hills covered with beautiful pines, an area with no "foundation" problems and no flooding. This marvelous Pleistocene land (now the sites of Mandeville, Madisonville, and Covington) is the result of faults in the earth's crust, which have allowed the material to "crop out." From the north shore of the lake, the material drops below the surface of the water, dipping gently southward, until it rests some 70 feet beneath the city of New Orleans. Because of this, no Orleanian would think of erecting a building of any height or weight without first sinking pilings to gain solid footing on the bedrock.

Except for levees, there is no natural land surface in the city that is higher than 15 feet above sea level. Canal Street meets the river at an elevation of 14 feet above sea level; yet Jackson Square, only 6 blocks downriver, is only 10 feet above sea level. The Tulane University area is a mere four feet above sea level, while the intersection of Broad and Washington (originally part of the backswamp, now Mid City) is two feet *below* sea level. All these facts, part of the geologic picture of the city's relationship with the river, helps us to understand many things about life among the natives of the city.

The earliest known waterways through the city of New Orleans are two abandoned distributaries of the Mississippi: Bayou Metairie and its eastern sector, Bayou Gentilly. Between 600 B.C. and 1000 A.D., Bayou Metarie wandered away from the Mississippi about 20 miles above the French Quarter, near today's Kenner, and strayed eastward toward the Gulf of Mexico, running more or less parallel to the river. The eastern portion of this distributary is shown on some old maps as Bayou Sauvage, on others as Bayou Gentilly. In time, the river abandoned these wanderers, leaving them to meander lazily through the marshes of the backswamp.

The course of these two connected waterways was, roughly, along Metairie Road and City Park Avenue, to Dumaine Street, across Bayou St. John, then left to Grand Route St. John, then right to Gentilly Boulevard, which becomes Old Gentilly Highway.

The Metairie-Gentilly Bayou was never important to the early settlers as a *water route*, but became important because alongside it, there developed a levee of well-drained soil which provided a flood-free *land route* into the city, from the west by Metairie Road, and from the east by Gentilly Road (or Chef Menteur Highway). There is another land route into the city from the west, along the river front from Baton Rouge, called the River Road. From the east, however, Gentilly

"Ridge" is the main road, for it carries both national highways (U.S. 90) and the main line of the Louisville and Nashville Railroad. During the Civil War, the federals used maps showing these highways as routes of entry into the city.

Over the centuries, the river builds delta land by depositing material where it empties into the sea, forming sandbars, which in time become islands. The islands split the river into two or more distributary channels. This is how the Metairie-Gentilly Bayous were formed. The same thing is happening today about 20 miles below Venice, Louisiana, where the river divides into three major distributaries: Pass L'Outre, South Pass, and Southwest Pass. Southwest Pass is deepest, and carries the largest volume of traffic.

Another method the river has of making delta land, which is more important to the development of the city, is by abandoning its lower course for hundreds of miles and lunging out to sea by an altogether different route. The river does this regularly, every several hundred years, leaving behind great gashes across its delta. The Mississippi as we know it today took up the diversion near New Orleans sometime between 1500 and 1600 A.D.

We are forced to wonder under what conditions a river jumps its banks. An understanding of how levees form might help to clarify. During flood time, the fast-moving waters of the river pick up heavy material and, spilling over their banks, deposit the material, systematically raising the banks, (or natural levees) with the flood. Artificial levees, which are built on top of these natural levees, may be 30 feet high and faced with concrete. They are among the most prominent landforms in New Orleans. The natural levee may be only 10 to 15 feet above sea level, but a mile or two wide, sloping downward from the river so gently that the decline would not be noticeable in a moving vehicle.

Natural levees end where they merge with the backswamp (lowland). Natural levees provide the only well-drained land in southeast Louisiana, which is the reason why most settlements, urban or rural, were located on natural levees (of either the Mississippi or smaller streams). For one thing, in colonial times, the settlers had *only* the Mississippi for transportation. For another, it was the only place to build roads and buildings that was fairly safe from floods.

So, for the first 200 years, the city was laid out along the natural levees of the Mississippi River and Bayous Metairie and Gentilly (Sauvage). The city came to an abrupt end at the backswamps.

Prior to 1700, Bayou Metairie was called Bayou Chapitoulas (or Tchoupitoulas) after an Indian tribe of that name, who lived near the stream's confluence with the Mississippi River. It was renamed Metairie (meaning farm) by the French settlers who established plantations there. Traces of the original bayou may still be found in Metairie Cemetery.

Bayou Gentilly, originally called Bayou Sauvage, was so named by the French since the French word *sauvage* meant savage, wild, or untamed, and was used to describe the Indians. Bayou Sauvage, therefore, meant Bayou of the Indians or Indian Bayou. It was renamed Bayou Gentilly about 1718, commemorating the Paris home of the Dreux brothers, early settlers along the waterway.

The "upriver" end of town is surrounded on three sides by the river, which sweeps in a giant semi-circle around that part of the city. The remainder of the upriver area is closed off by the lower natural levees of the abandoned Metairie distributary. Thus, a "bowl" is created, which is, of course, below sea level. (This area is now Mid City.) In the last century, a pump was invented to drain the water from Mid City and make it habitable, but in prehistoric times, when the "bowl" filled, it spilled over into the lowest place in the Metairie levees. Over the centuries, a channel formed there, small but immensely important to early New Orleans commerce. The channel was later called Bayou St. John, and it flowed northward into Lake Pontchartrain.

Long before the white man came to Louisiana, the Indians traveled from the Gulf of Mexico, through the Mississippi Sound, Rigolets Pass, Lake Borgne and Lake Pontchartrain into Bayou St. John, which the Choctaws called Bayouk Choupic or Shupik (Bayou Mudfish). Five and a half miles after entering the bayou, they got out of their bark canoes and carried them over a time-worn trail to the Michisipy (great river). The Choctaws called Bayou St. John "Choupithatcha" or "Soupit-catcha"—a combination of the Choctaw "shupik" (mudfish) and "hacha" (river).

The old Indian portage, which became a boundary of the city of New Orleans, can still be followed today. Beginning at Governor Nicholls and Decatur Streets near the Mississippi River, one would follow Governor Nicholls through the French Quarter toward the lake. At North Claiborne, Governor Nicholls becomes Bayou Road, and the street angles northeasterly, crossing Esplanade Avenue at North Miro. A few blocks farther, Bayou Road intersects with Grand Route St. John. A sharp turn to the left and an additional three quarters of a mile brings the traveler to the Shores of Bayou St. John. The route of the portage, called Bayou Road in French times, has varied through the years.

The Mississippi River, beginning in Lake Itaska, Minnesota, and ending in the Gulf of Mexico, is 2,340 miles long. It runs as deep as 217 feet, and at the foot of Canal Street, is 2,200 feet wide. It is the third largest river in the world, after the Amazon and the Congo. It drains 40% of 48 continental states, and has a basin covering 1¼ million square miles, including parts of 31 states and two Canadian provinces.

With a river of such enormity, any big flood can cause the water to break through its natural levee and spill over into the backswamp. Such a breakthrough is called a "crevasse," a natural disaster feared by early

Figure 2. Map showing drainage system of Mississippi River.

settlers because it could pick up miles of farmland and wash it into the backswamps. In addition, a crevasse made wide splits in the river road, paralyzing transportation and communication. A crevasse at the Sauvé Plantation in 1849 caused an uncontrolled flood into the mid city. The greatest danger of such a crevasse is that once the river jumps its banks, there might be no way of getting it back. The possibility exists that it might have permanently changed its course. The Sauvé Crevasse was brought under control, however, and the danger was averted.

There is geologic evidence that the Mississippi River has changed its course many times in the past 5,000 years, leaving old channels, each with its own delta. The oldest visible course is now occupied by Bayou Teche. A more recent ancestor of the Mississippi is Bayou Lafourche, which was apparently the last course it took before the one it now follows. Another early route is the St. Bernard Delta east of New Orleans.

The Mississippi has run its present course since the 16th century. It was on the verge of jumping again when explorers appeared on the scene. If such a jump were to occur now *below* New Orleans, it would require a whole new system of navigation from the Gulf to the city. But if it were to occur *above* New Orleans, the result would be disastrous. The largest port in the United States would no longer be on a river, but on a stagnant stream.

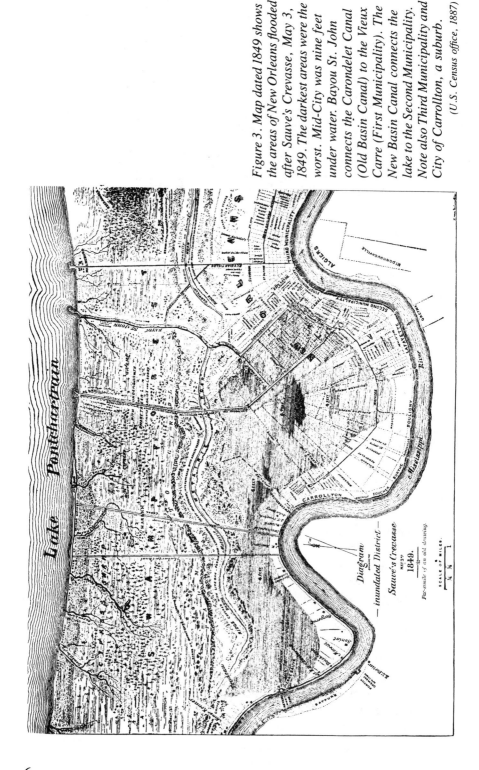

Figure 3. Map dated 1849 shows the areas of New Orleans flooded after Sauve's Crevasse, May 3, 1849. The darkest areas were the worst. Mid-City was nine feet under water. Bayou St. John connects the Carondelet Canal (Old Basin Canal) to the Vieux Carre (First Municipality). The New Basin Canal connects the lake to the Second Municipality. Note also Third Municipality and City of Carrollton, a suburb.

(U.S. Census office, 1887)

New Orleanians could recite a litany of difficulties they have lived with involving the river:

1) Most of the city is below sea level, while the river flows 10 to 15 feet *above* sea level.

2) The present Mid City area, lying as it does, in a "bowl," used to flood constantly, and was a breeding ground for yellow fever and malaria. The swamp teemed with snakes and alligators, and even when dry, was the consistency of glue.

3) The bedrock beneath the city, which is only compacted clay, is 70 feet below the surface in some places.

4) The only avenues into the city when the white man came were natural levees. During flood times, if crevassess occurred, the levees would be cut and transportation disrupted.

5) Hurricanes struck frequently from the Gulf, and still do, driving high tides ahead of them, often in the direction of the city.

In view of all this, one wonders why almost a million people live and work in New Orleans. But more than that, one wonders why Bienville chose such a site for his city. To Bienville, it was simple: it was the logical and necessary spot for a city.

It was clear to Bienville that the river demanded that a city exist at its mouth, but in all the 200 miles south of the site of Baton Rouge, it provided no place to put one. Naturally, the settlers wanted high ground, and the site of Baton Rouge met that requirement, but it was too far upriver to be convenient to ocean-going ships.

The site of the old Indian portage from the Mississippi River to Bayou St. John could be reached not only by coming up the river from the Gulf, but by traveling westward from the Gulf Coast through the Mississippi Sound through Lake Borgne and into Lake Pontchartrain. This was the place where Bienville decreed that the city of New Orleans would be built.

The Mississippi River Basin is shaped like a funnel, and the city that was to be founded on Bienville's "Beautiful Crescent" of land in the bend of the river would control the tip of that funnel. It would be gatekeeper to the richest river valley on earth. This was the destiny of New Orleans. Had there been nothing more than a sandbar in that bend of the river, Bienville would have urged his settlers to camp on it, fighting the elements until their own ingenuity provided the answers to their problems. This, of course, is what eventually happened, for the settlers did not leave. They endured with proprietary pride, and slowly, against indomitable odds, the city grew and prospered.

Almost every river in the world provides a site for a city near its mouth, where there is high ground to build on and where the river is narrow enough for land traffic to cross it conveniently. But not the Mississippi. At the mouth of almost every river, there is an embayment, where the sea has entered the mouth of the river and flooded it, forming a bay at the point where the river narrows. But the Mississippi does not narrow at any point. At the foot of Canal Street, it is nearly a half mile wide. It runs uniformly wide for hundreds of miles. It provides no site for a city south of Baton Rouge. It forms no bay, and it wildly jumps its riverbanks every five or six hundred years, aloof and indifferent to the needs of Man.

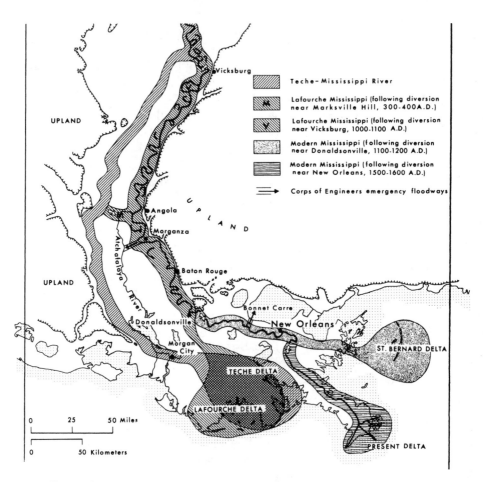

Figure 4. The Mississippi with its ancient deltas. In recent times, the river appeared to be threatening to jump its course again, either into Lake Pontchartrain at Bonnet Carre, or into the Atchafalaya at Morganza. Either would have been disastrous to New Orleans. The Army Corps of Engineers has built spillways at both locations to prevent flooding and to keep the river in its present course (H.N. Fisk, Geological Investigation of the Atchafalaya Basin and the Problem of Mississippi River Diversion *[Vicksburg: Mississippi River Commission, 1952]. Modified by William D. Thornbury in* Regional Geomorphology of the United States *[New York: John Wiley, 1965], p. 61. Used with permission of author and publisher.)*

8

The river last jumped its riverbed in the 16th century to follow a diversion near New Orleans, instead of near the city of Donaldsonville, to which it had diverted in the 12th century. So, in 1541, the scene was set for the discovery of the river in its present location, and into this chapter of history sailed Hernando DeSoto, a Spanish explorer, the first European to locate and describe the Mississippi River Valley.

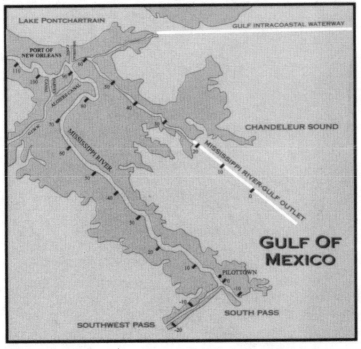

Waterway approaches to the Port of New Orleans from the Gulf of Mexico (lower right) and the Intracoastal Waterway (upper right).
(Courtesy Port of New Orleans)

Figure 5. De Soto's discovery of the Mississippi River, May, 1541.

CHAPTER II

Discovery and Exploration

The Indians spoke of a great river flowing through the continent, cutting it in two, and the white men jumped to the conclusion that it flowed east to west and could provide a western passage to China.

HERNANDO DESOTO

Hernando DeSoto is credited with having established the fact that there *was* such a river. DeSoto was a young man who had been with the Spanish army in the conquest of Peru, and had made his fortune there. As a result of that service, he was appointed governor of Cuba in 1538. Goaded by a desire to find still more gold, he set out in 1539 with 600 soldiers to explore Florida, which had been described to him as a "land of gold."

After landing in Tampa Bay in May, 1539, he and his men moved north, while a party he had sent west discovered Pensacola Bay. After crossing mountains and fighting off Indians for two years, he sighted the Mississippi River in May, 1541. The exact site of his discovery is in dispute. Some historians place it in Memphis, others in northern Mississippi. He described it as "wide and muddy and full of logs." He crossed the river into Arkansas, but returned to Mississippi, and in. 1542, died of fever. His men weighted down his body and buried it in the river.

DeSoto's explorations had taken him through the areas that are now the states of Florida, Georgia, South Carolina, North Carolina, Tennessee, Alabama, Mississippi, Arkansas, and Louisiana. After his death, his men, under the leadership of Luis de Moscoso built crude boats and continued down the Mississippi in 1543. They were the first white men to view the site of the city of New Orleans. Fighting Indians all the way, they eventually took refuge on the Gulf Coast.

MARQUETTE AND JOLIET

Over a century after DeSoto's death, the next chapter in the history of New Orleans unfolded. For 133 years, the lower Mississippi lay neglected by explorers. In 1673, a French Canadian fur trader by the name of Louis Joliet and a Jesuit missionary priest, Father Jacques Marquette, came down the Mississippi River toward the Gulf of Mexico.

In that year, Governor Louis Frontenac of Canada had ordered Marquette and Joliet to take an expedition party in search of a route to the Pacific Ocean. With five other Frenchmen and some guides, they left Lake Michigan, paddling canoes up the Fox River to the site of the present city of Portage, Wisconsin. They carried their canoes across land to the Wisconsin River which empties into the Mississippi. Going south on the Mississippi, they stopped for a peaceful meeting with the Illinois Indians who gave them a *calumet*, a peace pipe. Now they continued south as far as the Arkansas River, where they were surrounded by Indians with guns. It was only the calumet that saved their lives.

Some of the Indians now became friendly enough to tell them about some other white men, ten days farther south, who had given them the guns. Knowing this had to be a party of Spaniards, Marquette and Joliet decided that it was too dangerous to journey farther. They ended their trip down the Mississippi and returned to Canada by way of the Illinois River, passing the site of the present city of Chicago.

ROBERT CAVELIER de LASALLE

The real story of Louisiana begins with its third episode: the expedition of Robert Cavelier de LaSalle down the Mississippi River in the year 1682. LaSalle had been born of a wealthy family in Rouen, France. He had come to Canada in 1666, at the age of 23, to become a fur trader. To this end, he bought a piece of land eight miles from Montreal and established a trading post. He did much trading with the Indians, who taught him their language and customs, and told him stories about a great river called the Ohio, which flowed south to the sea. LaSalle believed this to be the much sought-after route to the Pacific Ocean. So, in 1669, at the age of 26, he sold his land and set out to explore the Ohio.

Four years later, in 1674, LaSalle was called to the French court to receive honors, on the recommendation of the governor of Canada. He used this opportunity to ask permission of Louis XIV to explore the rich Illinois country and whatever it would lead him to. This was a privilege which required royal sanction at the time. Permission was willingly granted since the king belived that colonies in the New World would add measurably to the prestige of France as a world power. His treasury, however, was depleted from war with England. LaSalle had to pay to have his own ship built.

In 1682, LaSalle led an expedition of 56 persons entering the Mississippi River from the Illinois River (which he left on February 6, 1682) to the Gulf of Mexico (which he reached on April 9, 1682). On this date, he disembarked, erected a cross on shore and a column inscribed with the name and the coat of arms of the king. Then he claimed all the land drained by the Mississippi for France and named the region Louisiana, in honor of King Louis XIV.

He then returned to France for supplies and settlers for a colony at

Figure 6. LaSalle claims Louisiana for France 1682.

(Courtesy Leonard V. Huber Collection)

the mouth of the river. In his company was an Italian adventurer named Henri de Tonti (or Tonty), who shared his dream of an empire stretching from Canada to the Gulf of Mexico. Tonti had long been his trusted companion and was to be the principal historian on the expedition. It is not difficult to imagine their excitement as they considered the possibility of developing a land area larger than the country of France, and then controlling trade on the only highway through this vast continent, since travel at the time was done almost entirely by water. The court of France, still in financial difficulty, agreed that the value of such a possession was inestimable.

LaSalle left France on July 4, 1684, on his way to the Gulf of Mexico with four ships, a force of marines, 100 soldiers, and 250 settlers, including women and children, all ready to be the first to live in Louisiana. Stopping in Santo Domingo to rest and refit their ships, they moved on in November, 1684, for the Gulf of Mexico.

Why LaSalle didn't return to the Mississippi River by his original route is not recorded. Perhaps he thought the southern route shorter. Perhaps he simply wanted to explore it. Undoubtedly, he was so heady with his earlier success that he expected no problem in finding the river from the South. How could anyone miss a river of such size? Now, anyone who had been out in the Gulf seeking an entry back into the Mississippi knows that the several mouths of the river look little different from the low grassy sandbars surrounding them, and that they *all* look exactly like the bayous which lead inland from the Gulf and then fade away. Few maps charted these estuaries, for white men had not sailed that way, so the probability of errors was great.

Then, too, LaSalle had never viewed the river from the South, so he had no points of reference. He became confused, lost his bearings, and made a few trial runs into the coast. Finally, the ships landed in Matagorda Bay on the Texas coast in February, 1685.

The bay was situated at the mouth of a large river emptying into the Gulf of Mexico. LaSalle knew by the curve of the coastline that he had missed the mouth of the Mississippi River. Beaujeu, his ship's captain, with whom he had argued constantly, left then to return to France, leaving LaSalle the brig *La Belle*. In this ship, LaSalle hoped to continue his search.

LaSalle built Fort St. Louis in Matagorda Bay, completing it in 1685. Then his brig was wrecked in a storm and he determined to return to Canada by land to get help for his colony. Although he had left Europe with four ships, he now had none. One had been captured by the Spanish in the Gulf of Mexico. Another had been lost when entering Matagorda Bay. Beaujeu had left with the third; and the last, *La Belle*, had been wrecked in a storm.

Some of the settlers agreed to stay in the fort, but with LaSalle on this incredible journey were his brother, his nephew, and a few companions, including a man named Joutel, who survived to relate the story. In 1687, the heroic LaSalle was murdered by his own men and buried in alien soil. We can only surmise that the assassins were exhausted and despondent after their unsuccessful adventure. The many months had taken their toll. Both ships and lives had been lost. The men were unsure of their position, without supplies, and fearful for their lives. It is understandable that on a long, difficult journey, violence would erupt. The survivors of the march continued on to Canada, where they told the sad story of "LaSalle's Folly." The colony that had been established in Texas was later destroyed by the Indians.

But another part of the story has not yet been told. Tonti, LaSalle's friend, had come down the Mississippi River from the Illinois country, planning to meet LaSalle coming northward from the Gulf of Mexico at the camp of the Bayogoulas (between New Orleans and Baton Rouge). Tonti waited as long as possible, then left a letter with an Indian chieftain, a letter that would not be delivered unit 1699, and then, not to LaSalle, but to Bienville and Iberville, the next French explorers in our story.

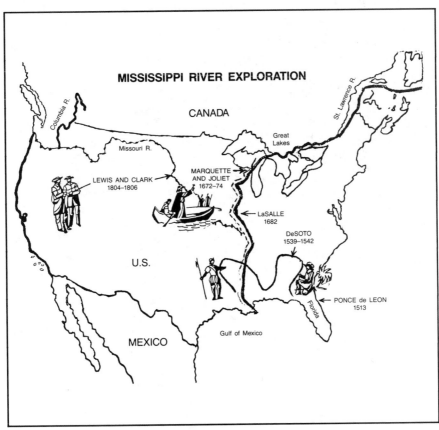

Map by Joan B. Garvey

Figure 7. One of the first views of the Place d'Armes was this watercolor made in 1726 by Jean Pierre Lassus.
(French National Archives, Paris. Courtesy Leonard V. Huber Collection)

The French Period

LaSalle was gone, but France's desire for empire was still strong. For ten years, France had been in no position to attempt further colonization. She had been involved in a war with England, which had just ended in 1697, and now she looked to the New World for empire. A favorable time had come for colonization plans to be presented at the court of France, and Pierre LeMoyne, Sieur d'Iberville, a young French Canadian, had his plans ready at the right time.

Iberville's father, Charles LeMoyne, was a successful fur trader with a wealth of eleven sons. Two of his sons, **Pierre LeMoyne, Sieur d'Iberville,** and **Jean Baptiste LeMoyne, Sieur de Bienville,** could foresee that the fur-trading business would not provide for them all. They had made other plans for their future. Iberville, the older of the two, had just distinguished himself in the war against England. He presented his plans to found a colony near the mouth of the Mississippi River to the king, who received them favorably. Iberville, however, needed more than just permission. He was not a wealthy man. Seeking a sponsor in this enterprise, he was fortunate in finding Louis de Phelypeaux, Comte de Pontchartrain, minister of marine.

Iberville left France in October, 1698, with two large frigates and two freight ships, a company of marines, and 200 settlers, including women and children, for his colony. In his company were his brother Bienville and Father Anatase Douay, a survivor of LaSalle's expedition.

Iberville had been commissioned to build forts at the mouth of the river to protect the settlement against British encroachments. In Santo Domingo, he was joined by the Marquis de Chateaumorant, in command of a war vessel, who presumably was to protect him in this venture. He sailed to Apalachicola Bay, Florida, and then followed the coast in search of the river. On January 29, 1699, he reached Pensacola, Florida, but the Spanish governor did not allow the Frenchmen to enter the harbor. They set sail again, and in February arrived at Mobile Bay, where the Indians told Iberville that the Mississippi was only a short distance to the west. Moving on, Iberville anchored before the

Chandeleur Islands. He landed on Ship Island, (which his men so named because it had a good harbor). He built some huts there, and then went on with his brother to explore the coast of what is now Biloxi and Ocean Springs. From there, he and his men set out in small boats to look for the river.

Iberville found many other islands. One they called Massacre Island, because there were so many bones there (later called Dauphin Island). Another was christened Horn Island because a powder horn was left there. There was Cat Island, so-called because of the many racoons, which they mistook for cats; and Deer Island, because deer were plentiful there.

On March 2, 1699, Iberville arrived at the mouth of the river, where there was fresh water and a strong current. The following day, Shrove Tuesday, they began their travels up the river. Finding a bayou 12 miles upstream, they named it for the day, Mardi Gras Bayou, and thus was Mardi Gras introduced to the Louisiana territory.

Father Anatase Douay said Mass the following Sunday for Iberville's company at the village of the Bayogoula Indians, who informed them that a letter had been left by Tonti to LaSalle in 1686. The letter was found in the possession of the Mongoulacha Indians. In addition to the letter, there was a prayerbook, a list of names of LaSalle's companions, and a coat of arms from LaSalle's expedition. At last, Iberville knew that he was on "LaSalle's River."

At the bluff above the river, which Iberville considered a good spot for a settlement, he saw a red stick, the maypole used by the Indians for hanging up offerings of fish and game. Iberville called the place Baton Rouge.

The Indians asked him if he would like to return to Ship Island by a different route. Enthusiastically, and with commendable courage, he agreed. The Indians knew that Iberville had come on a serious mission to establish settlements for white colonists. This could only work to their detriment. Iberville had no way of knowing they would not murder him and drop his body in the river. But curiosity is the essence of men like Iberville, and eagerly, he went with them.

From Baton Rouge, they took him south on the Mississippi River as far as Pass Manchac (which means "back door"), then by way of the bayou to the Amite River, and then through two lakes and into a bay before returning him to his fleet at Ship Island. Iberville named the larger lake Pontchartrain, for his benefactor; the smaller one Maurepas, for Pontchartrain's son; and the Bay, St. Louis, for the patron saint of the king.

Now, sailing on to Biloxi Bay, Iberville established colonies at Ocean Springs and Biloxi in March, 1699. Then, having sewn the seed of his Louisiana colony, Iberville made a trip back to France, leaving command in the hands of Sieur de Sauvole, a brave and capable young French officer.

ENGLISH TURN

In his brother's absence, Bienville often left the fort at Biloxi to explore the Mississippi. On September 15, 1699, on returning from such an exploration with a small band of friends, he was surprised to encounter the English corvette, *Carolina Galley,* towering over him. The ship, loaded with settlers bent on colonization, had dropped anchor some 28 leagues (approximately 75 miles) from the mouth of the river. The British officer in charge asked Bienville for directions to the Mississippi River. Bienville told the officer that the Mississippi was much farther west, that he was in French territory, heavily guarded by forts, and that he was in danger in those waters.

The British vessel weighed anchor, and, turning around, sailed to the Gulf. The bluff had worked. To this day, the point in the river where the meeting took place is call English Turn. It is about 10 miles below New Orleans. It was an unlucky day for the British, that they chanced to meet Bienville in that place. Had they not, it might have been the English who headed up the river and founded a city at the site of New Orleans, instead of the French. A century later, not far from English Turn, the Battle of New Orleans was fought, and once again, the British were turned back.

By 1700, Bienville's colonists had built Fort Boulaye as a protection below English Turn. On Biloxi Bay, they built Fort Maurepas, one of the few forts in North America that was stoutly built, according to the European style. It has out-lasted all the others in the area. For 24 years, from 1699 to 1723, the capital of Louisiana remained on the Gulf Coast.

Settlers came from France and Canada, some disembarking at Ship Island, Cat Island, and Dauphin Island, where they were to remain until a more permanent settlement had been established. The land was hard on the newcomers. Sandy soil made farming difficult, and fresh water was in short supply. An account by Sauvole, himself, tells of the beauty of the white beaches on the Mississippi Sound, the magnolia and oak trees, and the infertility of the soil, but it adds that "the colonists, for several years, paid little attention to the tilling of the land and counted for sustenance on the provisions sent from France."

It was not so difficult for the Canadian fur traders and trappers who were used to an outdoor life, but those who came from France were often debtors and vagrants, unaccustomed to the wilderness and to farming. In France, if a citizen was out of work three days, he was given a free trip to Louisiana. Women of the streets, thieves, smugglers, dealers in contraband, vagabonds, and even prisoners were sent to populate the colony. Some had been imprisoned for little or no reason, but they still preferred Louisiana to the Bastille. Passengers on those first ships to arrive were not revered by their descendants, like those who came over on the Mayflower.

Advice coming from France wasn't much help, either, since it was "to search for mines and pearl fisheries, to domesticate the buffalo for their wool, and to raise silkworms." Tormented by mosquitoes, suffering from the heat, and itching from the sandy soil, the settlers profited little from such advice.

Members of the French court didn't like the exotic names of the colonies: Biloxi, Natchez, Massacre Island. They thought Mobile suggested instability. It is written that Bienville even considered changing the name to Immobile.

Iberville returned to the colony in 1700, accompanied by the Jesuit priest, Father Paul Du Ru, who was to found missions among the Indians on the Mississippi River. Iberville ordered a fort built in the Natchez country, which he could call Fort Rosalie, (for the beautiful Duchess de Pontchartrain). He gave command of Fort Maurepas and the Ocean Springs settlement to Bienville, who stayed there until the death of Sauvole in 1701, when Bienville became commander of the Louisiana Territory at the age of 22. The seat of government was changed from Biloxi to Fort Louis de la Mobile, which was established in 1702.

Iberville, the Father of Louisiana, died of yellow fever in 1706 in Havana, leaving Bienville the acting governor of Louisiana.

Very little help was now forthcoming from France, and Bienville was often obliged to scatter his men among the Indians, who took good care of them. Penicaut, Bienville's young friend, who was a carpenter and an Indian interpreter, took a few colonists and went to live with the Acolapissa Indians on the north shore of Lake Pontchartrain for a year. He leaves a description of dining on buffalo, bear, geese, and ducks, fruits of the season, and dishes prepared with corn. At evening parties, his friend played the violin, and the French danced with each other, while the Indians tried to imitate the minuet. Penicaut dined with the Chief on sumptuous meals, and repaid the hospitality by giving the Chief's daughter French lessons.

In 1705, the first commercial cargo came down the Mississippi, passing the site of the future city of New Orleans. It was a load of 15,000 bear and deerhides, which came from around the Wabash River in the upper Mississippi through the lake passages: the Amite River, Pass Manchac, Lakes Maurepas, Pontchartrain and Borgne to the Mississippi Sound, to the settlement at Ocean Springs and then to France.

In 1707, word reached France that the limited supplies on Dauphin Island, which had been sent from France to support the garrison, were being sold for six times their worth. Martin d'Artaguette d'Iron was sent from France as Commissary General of Louisiana to investigate, and Bienville lost his position as commandant and acting governor. His replacement, Nicholas Daneau, Sieur de Muy, died en route, however, and Bienville was reinstated, but d'Artaguette stayed on to supervise the affairs of the colony.

20

In November, 1708, the first concessions of land in what was later to be the city of New Orleans were made on the west bank of Bayou St. John. Bienville granted this tract to Louis Juchereau de St. Denys, a friend from Canada, and an outstanding figure in Louisiana history. He was one of the first settlers in Louisiana, arriving on his second visit with Iberville in 1699 at the age of 23. He later founded the city of Nachitoches, the oldest in Louisiana. The St. Denys Concession is shown on a map drawn by Allou d'Hemecourt, which is in the Louisiana State Museum Library.

Other concessions along the Bayou were granted to Antoine Rivard de LaVigne . . . 2½ arpents; Nicolas "Alias Delon" . . . 2½ arpents; and Baptiste Portier . . . 3 arpents; three others were granted the same day, but were not recorded. "These concessions had narrow water frontages 2½ to 3 arpents each. They were long, narrow ribbons of land extending from Bayou St. John to Bayou Gentilly, granted by the French Colonial Government at Mobile."[1]

The village of Bayou St. Jean, as the French called it, and the suburb of Gentilly, which built up on the natural levees of the Metairie-Gentilly distributary, were the earliest habitations and plantations in the region. Bayou St. John, in its present form, came into being 400 to 600 years ago, when all flow activity in the Metairie-Gentilly distributary ceased.

By the year 1712, the Louisiana colony as a whole had not prospered. The sites were not self-supporting and war between France and Spain made it difficult for France to maintain a colony so far away, scattered over such an immense territory and protected by five forts. Therefore, Louis XIV, in 1712, transferred control of Louisiana to a wealthy banker named **Antoine Crozat** for a period of fifteen years.

In 1713, Crozat replaced Bienville with **Antoine de LaMothe Cadillac,** the founder of Detroit, who was to be the governor of Louisiana. In his new position, Cadillac failed miserably. He lacked tact in dealing with the Indians, and the first Natchez war broke out in 1716.

The Natchez were a brilliant tribe of Indians. They worshipped the sun and kept a fire burning perpetually in their temple. The story of Noah's ark was part of their culture. In 1716, they rose against the French, and Bienville was sent to fight them. With only a few men in his detachment, he put two of them to death and made terms with the others. In the same year, 1716, Bienville built Fort Rosalie on the site which had been selected by his brother years before.

In 1717, just five years after Crozat was granted his charter, he gave it up. Trade with the Spanish in Mexico had not materialized, and trade

---

[1]Freiberg, Edna B., *Bayou St. John in Colonial Times (1699–1803)*, p. 30–1. A linear arpent = 191.835 feet. A square arpent = 85% of an English acre.

with the Indians was not profitable. He declared that he had spent four times his original investment, and had seen no profit.

Louisiana, then a colony of 700 people, was transferred to the Company of the West (called the Company of the Indies after 1719), which was to have authority in the colony for 25 years, to enjoy a monopoly of trade, to name the governor and other officers, and would in turn be obliged to send to Louisiana 6,000 white colonists and 3,000 blacks within 10 years. The president of the Company was the famous **John Law**, private advisor to Philippe, the Duc d'Orleans.

JOHN LAW, IMPRESARIO OF HIGH-PRESSURE

John Law was a Scotsman, a professional gambler, and a financial genius. He had escaped Great Britain fifteen years earlier after killing a man in a duel, and had spent the intervening years traveling all over Europe, trying to develop his "great plan."

Law was a well-known manipulator. It is therefore easy to understand that he sought and secured the good will and confidence of Philippe of Orleans, regent of France after the death of Louis XIV. Like Law, Philippe was a gambler and a womanizer, and the friendship of the two rogues was inevitable. In time, Law became the advisor to the regent, and with his aid and encouragement, started his campaign to populate the Louisiana colony in record time, and to make himself a fortune in the bargain.

His fraudulent scheme called for the combining of the Bank of France and the Company of the West, an arrangement which he successfully managed. The Mississippi Bubble, a name later given his plan, still incites the envy of high-pressure salesmen everywhere. The plan was 1) to induce noblemen and rich middle class businessmen to buy shares of stock in Louisiana land, and also to purchase some land for themselves; and 2) to entice (or to force) the poor of Europe to become *engagés,* hired field hands for the Company or for the concessionaires. Shareholders would prosper, Law promised, when the gold, silver, diamonds and pearls were found in the New World. With nothing but gaudy promises to back his "shares," Law found himself inundated by the demands of the speculators. He could not print the shares fast enough.

In 1716, Law had signed a contract with the government of France, (with the blessing of Philippe) allowing him to establish a private bank, which would provide him with all the credit he needed. Then, in 1717, he replaced the governor of Louisiana, Jean Michiele, Seigneur de Lepinay, with the man of his choice, Bienville, who then began his second term of governor at the age of 37.

A brilliant, ruthless sales campaign followed, unprecedented in Europe. Posters and handbills flooded France, Germany and Switzerland, offering free land, provisions, and transportation to those who would volunteer to emigrate to the New World. They were told that the soil of Louisiana bore two crops a year without cultivation, and that the Indians so adored the white man that they would not let him labor, but took that burden from him. In addition, they were promised the imaginary gold mines, the pearl fisheries, as well as a delightful climate where there was no disease or old age.

Many paupers who strayed into Paris, or prisoners who would not volunteer were kidnapped and shipped, under guard, to fill the emptiness of Louisiana. Prostitutes, and the inmates of jails and hospitals, were all sent to populate the colony and to start the flow of wealth to the stockholders.

Franz, in his "Kolonisation des Mississippitales" (Leipzig, 1906), writes:

> "The company even kept a whole regiment of archers which cleaned Paris of its rabble and adventurers, and received for this a fixed salary and 100 livres a head . . . . Five thousand people are said to have disappeared from Paris in April, 1721, alone."

> "Prisoners were set free in Paris in September, 1721 . . . under the condition that they would marry prostitutes and go with them to Louisiana. The newly married couples were chained together and thus dragged to the port of embarkation."

Meanwhile, Bienville set his men to work, clearing forests and erecting sheds and barracks at the site of the Indian portage which he had selected back in 1699 on his first visit to Louisiana with Iberville. The portage was, roughly, where Esplanade Avenue is today. It is a trail from the river to Bayou St. John (Bienville had named the bayou in honor of his patron saint). The trail led through cypress swamps, teeming with snakes and alligators, near a fortified Indian village called Tchoutchouma. It was at this point, where the river comes closest to the lake, that Bienville had decided to build his city. This "beautiful crescent in the river" would be the site of his new trading post.

He wanted the spot for two reasons. First, it was the half-way point by water between Natchez (Fort Rosalie) and Mobile (Fort Louis). Secondly, it was a spot "safe from Hurricanes and Tidal Waves," according to an early account of the city.

Bienville had to argue for the site, with Pierre Le Blond de La Tour, the royal engineer; with Adrien de Pauger, assistant engineer; and with John Law, president of the Company. They all thought it absurd to select a site in the midst of a swamp, but Bienville persevered, and the "beautiful crescent" became the city of Nouvelle Orleans.

In June, 1718, Bienville wrote in his diary:

> "We are working at Nouvelle Orleans with as much zeal as the shortage of men will permit. I have myself conveyed over the spot

to select the place where it will be best to locate the settlement . . . . I am grieved to see so few people engaged in a task which requires at least a hundred times the number. All the ground of the site, except the borders, which are drowned by floods, is very good, and everything will grow there."

John Law ordered a garrison, a director's building, and lodging for the director's staff to be built to establish the beginnings of trade.

Some inhabitants of the city in 1718 were Bienville, his Intendant (the head of civil affairs), surveyors (the Lassus brothers from Mobile), carpenters, troops, and a few concessionaires. There was de la Tour, the Royal engineer; Pauger, second engineer; Ignace Broutin, who built the Ursuline Convent; doctors and priests and soldiers. French soldiers

Figure 8. Costumes of French soldiery early in the eighteenth century.
(Courtesy Leonard V. Huber Collection)

24

usually had another trade. Some were wigmakers, ropemakers, weavers, gardeners, shoemakers, laborers, brewers, locksmiths, bakers, papermakers, and the largest group were cabinet-makers.

In June, 1718, the first wave of European immigrants began to arrive in response to John Law's campaign, at the same time that Bienville was supervising the work in New Orleans. Three hundred came in three ships, accompanied by five hundred soldiers and convicts, a total of 800 coming into a colony where only 700 lived, thus doubling, in one day, the population of Louisiana.[2]

They were dumped, for lack of a better place, on Dauphin Island. They were crowded, unsheltered, hungry and wretched. Many starved and died, but there was no place else to go, until Governor Bienville could come for them with his few boats and his few men, to distribute them around the countryside. Some he sent to Natchez, some to the valley of the Yazoo River, and some to New Orleans, where they were crowded into tents and rough sheds.

John Law's career ended with his flight from Paris as a bankrupt and a fugitive on December 10, 1720. He fled to the Belgian frontier in a coach lent him by Madame Brié and with escorts provided by the Duc d'Orleans.

THE GERMAN LAW PEOPLE

During the years of the John Law promotion, 10,000 Germans left their homelands to come to Louisiana. The Jesuit priest, Father Pierre Francois-Xavier de Charlevoix, who came from Canada to Louisiana in 1721, wrote of passing by the "mournful wretches" who had settled on John Law's grant on the Arkansas River. These Germans were originally from the Rhine region, which had been devastated in the Thirty Years War between France and Germany (1618–1648). After the war, Louis XIV had seized Alsace and Lorraine. Both Germans and French in the area suffered the consequences of war: pestilence, famine, and religious persecution. There is little wonder that the glorious picture painted of the New World enticed them to emigrate.

Only a small percentage of the German Law People, as they were called, ever reached Louisiana. Of the 10,000, only about 6,000 actually left Europe. They lay crowded in French ports for months, awaiting the departure of vessels. They starved, fell ill with disease and died in the ports. Many survivors died on the "pest ships" from lack of food and water or diseases contracted when the ships stopped in Santo Domingo. Only about 2,000 reached the New World. They disembarked in Biloxi and on Dauphin Island, and still more perished.

---

[2]Deiler, J. Hanno, *The Settlement of the German Coast of Louisiana*, p. 18

One important group of Germans was led by Karl Freidrich D'Arensbourg. They arrived in Biloxi in June, 1721, where they met the survivors of some of the "pest ships." D'Arensbourg organized the survivors, and they settled on the banks of the Mississippi, about 25 miles upriver of New Orleans.

Meanwhile, an earlier group of Germans who had settled on the Arkansas River in 1720, had been too ill and too busy providing shelter to have produced a crop by 1721. No financial help came from the bankrupt John Law. So, in January, 1722, they abandoned their concession and descended upon New Orleans, where they demanded passage to Europe. Bienville tried to induce them to remain. They were given rich lands near the "D'Arensbourg Germans" in the area that is today called the German Coast (the parishes of St. Charles and St. John the Baptist).

Professor Deiler tells us that these "Arkansas Germans," on their descent to New Orleans, must have met their fellow countrymen (the D'Arensbourg Germans) who had just settled there. This was undoubtedly a determining factor in their decision to accept Bienville's offer of the land in the area. The descendants of those early settlers still live in the area, first called "La Côte des Allemands," and later, "Des Allemands." These early German settlers brought much stability to the colony with their successful farming and were better able to endure the climate than the French were.

There was a shortage of unmarried women in the colony, and the men were forced to take Indian squaws as brides.

"Send me wives for my Canadians," Bienville wrote to Paris. "They are running in the woods after Indian girls." In 1721, 88 girls from a house of correction in Paris, ironically called *La Saltpêtrière,* arrived in the city, under the care of three Gray Sisters and a midwife, who was nicknamed *La Sans Regret.*

Within a month, 19 had married, and 10 had died, leaving 59 to be cared for, not an easy task, for they were girls who "could not be restrained." They are to be distinguished from the Casket Girls, who did not arrive until 1728. The latter came to Mobile and Biloxi to be wives to the settlers. They were from good middle class families, and they were skilled in housewifely duties and excellent of character. The Ursuline nuns claim that there is no historical basis for the story that they came to New Orleans.

Some of the concessionaires that came to work their own land are worthy of mention.

The **Marquis de Mezieres** from Amiens, France built his home in 1720 at the present site of the Petite Salon on St. Peter Street.

Villars Dubrieul and his family arrived in New Biloxi in 1721. He later settled in the Tchoupitoulas, near the location of the present Ochsner Hospital. There, with his family and ten servants, he grew rice and indigo. By 1724, he had an avenue of trees, and by 1725, two indigo factories, which produced ink and dye. He became contractor for the Mississippi Valley. He built the first levee in New Orleans and a canal between the Mississippi River and Bayou Barataria, the location of the present day Harvey Canal.

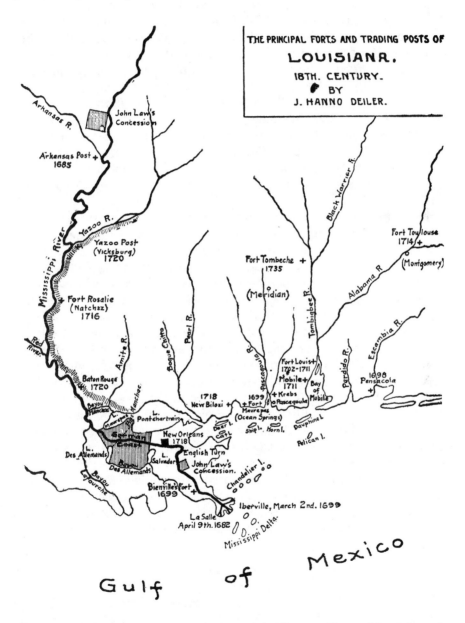

Figure 9. Map from The Settlement of the German Coast of Louisiana, *by Hanno Deiler, University of Pennsylvania, 1909.*

Antoine Simon LePage DuPratz, (1695–1775), was born in Holland and came in 1718 to Dauphin Island, after having served with the French army in Germany. In his three-volume work, *Histoire de la Louisiane,* he tells of settling a plantation on Bayou St. John, then moving on to the Natchez country, where he spent eight years. He wrote of their lives and customs, leaving the most accurate account we have of these original inhabitants of Louisiana. After 16 years in America, during which time he served as manager of the Company of the Indies and manager of the King's Farm, which dealt in slave trade at Algiers Point, he returned to France where his books were published in 1758. They were, and still are, a treasure-trove of early Louisiana history.

Antoine Philippe de Marigny de Mandeville, born at Fort Louis de la Mobile in 1772, was the stepson of Ignace Broutin, the royal engineer. He built a beautiful summer home in 1788 in Mandeville, a town north of Lake Pontchartrain which bears his name. His grandson was Bernard de Marigny, a colorful Creole of New Orleans.

Other names of early settlers were Villere, de la Ronde, and Delery.

It is interesting to note that most settlers were under five feet, three inches tall. The average height was five feet. The average age was 21 years old. There were few over 50, and few in their teens.

Before the hurricane of 1721, the city is described by Father Pierre de Charlevoix, in one of the first letters written from New Orleans. He wrote that there were a "hundred barracks," placed in no particular order, a wooden storehouse, and two or three houses "which would be no ornament to a village of France . . . ." He also wrote that he felt the city would be the "future capital of a fine and vast country."

The city of which he spoke consisted of 470 people, living on three streets which had been laid out by Pauger. The hurricane of 1721 devastated the town, destroying all the buildings.

In April, 1722, the first complete plan for the city of New Orleans was signed by Pierre Le Blond de La Tour, who dispatched Adrian de Pauger to supervise the construction of the city. The area on which La Tour planned to build was scattered with wooden houses built by immigrants from Illinois. Pauger cleared a strip of land on the river wide enough and deep enough to put the plan into execution. The hurricane of 1721 had taken care of most of the original buildings, which were not in keeping with the engineer's plans, and would have had to be removed, in any case.

> "Then with the help of some *piquers*, he traced on the ground the streets and quarters which were to form the new town, and notified all who wished building sites to present their petitions to the Council. To each settler who appeared, they gave a plot of ten fathoms front by twenty deep, and as each square was fifty fathoms

Figure 10. The first parish church of St. Louis, designed by de Pauger in 1724, dedicated on Christmas Eve, 1727, on site of the St. Louis Cathedral. Drawings reconstituted from plans in French National Archives.

(Courtesy Leonard V. Huber Collection)

29

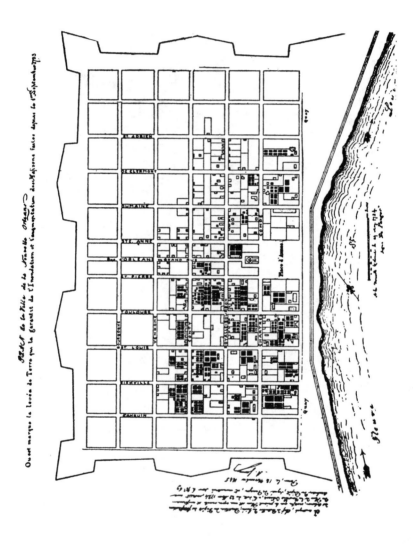

Figure 11. Map by Adrien de Pauger, May 26, 1724. It was De Pauger who laid out the original city in 1721. This shows the additional houses constructed after the overflow of September 1, 1723, the shaded houses being the first erected.

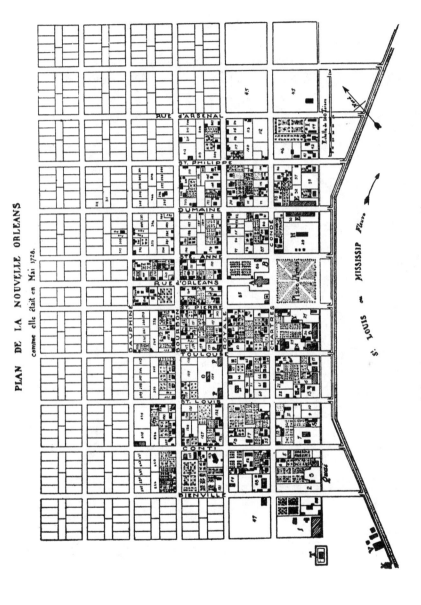

Figure 12. New Orleans, May 15, 1728. From the original map by N. Broutin deposited in office of Marine and Colonies, Paris, France.

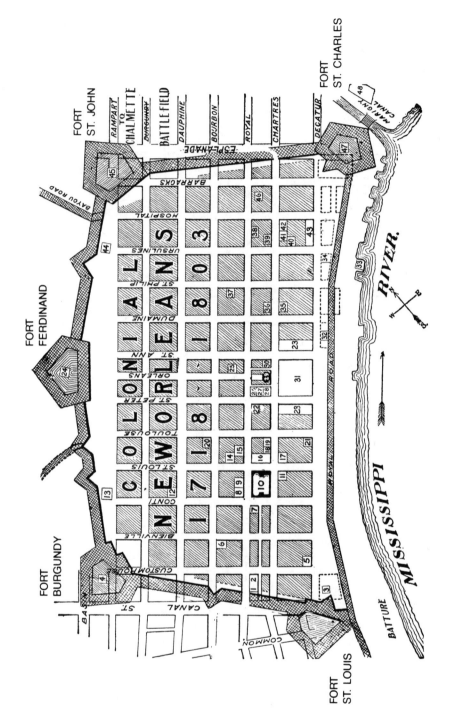

Figure 13. Map of New Orleans, 1803.

front, it gave twelve plots in each, the two middle ones being ten front by twenty-five deep. It was ordained that those who obtained these plots would be bound to enclose them with palisades, and leave all around a strip at least three feet wide, at the foot of which a ditch was to be dug, to serve as a drain for the river water in time of inundation." (From the Memoirs of M. Dumont, found in *Historical Memoirs,* by B. F. French.)

The streets were laid out in a grid pattern, and they were straight, not conforming to the curve of the river. The exact site of the Vieux Carré today is the place Bienville chose in 1718, and the spot where the St. Louis Cathedral is today was the location of the St. Louis Parish Church. The wooden church was blown down in 1723, but in 1724, construction of a brick church was begun on the spot.

The map shows the plan of the city, with its limits and its street names. From left to right, vertically, the streets were Canal, Iberville, Bienville, Conti, St. Louis, Toulouse, St. Peter, Orleans, St. Ann, du Maine, Clermont (changed to St. Philip), Rue Arsenal (changed to Ursulines), Hospital (changed to Governor Nicholls), Barracks, and Esplanade. The original city ended at Iberville Street. (Our present Vieux Carre Commission had no jurisdiction past Iberville.) The streets Conti, Toulouse, and du Maine are the names of King Louis XIV's illegitimate sons.

Reading from top to bottom, horizontally, the streets were Rampart, Bourgogne (changed to Burgundy), Vendome (changed to Dauphine), Bourbon (family of the king), Royal, Condé (an extension of Chartres, later changed to Chartres also), and Rue de la Leveé (changed to Decatur).

MAP OF VIEUX CARRE

The Place d'Armes fronts the church, jail, and the priest's house, (now the Cathedral, flanked by the Cabildo and Presbytère). Barracks were on either side of the square, moved by a later governor to a location beyond the Ursuline Convent on Barracks Street.

New Orleans was a city bounded on three sides by swamps and on the fourth by the river. A levee was built on the river side, and drainage ditches were dug to allow the water from the river to drain around the city to "Back of Town."

A description of 18th century New Orleans, from *History of Regional Growth*:

"At high tide, the river flows through the streets. The subsoil is swampy. New Orleans becomes famous for its tombs. Buried coffins must have holes so that they do not float to the surface when the land is flooded. Dikes have to be built along the river. . . .

Those living in the city dedicated to the Duke of Orleans feel as if they were living on an island in the middle of a mud puddle."

Alongside the river were high banks covered with great cypress forests, occasionally broken by the home of a concessionaire or an Indian village. Buildings were constructed of thick wood with sloped roofs like Norman houses in Canada. Galleries were later added for cool comfort and the protection of the exterior against decay.

The French in Louisiana, gregarious by nature and possessing a remarkable ability to adapt, settled in groups instead of seeking solitude, as much for sociability as for safety. They were predominantly traders, not farmers. Unlike the American frontiersmen, they built substantial houses of hewn timber or brick, large and comfortable. They were survivors, and they were here to stay. Their attitude is reflected in the types of homes they built.

CODE NOIR, 1724

In 1719, the Company of the West caused an influx of slaves in Louisiana. By 1724, there were so many Negroes in the colony that the French government enacted a set of laws called the *Code Noir*, or Black Code, whose purpose it was to protect the slaves and the free blacks, and to define and limit their activities. It governed the treatment of slaves by their masters. Slaveowners were ordered to have their slaves baptized Catholics. They were not to work their slaves on Sundays or holidays, except for marketing.

The Code was not as cruel as it is often made to appear. It provided more lenient treatment of slaves than could be found almost anywhere else in the South. It was the basis of Louisiana slave laws until the late 1820s, when the state adopted parts of the much more severe slave codes of the southeastern states (Joe Gray Taylor, Louisiana, *A Narrative History,* p. 12).

NEW ORLEANS, THE CAPITAL OF LOUISIANA

Bienville had tried as early as 1719 to have the Louisiana seat of government moved to New Orleans, but the Superior Council argued that it should be transferred back from Mobile to Biloxi. The Council won. Biloxi, however, had just burned down and was abandoned for the other side of the Bay. In 1722, three commissioners arrived in the colony, charged with the administration of the Company's affairs, after John Law's failure. In 1723, the commissioners allowed Bienville to make New Orleans the capital of Louisiana.

THE URSULINE NUNS ARRIVE

It was Bienville who had laid the groundwork for the coming of the

Ursuline nuns, although he was "between terms" and not in the colony when they finally arrived. A school for boys had already been started by a Capuchin monk, Father Cecil, where the Place d'Armes Motel stands today on St. Ann Street, across from the Presbytère. Bienville tried to get the *Soeurs Grises* (Gray Sisters) from his native Canada to come to New Orleans to teach the girls, but he failed. He consulted Father Beaubois, Superior of the few Jesuits in Louisiana at the time, who advised him to try to procure the services of the Ursuline nuns. Bienville did so, and twelve nuns arrived August 7, 1727. Their Superior was Mother Tranchepain, and among them was the talented Madeliene Hachard, to whom we owe a charming description of the journey and the city in 1727. Their first convent was built in 1730.

In February, 1724, Bienville was ordered to return to France, to render an account of his conduct. Disagreements between Bienville and his Superior Council had always existed, and the officers were successful in having him recalled. During his second administration, he had taken Pensacola in 1719 (it was returned to Spain in 1723), he had undertaken a war against the Natchez and defeated them, and he had begun negotiations for the coming of the Ursuline nuns. Nevertheless, he was replaced by Governor Etienne de Périer, who arrived in 1725.

Figure 14. The Old Ursuline Convent.

THE NATCHEZ MASSACRE

During Périer's administration, a great war with the Indians took place. In 1729, the Natchez were ordered by the commandant of Fort Rosalie, a vile little man named Chépart, to abandon one of their finest villages, the White Apple, in order that he might establish a plantation there. The Natchez Indians decided that they would never have peace until they destroyed the French at Fort Rosalie. On November 28, 1729, they surprised the fort, killing 200 men. They took women, children, and Negro slaves prisoners.

The Choctaws allied themselves with the French, killing many of the Natchez, and recovering some of the prisoners. Then the Choctaws dispersed.

The Natchez entrenched themselves and resisted for some time. Finally, they escaped to a mound in the Black River, leaving their prisoners behind. On November 15, 1730, Périer left with 650 soldiers and 350 Indian warriors for the Black River. He brought back 427 prisoners, who were sent to Santo Domingo and sold as slaves. The rest of the tribe was adopted by the Chickasaws, and the Natchez name was lost forever.

When the children who had been orphaned in the Indian War arrived in New Orleans, the Ursuline nuns began their orphanage. They also put bars on the windows of their convent (which still remain today) in fear of a similar Indian attack in New Orleans.

The war with the Indians had been too costly. In 1731, the Company of the Indies gave Louisiana back to France. In April, 1732, Louisiana became, once again, a royal province. The population at this time was 5,000 whites and 2,000 blacks in the entire territory. France removed the duty on goods coming from France to Louisiana, in order to stimulate trade.

In 1732, Bienville returned for his third term as governor. This third administration was a disaster because of war with the Indians. Bienville was forced to make war on the Chickasaws, and hostilities did not end until April, 1740. In 1743, Bienville asked to be relieved of his command, and returned to France. He was 62 years old, and had been about 44 years in Louisiana.

MARQUIS DE VAUDRIEUL

His successor was **Pierre Rigaud, the Marquis de Vaudrieul**, called the Grand Marquis. While it is true that he brought culture, elegant manners and elaborate entertainment to the colony, such pleasures were availabe only to the wealthy. His administration was filled with nepotism in political appointments, misuse of army provisions for personal profit, trade monopolies, and general negligence of duty. His wife, the Marquise de Vaudrieul, looked quite elegant driving her "imported from Paris" four-hourse carriage around New Orleans, but once inside the governor's palace, she engaged in the selling of drugs, and the governor shared in the profits.

A good picture of the times is painted in the report of the ceremony honoring Vaudrieul's appointment as governor of Canada. Kerlerec was host at a dinner for 200 guests followed by a remarkable show of fireworks. To ignite the display, two doves were released by Madame Kerlerec and Marquise de Vaudrieul. In their beaks, the doves carried lit tapers to set the extravaganza ablaze.

And so, a more accurate account of Vaudrieul's term would be ten years of political corruption and Indian wars. He kept up the enmity between the Chickasaws and the Choctaws, and civil war broke out among the Choctaws. Receiving reinforcements from France, he undertook an expedition against the Chickasaws in 1752, which accomplished little except for the devastation of their country.

Vaudrieul was, however, the first governor to establish a real levee system in New Orleans, which offered some relief and protection from floods. He also suggested *columbage* as a method of construction. This method employed a heavy framework of squared timber filled in with either bricks *(briqueté entre poteaux)* or a mud-and-moss mixture called *boussilage*. You can still see evidence of this *boussilage* construction in French Quarter buildings. He suggested that buildings be placed three feet off the ground, that they be built no higher than two stories, and constructed with galleries.

At the time of Vaudrieul's administration, the Jesuits had settled on the plantation Bienville abondoned when he returned to France. It ran from Canal to Felicity Street and included the site of the present Jesuit Church on Baronne Street. It was in that area, in 1751, that they planted sugar cane sent to them by the Jesuits in Cuba.

In 1753, Vaudrieul left to become governor of Canada. He was replaced as governor of Louisiana by **Louis Billouart, Chevalier de Kerlerec.** Kerlerec was nicknamed Chef Menteur (Chief Liar) by the Indians. This was the name originally given to the stream that meandered beside the present highway of the same name through the Rigolets to the Lake and on to the Gulf. It was the "Chief Liar" among streams because its current flowed deceptively either way with the tide. The Indians seemed to know Kerlerec very well.

Governor Kerlerec had violent disputes with his Commissary-Commissioner Vincent de Rochemore, who accused him of being a dictator and of robbing the treasury. Kerlerec, in turn, accused Rochemore of theft and neglect of his duties. These conflicts, together with a *laissez-faire* attitude toward the colony, made progress impossible. The unsuccessful wars of Louis XV limited the help that could be given Louisiana, and the poor financial policy of the colony caused instability in the currency. In 1761, Kerlerec was recalled to France and thrown in the Bastille, but his friends managed to secure his release.

The French and Indian Wars had been going on in North America since 1689. The last of these four wars, 1754 to 1761 (although the treaty was not signed until 1763), was a conflict involving French and British possessions in the New World. In this war, Colonel George Washington fought against the French in the Ohio Valley. Louisiana was almost a forgotten territory. No new colonists came. Few ships or supplies arrived.

THE ACADIANS

In Acadia (later called Nova Scotia), which had been won by the British at the end of Queen Anne's War in 1713, the British and the French Acadians had been living side by side in peace for half a century. Now, the British feared that if Acadia were invaded, the French Acadians would fight against them. Therefore, the governor demanded that the French Acadians swear allegiance to the British crown and give up their Catholic religion. They refused and were exiled. Many of these excellent farmers, after a lengthy odyssey, found new homes in Louisiana, during the period of Spanish domination.

The war ended disastrously for France, causing her to lose all her colonies in America and nearly all in India. Her loss of Canada made the Louisiana colonists fear that there would soon be a change in domination. Indeed, on November 13, 1762, the king of Spain, Charles III, accepted, by the secret treaty of Fountainbleau, the gift of Louisiana from his cousin, Louis XV, the king of France.

Once before, in 1761, Louis had tried to give Louisiana to Spain, in exchange for a loan and on the condition that Spain would enter the war against England. Spain had refused. Now, in 1762, England declared war on Spain, and was wreaking havoc with Spain's colonial possessions. France wanted peace with England, but this was impossible as long as England and Spain were at war. So, once again, in 1762, Louis offered Louisiana to his cousin Charles III, but this time, not to *enter* the war but to *end* it. When England took Havana and invaded Florida, Spain accepted the offer. Louis truly believed that he was giving Spain something of little value. France had owned Louisiana since 1699 and had received no profit from it. In fact, France had spent huge sums of money on the territory. The king considered this loss one that would bring him little sorrow.

The treaty was kept secret and, on February 10, 1763, the Treaty of Paris was signed, ending the French and Indian War. In this treaty, Louis XV ceded to England all of Canada and everything east of the Mississippi (except the Isle of Orleans which had already been secretly given to Spain). Britain returned to Spain the Philippine Islands and Cuba, in return for both East and West Florida. (After 1763, the British settled in Florida and the portion of Louisiana east of the Mississippi. This included the territory from Baton Rouge eastward through the Florida parishes to the Perdido River [north of Lake Pontchartrain]. Great Britain divided these colonies into East and West Florida.)

The fact that New Orleans had been ceded to Spain remained unknown to the people of the city for almost two years. In truth, they were not too interested. During Kerlerec's loose administration, they had done pretty much what they wanted. They had traded with the Americans, English, Spanish, whoever suited their purposes. They weren't interested in being governed by anyone. France had been negligent in its controls, and while the people of New Orleans had no great desire for independence, they did have a great desire for non-interference.

As we leave this period of French colonialism, we find Louisiana an area with great style and little substance, relatively speaking, still in need of farmers for food supplies and products for export. The people still depended on trade for most of their other needs. The colonists of New Orleans were traders, not farmers. They preferred bargaining for their food to growing it.

The historian Joe Gray Taylor titled this period "a study in failure." This seems a trifle harsh. John Law, on the other hand, had touted Louisiana "a little Paris." A Paris it was not, but it was not too different from other infant colonies. One remarkable characteristic of the French in Louisiana was the "staying power" of their language, their customs, and their culture. Their influence on New Orleans has never been lost, though many other ethnic groups have settled in large numbers.

The feeling, the flair, and the style of the city always were, and are now, French. The love of balls, celebrations, and holidays is still part of its lifestyle. It was this lack of restraint that shocked the Spanish and surprised Americans coming into the city in the years to follow. The loose keeping of the Sabbath and the easy interpretation of religion that the French Catholics allowed themselves amazed these newcomers, who jokingly remarked that "it was caused by the humidity."

The colony had not been fortunate in its governing officers, however. Again, Joe Gray Taylor tells us, "Probably the origin of chronic corruption in Louisiana government can be traced back to the French attitude that political office was a form of property from which the holder should profit."

All of these harsh words were directed against French colonialism because the French approached Louisiana as a money-maker. It was never that, and so, in one way, it must be admitted that it was a failure. But a city *was* established, trade *was* begun, and New Orleans was a living, breathing, seductive lady, to whom much had happened. Now, the lady was to become Spanish, or so the treaty said.

Figure 15. General Alessandro O'Reilly, sent to take over Louisiana for Spain in 1769. *(Courtesy Leonard V. Huber Collection)*

40

The Spanish Period

"Seldom in history has a dominant power been so lenient with colonials of another nationality, and seldom has a ruling nationality been so completely dominated and assimilated by that held under control."[3]

The city of New Orleans was *never* Spanish, in its customs, culture, or language. Throughout the period of Spanish domination, it remained tenaciously French. The French language was spoken in schools, in business, even in the newspapers. There was never a Spanish newspaper printed in the city. The people of New Orleans never became Spanish-speaking people until the Cubans began arriving in the 1960s.

When the French colonials came to Louisiana, they brought their wives and families, and so their heritage remained intact. When the Spanish settlers came, they came in smaller numbers and the men often came alone and married Creole girls, natives of Louisiana. The language spoken in most of their homes was, therefore, French, as were the customs and traditions. The Spanish were assimilated into the already-established French way of life and made little change in the people they controlled. They were, perhaps, more sober in their Catholicism than the pleasure-loving French Creoles, but in time, the French even managed to convert them to a more lethargic religious life.

The word "Creole" derives from the Spanish *crillo*, "a child born in the colonies," according to John Chase (*Frenchmen, Desire, Good Children* . . .). Therefore, native-born Orleanians of Spanish and French descent were designated Creoles.

Only one group of Spanish settlers arrived *en masse* to stay. They were the Canary Islanders who settled in St. Bernard Parish in 1778.

---

[3]Davis, Edwin Adams, *The History of Louisiana*

Colonists migrated to Louisiana from Spanish Florida and settled in the parish called New Iberia (New Spain).

The most indelible impression left by the Spanish from their 40-year rule (1762–1800) is the Spanish style of architecture with which the Vieux Carre is stamped. Even this was the outcome of accident, not of purposeful design, as we shall see.

As to the beginning of Spanish rule, it is well to say at the outset that the change in administration was not made without a struggle. The transfer of Louisiana from France to Spain had been legalized in the Treaty of Fontainbleau on November 23, 1762, but the treaty had been kept secret to all but the Spanish. The king of France continued to act as sovereign over Louisiana.

In 1763, because of problems with the hierarchy of the Church, the Jesuits were expelled from the province of Louisiana and from all the French Empire. The Jesuit Order was disbanded throughout the world. The property of the Jesuits in New Orleans was confiscated, including land that had once been part of Bienville's plantation. The Jesuits were reinstated by Pope Pius VII in 1801, and in 1837, began the first Catholic college for boys, St. Charles College in Grand Coteau. By 1847, they had established the second college in New Orleans, the College of the Immaculate Conception. Later, the confiscation of their property (1763) was questioned by a Jesuit ex-student, Thomas J. Semmes, because the French had ordered the confiscation when, by treaty, Louisiana had already been ceded to Spain. Semmes was right, but the Jesuits wisely dropped the suit since it would have involved most of downtown New Orleans.

On April 21, 1764, Louis XV sent a letter to **Jean-Jacques Blaise D'Abbadie,** governor of Louisiana, informing him and the colonists of the formal transfer of Louisiana to Spain. Both governments seem to have been responsible for the delay in transferring the colony. The Spaniards felt that they needed a larger contingent of troops to take possession of Louisiana. The French Minister of State, the Duke of Choiseul, suggested that the French soldiers in Louisiana enlist in the Spanish army. Spain agreed, and the obstacle seemed to be overcome.

When the colonists heard, in October, 1764, of the cession to Spain, they were despondent. They had had a great affection for France in spite of the infamous Louis XV. But more than that, they had enjoyed the *laissez-faire* type of government and the freedom of trade they had been allowed. (Many colonists left West Florida when it was ceded to England in 1763 and came to New Orleans hoping to remain Frenchmen.) A meeting of the Superior Council was held, to which prominent colonists were called to discuss the event. At the meeting, the attorney-general, Nicolas Chauvin de Lafrenière, suggested that a representative be sent to Louis XV to ask him to revoke the act of cession. Jean Milhet, a wealthy merchant, was sent on this mission.

In Paris, Milhet visited Bienville, then 84 years old. Together, they called on the Duke of Choiseul who refused to let them see the king, expressed his sympathy, and told them that the cession was a *fait accompli*. Milhet was not to return to New Orleans until 1767 to report the news. For a while, the citizens of New Orleans had begun to hope that the Spanish king would not take possession of the colony. He had not appreared anxious to do so. More than three years had passed since the Treaty of Fountainbleau, and no Spanish official had yet appeared on the scene.

DON ANTONIO DE ULLOA

On July 10, 1765, however, **Don Antonio de Ulloa** wrote to the Superior Council of New Orleans from Havana to inform that body that he had been appointed governor of Louisiana by Charles III of Spain. He arrived in New Orleans March 5, 1766, and was greeted by the French Commandant and the acting governor, **Charles Philippe Aubry**, who had succeeded D'Abbadie on his death in February, 1765.

Ulloa did not assume authority in a public way. He had with him only two companies of infantry (90 men), since he had anticipated many enlistments among the French soldiers in Louisiana, but the French troops were unwilling to enlist in the Spanish army.

This remained one of the problems that plagued Ulloa throughout his stay in the colony. Another important obstacle to good relations with the colonists was the decision of the Spanish court to enforce typical Spanish mercantile restrictions on trade in Louisiana. Two such decrees (in 1766 and 1768) prohibited trade with any country except Spain and its colonies. The colonists had long been free of such restrictions and were unwilling to submit to these hardships. A third conflict arose when Ulloa offered to exchange French currency for Spanish at 75% of its value, a ratio established by Louis XV. The colonists were furious, but powerless.

Never during his stay did Ulloa have sufficient funds to operate the government of the colony. The allotment was set at 150,000 *pesos* annually for the Louisiana colony from the treasury of New Spain. Repeatedly, Ulloa wrote letters, pleading for additional funds, as he was unable to pay salaries to those in the employ of the Spanish government, but funds were not forthcoming.

Trouble between Ulloa and the Superior Council arose almost as soon as he arrived in Louisiana. Acting on Aubry's advice, Ulloa refused to present his credentials to the Superior Council, even when they demanded to see them. The document of transfer, turning over the government of the colony to Ulloa, was signed by Governor Aubry only, and not in the capital city of New Orleans, but at the fort of La Balize at the mouth of the river. No member of the Superior Council was present.

All this was done in La Balize because Aubry warned Ulloa that the transfer could never be made in New Orleans without a large contingent of troops. Spanish control of the colony would not be recognized, in any case, until the Spanish flag flew over the Place d'Armes in New Orleans, but the status of the colony was never in doubt after 1764. The colonists reconized Ulloa as their governor, even if they did so half-heartedly. The use of Spanish currency was proof enough that the colony was a Spanish possession. Nevertheless, the colonists were prepared to oppose Ulloa and the Spanish government in every way possible.

Actually, Ulloa was a man of merit, a former naval officer and a distinguished scientist. Until 1764, he had been in Peru as governor of Huancavelica, where he undoubtedly met the Peruvian Marchioness d'Abrado, whom he married by proxy. The historian Gayarré describes Ulloa as a man "of medium stature, with stooped shoulders and pale cheeks . . . tactless, highly sensitive to criticism . . . retiring and unsociable." It is no wonder the Creole colonists considered him haughty and "strange." Even today, it seems strange that he waited in the fort at La Balize for seven months for his Peruvian bride without once coming to the city of New Orleans. In truth, it was through Aubry that Ulloa governed Louisiana during his entire stay in the province.

In 1767 Milhet returned from France with the story of his failure. This news, in addition to the hostility aggravated by the trade restrictions, brought about an event known in history as the Revolution of 1768.

It began with the signing of a petition by 560 influential colonists, asking the Superior Council to order Ulloa to present to this body his credentials, proving the legitimacy of the Spanish regime he headed, or face banishment as a disturber of the peace. Ulloa refused, considering himself the legal governor and therefore not subject to the demands of the Council. An impasse had been reached.

After this, armed bands of colonists, including Acadians and Germans led by Joseph Villere from the outskirts of the city, arrived in New Orleans. Fearing for Ulloa's safety, Aubry convinced the governor to take refuge on board the Spanish frigate *El Volante* anchored in the New Orleans harbor, while Aubry tried to calm the rebels. On November 1, 1768, Ulloa set sail for Havana. Legend has it that his ship was set adrift by drunken patriots returning from a wedding party. The Spaniard was thus expelled from the colony, and the revolution appeared to have succeeded.

The colonists continued in their opposition. They had the Superior Council draw up a "Representation to Louis XV" which was carried to France by Ensign Bienville de Noyan (a nephew of Governor Bienville) and other delegates, but the king refused to see them. It was becoming clear that Louis had disowned his subjects in Louisiana. The colonists in

New Orleans, now numbering only 3,190, including slaves, could no longer resist the power of the king of Spain.

GENERAL O'REILLY

At this time, **Don Alejandro O'Reilly**, an Irish soldier of fortune, an exile from religious persecution in his native country, now in the service of the king of Spain, was appointed governor and captain general of the province of Louisiana. O'Reilly is called the Father of Spanish Louisiana.

O'Reilly had an extraordinary military background. Because of his outstanding service in the Seven Years' War, and later in the reoccupation of Havana in 1763, he was recalled to Madrid. With his excellent record, he was made lieutenant-general on July 15, 1767. Such zeal as he had exhibited in the service of King Charles did not go unnoticed. The king believed him the right man to suppress the rebellion in Louisiana.

King Charles sent O'Reilly with a *cedula* appointing him commander of the expedition to bring Louisiana to order, "to take possession of it in my Royal Name . . . and punish according to the law, the instigators and accomplices of the uprising which occurred in New Orleans . . . I give you . . . such power and jurisdiction as shall be necessary . . . ."

O'Reilly arrived at La Balize on July 20, 1769, on a frigate, accompanied by 20 other ships and 2,056 soldiers, 46 cannons of various sizes, mortars, a large supply of arms and ammunition, medical provisions and food. He sent his aide-de-camp, Lt. Col. Bouligny, with a letter to Charles Aubry, notifying the French of his arrival, informing Aubry of his Royal commission to take possession of the colony, and asking his cooperation. Bouligny was greeted in New Orleans by a large crowd, including three Spanish officers who had been detained by the colonists as security for debts owed them by the Spanish government. He proceeded to Aubry's home to deliver the letter. Aubry now promised his cooperation and assembled the colonists in the Plaza to inform them of O'Reilly's arrival.

Three representatives were sent to greet O'Reilly. They promised submission, explained that their rebellion had been brought about by the "severe nature of Don Antonio and the subversion of privileges which had been assured in the act of cession . . . ."[4] Then, they asked for time sufficient for those who wished to emigrate, to do so.

O'Reilly replied that he wanted to become well informed about the events that had occurred before he acted. The men dined with him and then returned to New Orleans, full of admiration for O'Reilly.

[4]David Ker Texada, *Alejandro O'Reilly and the New Orleans Rebels,* 29

During the night of August 16, 1769, the Spanish convoy moved quietly into the city of New Orleans, and the colonists were awakened on the 17th by cannon shot from the flotilla. When they arrived at the river, they found the Spanish fleet at anchor.

On August 18, possession was taken in the Plaza. O'Reilly walked to the center of the Square and presented Aubry with the letter from the king. Aubry placed the keys of the city at O'Reilly's feet. Spanish flags were run up in all parts of the city, and artillery was fired. Then all retired to the Cathedral to say a *Te Deum* in thanksgiving.

Following the ceremony, O'Reilly consulted privately with Aubry, demanding that he prepare a complete account of the events surrounding the rebellion. The French governor, obeying the orders of his new sovereign, wrote a complete report. As a result of his information, O'Reilly arrested Lafrenière, Foucault, Noyan, and de Boisblanc, members of the Superior Council; and Braud, the printer. Each of these men was summoned separately to his home. Later, Marquis, an officer of the troops; Doucet, a lawyer; Petit and Mazant, planters; Jean and Joseph Milhet, Caresse, and Poupet, merchants, were also arrested.

According to historian Gayarré, Joseph Villere, who had led the Germans to join the rebels, was on his plantation on the German Coast when he received a letter from Aubry saying that he had nothing to fear from O'Reilly and that he could come to New Orleans in perfect safety. Villere descended the river to New Orleans and found himself arrested. Outraged, he struck the Spanish officers, who pierced him with bayonets. He lingered and later died in prison, awaiting trial (Gayarré's *History of Louisiana II*, 304).

Without a jury or a hearing in public court, in keeping with Spanish law, the defendants were interrogated separately. Their sentences were pronounced by O'Reilly October 24, 1769, and on the following day, October 25, five rebels: Lafrenière, Noyan, Caresse, Marquis, and Joseph Milhet were shot to death by Spanish soldiers, there being no hangman in the colony. Petit was to be imprisoned for life; Mazant and Doucet were sentenced to imprisonment for ten years; de Boisblanc, Jean Milhet and Poupet to imprisonment for six years, all in the Castle Morro in Havana. Braud, the printer of the petition, was discharged. Shocked into submission, the rest of the colonists gave up the fight.

The French Creoles never forgave O'Reilly for his act. Henceforth, he was to be known by them as "Bloody O'Reilly," and as such he has taken his place in the history of Louisiana.

The question of whether O'Reilly was cruel or justified in his treatment of the rebels continues to be a matter of dispute among historians. Francois Barbé-Marbois said that "King Charles secretly disapproved of these acts of outrage." Historian Judge Francois-Xavier Martin said that "posterity . . . will doom this act to public execration. No necessity demanded, no policy justified it."

On the other hand, if it *was* treason, it was at the time considered a most grievous crime by *all* nations, and punishable by death.

Historian Henry Edward Chambers puts the blame for the execution of the rebels on the shoulders of Governor Aubry. O'Reilly, he says, came to the colony with orders from the king to suppress the rebellion and punish the leaders. "(He) . . . was compelled . . . to make an example of the leaders . . . lest other Spanish colonials follow the Louisiana example." Aubry, he feels, kept Ulloa and the colonial leaders from coming to terms. "He inserted a wedge of mutual antagonism," thus causing a rebellion.

O'Reilly began his administration by abolishing the Superior Council and substituting a Cabildo, composed of six *regidors* (council-men) and *alcaldes* (mayors), an attorney-general and a clerk, all presided over by the governor. The laws of Spain were substituted for those of France.

Under his Cabildo Governing Council of Louisiana, O'Reilly abolished Indian slavery. He permitted many French officials to stay in office, and helped farmers by establishing land titles. Under O'Reilly's Ordinance of 1770, a system of homesteading land was established, allowing an owner a parcel of land 6 to 8 arpents fronting on a river or bayou, and 40 arpents in depth, if he occupied the land and enclosed it within three years. The front of the land was to be cleared.

During his rule, roads and levees were installed. The only religion tolerated was the Catholic religion, which worked no hardship on the Creole Catholic population. Medicine was divided into three disciplines during his term: Medicine proper, Surgery, and Pharmacy. (An Ursuline nun was the first pharmacist in Louisiana.)

LUIS DE UNZAGA

As we can see, O'Reilly's administration was not without merit. He left Louisiana in 1770, turning over the reins of government to **Don Luis de Unzaga y Amezaga,** a successful, well-liked man whose rule was mild and paternal, as was that of every other governor during the next three decades of Spanish domination. Unzaga married a Creole native of Louisiana. As governor, he did whatever was needed to make the colony successful. Expediency was the byword of the Spanish Domination. Unzaga winked at smuggling and allowed the British traders to have commerce with the Spanish settlers along the Mississippi, because the colony needed what they supplied.

During Unzaga's administration, the American Revolution began. Unzaga helped the colonists in their struggle for independence of British control by conniving for the purchase of arms and ammunition for the Americans in New Orleans. He also beefed up the defenses in Louisiana, in case the British had any idea of trying to move in.

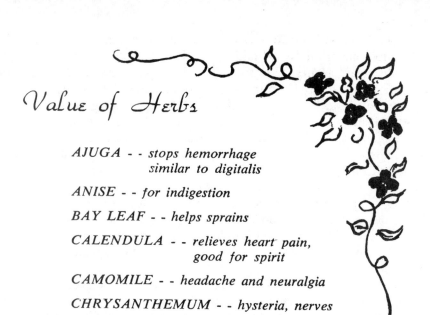

Value of Herbs

AJUGA - - stops hemorrhage
        similar to digitalis

ANISE - - for indigestion

BAY LEAF - - helps sprains

CALENDULA - - relieves heart pain,
        good for spirit

CAMOMILE - - headache and neuralgia

CHRYSANTHEMUM - - hysteria, nerves

DILL - - for soothing sleep

LAVENDER - - makes wash white

MARJORAM - - convulsions

OREGANO - - reduces rheumatic swelling

PEPPERMINT TEA - - for nausea

PARSLEY - - removes smell of garlic

ROSEMARY - - is a disinfectant

RUE - - for vision

SHALLOT - - for strength

SAGE - - helps nerves, puts fever to flight

VIOLETS - - skin disorders, roots used
        as a purgative.

SISTER XAVIER, O.S.U.
1st woman pharmacist in U.S.A.
Old Ursuline Convent

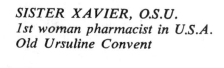

Figure 16. Value of Herbs.

One of the most well remembered Spanish immigrants to come to New Orleans during this period was **Don Andres Almonester y Roxas**, who came from Andalusia, Spain, in 1769, at the age of 44. A widower, whose wife and child had died in Spain, he had been appointed Royal Notary for the king of Spain. At his first meeting with the Cabildo (Council), he was also appointed clerk and notary to Governor Unzaga and his Intendant, and Royal Notary for Louisiana. Almonester was later to prove himself a real estate genius, New Orleans' greatest benefactor, and was to become the father of the celebrated Baroness Pontalba.

DON BERNARDO DE GALVEZ

In 1777, **Don Bernardo de Galvez** took over the duties as governor. Galvez was only 21 years old, a member of an influential family, and another Spanish governor to marry a Creole girl from Louisiana, Felicie de St. Maxent d'Estrehan. He proved himself to be extraordinarily heroic and admirable. He allowed great freedom to the colonists in their commerce, and gave help openly to the American Revolutionists. Spain declared war on England May 8, 1779, and on July 8, Charles III authorized his Louisiana subjects to take part in the war.

With a small fleet and an army of 1,430 men, Galvez led successful attacks against the British outposts at Baton Rouge and Natchez, capturing Fort Manchac along the way. In 1780, he conquered Mobile, and then undertook a lengthy attack against Pensacola. The English commander capitulated May 9, 1781, an act by which the province of West Florida was acquired by Spain.

The Treaty of Peace was signed in Paris, January, 1783, acknowledging the independence of the United States, with a southern boundary line of 31 degrees latitude. The description was important, since it became the dividing line between the United States and the Spanish colonies. Both Floridas thus passed to Spanish control.

In 1785, Galvez was made captain-general of Cuba, Louisiana, and the two Floridas. The same year, he succeeded his father as viceroy of Mexico. Galvez died in Mexico in 1794, at the age of 38. He remains one of the most romantic figures in colonial Louisiana history. A statue of Galvez stands at the foot of Canal Street.

Don Esteban Rodriguez Miro succeeded Galvez in 1785. He, too, married a native Creole girl, Marie Celeste Elenore de McCarty. It was during Miro's time that the 5,000 French Acadian exiles began arriving in Louisiana. During the French and Indian War, they had refused to swear allegiance to England, and had therefore been exiled. They were shipped to different points along the Atlantic coast and to far-flung ports of England and France. At one port in France, 375 families arrived (1,574 people).

Since the Spanish needed farmers to provide food for the colonists in Louisiana, bowing once again to expediency, they transported the Acadians on Spanish ships from the ports of France, to make their homes in Louisiana. The Acadians settled in the Lafourche-Teche area, where they would become substantial farmers and permanent inhabitants of the region. The Spanish gave them land grants, livestock, and grain to begin their new lives in southwest Louisiana. To Louisiana, they brought warmth and gaiety, love of home and family, and a love of the land. Like the Germans, they provided food for the tables of the colonists. But unlike the immigrants who eventually amalgamated, they stayed to themselves in the bayou country, working their land and establishing their homes. They spoke almost exclusively to one another, using the 17th century French of their forefathers. Few of them spoke anything but French until the First World War.

THE DISASTROUS FIRES

In 1788, during Miro's administration, the first of two terrible fires in New Orleans occurred. On Good Friday, March 21, 1788, Don Vincente Jose Nunez, the military treasurer, was in his private chapel in his residence on Chartres Street near St. Louis. It was a very windy day, and a candle fell from the altar, setting the chapel on fire. Flames spread, engulfing the entire city. Residences and business places burned to the ground. The fire spread around the Plaza, igniting the town hall, the arsenal, the parish church, and the quarters of the Capuchins, all of which disappeared. Prisoners were released from jail, just in time to escape the flames. In the morning, tents covered the plaza and the levee, and only chimneys remained of the 856 buildings that had been lost. Nearly half the town was in ashes.

Six years later, in 1794, some children, playing on Royal Street, accidentally set fire to a hay store. Within three hours, 212 stores and houses had burned down. The new buildings that had been built at the bottom of the Plaza escaped, but only two stores were left standing, and once again, the levee and the Plaza became camping grounds for the city's inhabitants.

From this time on, buildings were erected with sturdier material. The tile roof came into general use. Homes now displayed Spanish-American features, and the beauty of the town, as well as its safety, was improved. The new buildings stood shoulder to shoulder with party walls, each a different color of stucco over brick. The overall effect was Caribbean, from which area much of the architecture was borrowed.

An ordinance had been passed that buildings of more than one story be brick. Walls were designed with lovely arcades, and patios came alive with the plangent sounds of fountains. There were ponderous doors and windows, heavy iron bolts and gratings, all adorning sturdy structures. And as a finishing touch, magnificent wrought-iron lacework decorated the balconies of the two- and three-story dwellings. The French called the inner yards "courtyards," for they were the heart, *la coeur*, of the household. The Spanish called them *patios*, a word that sounded like horses' hoofs on the cobblestones.

Charles III of Spain had died in 1788, succeeded by Charles IV, a weak and ineffectual ruler. Soon after, **Father Antonio de Sedella** was sent to Louisiana as a representative of the hated Inquisition, to introduce this tribunal to New Orleans. Governor Miro had the Commissary of the Inquisition arrested at night, put on board a ship and taken back to Spain. In his official dispatch to the Spanish government, Miro commented: "When I read the communication of that Capuchin, I shuddered . . . . The mere name of the Inquisition uttered in New Orleans would not only be sufficient to check immigration . . . but would also be capable of driving away those who have recently come . . . ."

Father Antonio (Père Antoine) returned in 1795 and spent the rest of his life in New Orleans, where he assumed the role of pastor. Although he was a thorn in the side of the hierarchy, he was much loved by his parishioners. He died in 1829 at the age of 81, mourned by Protestants and Catholics alike.

A census taken in 1788 showed Louisiana (including West Florida) to have 19,500 whites, 1,700 persons of color, and 21,500 slaves, a total of 10,000 persons over the preceding three years.

In 1789, the foundation of the new St. Louis Cathedral was laid, to be built by the munificence of Don Andres Almonester. The Cathedral, built at a cost of 100,000 pesos, was designed by the French architect Gilberto Guillemard. The central tower was built in 1819 by Benjamin Henry Latrobe to house the clock. The bell in the Cathedral is inscribed to commemorate the Battle of New Orleans in 1815. In 1825, Zapari, an Italian, decorated the interior of the Cathedral.

Labor on this and other philanthropic projects sponsored by Don Almonester was done by his slaves who were masons, carpenters, blacksmiths and brickmakers. Much of the raw material, such as lime and timber, came from his own forests.

Also, due to the generosity of Almonester, the new Charity Hospital of St. Charles, named in honor of the Spanish king, costing over 100,000 pesos, was completed in 1786. Almonester endowed it with property, rents and slaves, and drew up a list of hospital regulations which were very advanced for the day:

"The doctors must have studied at the colleges of Cadiz, Madrid, or Barcelona . . . . Special attention was to be given to the 'poor in real distress' . . . . Incurable or infectious patients were not to be admitted . . . . All patients were to be supplied with a wooden bed, a table, bed clothing and garments for hospital wear. Almonster prepared a complete list of menus, which included a ration of meat.

Treatment of disease . . . was designed to rid the body of corruption . . . and depended largely upon bleeding, sweating, blistering, purging, and vomiting."[5]

Physicians seemed to believe that the more loathsome the remedy, the quicker the cure. "Such remedies as crabs eyes, dried toads, and urine were prescribed along with mercury, arsenic, antimony, camphor, opium, ammonia, alum, quinine, calomel, epicac, hemlock, much wine and brandy, rhubarb, licorice, and myrrh."

The cost of bleeding a patient was 50¢; purging, $1; dressing a wound, 50¢; liquid medicine 25¢ to $1.[6]

The disease of leprosy reached serious proportions in the early 1780s. On Miro's recommendation, a leper hospital was built on Metairie Ridge behind New Orleans in 1785, to which Almonester contributed generously. The wild, primitive area soon came to be known as "La Terre des Lepreux," Lepers' Land. By the end of the Spanish period, the disease had almost completely disappeared.

BARON DE CARONDELET

In 1791, **Francisco Luis Hector, Baron de Carondelet,** known in Louisiana history as the "City-builder," began his administration. The civic improvements made during his term were many. A lighting system was created for New Orleans, and a night police force established, which was, necessarily, bi-lingual. To meet these expenses, a tax of $1.12½ was laid on every chimney. Consequently, the same chimney was used on all floors of a three-story house, thus stamping the Quarter, now being rebuilt after two fires, with a homogeneous feature of architecture.

Carondelet built the Carondelet Canal (later called the Old Basin Canal), with turning basin behind the present site of the Municipal Auditorium, which connected New Orleans with Bayou St. John, and thereby Lake Pontchartrain, facilitating trade with Gulf Coast cities that had been founded about the same time as New Orleans.

To guard the city against attack, Carondelet built forts, redoubts, batteries, and deep ditches around the city. He made treaties with the Indians in the area, established a policy of free trade, and began the first newspaper in Louisiana, *Moniteur de la Louisiane.*

The year 1795 saw the beginning of the granulation of sugar by

[5]Davis, Edwin Adams, *Louisiana: A Narrative History,* 148
[6]Ibid, 48

Etienne deBoré, whose plantation was about six miles above New Orleans, the site of the present Audubon Park. Sugar cane had first been introduced in 1751 by the Jesuits. From it, syrup was made and a liquor called *taffia*. Granulation now opened up a tremendous market for sugar.

In 1797, Carondelet left the city, having governed with outstanding ability. His successor, **Brigadier-General Manuel Luis Gayoso de Lemos,** died of yellow fever in July, 1799, and is the only Spanish governor buried in New Orleans.

The Spanish governors after Gayoso were **Marques de Casa Calvo**, who served as acting governor from 1799 to 1801 and **Don Juan Manuel de Salcedo**, who served from 1801 to 1803, although the Treaty of San Ildefonso had been signed in 1800, giving Louisiana back to France.

THE TREATY OF SAN ILDEFONSO — LOUISIANA RETROCEDED TO FRANCE

Napoleon Bonaparte, after his glorious campaigns of 1796 and 1797, returned to France in 1799. He gathered an army, crossed the Alps into Italy and in June, 1800, defeated the Austrian army. Peace with Austria followed, and it seemed certain that peace with England would come soon.

Napoleon now wished to revive France's empire, chiefly Louisiana, which had been ceded to Spain by Louis XV. On October 1, 1800, by the Treaty of San Ildefonso, Charles IV, king of Spain, retroceded Louisiana to France. Historians are not clear as to *why* Charles agreed, but it was a demand made by a powerful ruler with recent conquests to his credit which could not easily be denied. For whatever reason, this treaty, too, was kept secret, as peace had not yet been declared between France and England.

In October, 1801, preliminaries of peace were signed between England and France, and the retrocession of Louisiana to France became known in the United States. The news caused great excitement in the colony. Then, later, when the Peace of Amiens was signed between England and France (March, 1802), Napoleon began to prepare for the occupation and government of Louisiana.

In the last decade of Spanish rule there were forts on the four corners of the city and behind the Cathedral. Later, in the 1800s they were demolished, but at this time, there were mounted guns in each fort and a moat (either natural or man-made) and barracks for 100 men. When the forts were in use, the gates were closed at nine each night. The back gates led to the suburbs, which were almost as big as the city (200 to 300 houses). The Bayou Gate led to Gentilly, Metairie, and Grand Bayou. Metairie (meaning Little Farm) was a "moi-toi" (you and me) partnership between owner and farmer.

The streets of the Vieux Carre were wide and straight, thanks to Pauger. Houses were made of wood, until the two fires, then of brick. In the suburbs, there were generally beautiful houses belonging to people from all over the world. The Creoles dominated society and business, but within the next decade, the Americans would begin to control more trade and commerce than the Creoles. In the 1790s, there were ocean-going vessels in the river, as well as coastal schooners, barges, and pirogues (the cypress dugout canoe adapted from the Indians).

THE RIGHT OF DEPOSIT

The Right of Deposit, the right to place goods on the docks in New Orleans awaiting shipment to Europe and South America, was vital to American merchants. Spain and the Americans had been on the verge of war ever since the Treaty of Paris in 1783, when Great Britain gave the Americans the right to free navigation on the Mississippi, a right which Spain did not consider theirs to give, since the mouth of the Mississippi was in Spanish Louisiana. Hostilities grew worse, and in 1784, trade was ordered to cease between Spain and the Americans. Governor Miro, however, disregarded the orders, knowing that his colonists needed what the Americans had to sell. In this matter, he was in constant conflict with his intendant, Juan Morales.

THE TREATY OF SAN LORENZO

In 1795, Spain and America signed the Treaty of San Lorenzo, in which Spain granted Americans the right of free navigation on the Mississippi River and the right of deposit at New Orleans for three years. Although the right of deposit expired in 1798, the privilege continued until 1802, when Morales, Miro's Intendant, ordered it stopped.

FLATBOATSMEN AND KEELBOATSMEN

After the American Revolution, much of the goods coming into New Orleans and subject to the "right of deposit" was carried in on the keelboats and flatboats of the new Americans. They were called "Kaintocks" by the Creoles and they were a dirty, noisy bunch of rogues and scalawags. For over four decades, keelboatsmen were on the river, bringing flour, coffee, soap, textiles and shoes to the people of New Orleans.

They traveled in canoes, rafts, ferryboats and scows, all manpowered, or pulled by mules on the river banks. They came from Kentucky, Tennessee, Mississippi, and Ohio, areas whose population was increasing rapidly. They were strong, practical and tough. Physical strength was needed to push, pull, and maneuver the loaded ships to their destination. Flatboats were propelled with two great oars. Keelboats were moved by one long oar in the center of the boat. Crewmen also used poles to push the boat along, and it was steered by a giant rudder. These men often sold their boats *with* the goods, and then traveled back upriver on horseback, following the old Indian trail, the Natchez Trace.

Their flatboats were then broken up and the gunwales, the long fore-and-aft planks, were sold for paving streets and *banquettes*, and for house construction. The rest of the timber was sold for firewood.

Keelboatsmen had appetites to match the roughness of their trade. On reaching port, they sold their merchandise. Then, they were ready for their whiskey, women, and gambling. Dens of vice, such as those on Tchoupitoulas Street near the river, on Gallatin Street, and in the "Swamp" on Girod Street at the river's edge, supplied their needs. Fistfights were inevitable. The Creoles deplored these men. They considered *all* Americans to be like the "Kaintocks" in the beginning. And thus the battle lines were drawn between the Creoles and the Americans.

INSURRECTION IN SAINT DOMINGUE

Until now, we have used the name Santo Domingo to refer to the island of Hispaniola, discovered by Columbus in 1492 and claimed for Spain. The Spanish called their colony Santo Domingo. In the 1600s, French colonists settled the western part of the island, which Spain gave France in 1697 by the Treaty of Ryswick. The French called their colony Saint Domingue. It was a sugar-growing colony, where a bloody insurrection occurred in 1791.

The successful slave uprising was led by Toussaint L'Ouverture against the white plantation owners, whom they outnumbered, ten to one. After a Voodoo ceremony of crazed dancing and the drinking of animal blood, a half million black slaves revolted against 50,000 whites and an equal number of privileged mulattoes. Plantations were destroyed, and 2,000 white islanders were killed.

By 1804, shiploads of whites and free men of color from the island poured into New Orleans. Many of these *gens de couleur libres* were artisans, craftsmen, and sculptors, who would add to the talent and literacy of the city's population, and help to build the beautiful monuments, tombstones, and cast-iron balconies that still grace its streets. The quadroon women were to become the beautiful concubines of song and story, so desired by the Creole men of the city.

Living standards were high for those who could afford them. There were handsome houses, lavish furnishings and elegant clothes. The most important piece of furniture in the Creole household was the *armoire*. The next in importance, the iron or brass bed. In fact, part of the volunteer firemen's equipment was a large key which he wore on his belt to unlock the bed, so that it could be removed in case of fire. The *armoire* was made to come apart so that it could be taken out of the house in pieces by one man.

We might mention here some attempts at fire prevention in the period. Each house was required to have at least one good leather bucket and a ladder long enough to reach the top of the house. The first fire insurance was a *donation* of money to a volunteer fire group, in exchange for a fire mark, which the donor displayed prominently. In case of a general fire, which most fires were in those days, the volunteer firemen would concentrate their efforts on the houses displaying the fire mark of their group.

In 1798, Gayoso had three visitors from the Court of France: Louis Philippe, Duc d'Orleans, future king of France; and Duc de Montpensier; and the Comte de Beaujolais, all brothers and all great-great grandsons of the namesake of New Orleans, Philippe, Duc d'Orleans. Entertaining these guests was Pierre de Marigny de Mandeville, who arranged lavish dinners for them. A story is told that special gold tableware was used, which was thrown into the river after one such elaborate meal, indicating that no one else was worthy of using it. De Marigny placed both his home and his purse at their feet, and they accepted both. Grace King, historian, tells us that later on, Bernard de Marigny, in financial straits, appealed to the court of France for the return of some of his money.

There was a tremendous increase in the value of exports in Louisiana during the Spanish rule. In 1767, the exports consisted of indigo, deerskins, lumber, naval stores, rice, peas, beans, and tallow, valued at $250,000 annually. By 1770, the yearly total had risen to $600,000, and by 1802, had multiplied several times.

In 1790, wrought iron was brought from Spain. It required no painting to protect it against the elements. The date is significant because it was midway between the two fires, the last of which caused the whole town to be rebuilt, and wrought iron decoration was an outstanding feature.

By the end of the Spanish period, Louisiana was more self-sufficient in foodstuffs. Natives had also been encouraged to cultivate indigo, tobacco, flax, hemp and cotton, as commercial crops. (Périque tobacco was grown in St. James Parish only.) Louisiana was exporting 125,000 pounds of tobacco annually. Indigo production increased for a time, but later declined, because of a bug that infested it. Handling it over a period of five years had proved fatal to slaves.

The population had increased sixfold in Louisiana during the Spanish period. Settlers trickled down from the North until the end of the American Revolution, after which the trickle became a torrent. This flood of people lasted until the end of the 1700s, when the population had reached the 50,000 mark in Louisiana. Many people came from

West Florida (acquired by the British in 1763) because they did not want to be under British rule. The Acadians began coming in the 1750s and continued to come throughout the Spanish period.

It was during the Spanish period that Almonester rebuilt the St. Louis Cathedral and the Cabildo, and built the first floor of the Presbytère as a domicile for the clergy. He contributed to a retreat for lepers, and rebuilt Charity Hospital when it was blown down by a hurricane in 1779. In 1789, he gave the Ursuline nuns a chapel for their convent.

Our Spanish ancestors are to be thanked for three decades of stable government, for the city's first fire and police protection, for the Old Basin Canal, and for the first attempts made at establishing public schools in 1771. They are to be thanked for a reconstructed Vieux Carre, with its Hispano-American architecture, which is a monument to the period of Spanish domination.

Credit goes to them for roofing the Indian Market on the riverfront. The market had always been a vital place of business and continues to be today. It has always been called the French Market, although it was originally an Indian Market, roofed by the Spanish, supplied by German farmers, and later on, run by Italian vendors, a typical New Orleans amalgamation.

Figure 17. Andrew Jackson. From a miniature presented by Andrew Jackson to Edward Livingston, March 1, 1815, painted by Jean François Valle in New Orleans, by Jackson's orders.

Mr E Livingston is requested to accept this picture as a mark of the sense I entertain of his public services, and a token of my private friendship and Esteem.

Head quarters N orleans,
Mar 1st 1815
          Andrew Jackson

Facsimile of note from Andrew Jackson to Edward Livingston.

CHAPTER V

On Becoming American: 1803–1815

On April 30, 1803, when Thomas Jefferson was America's third president, the territory of Louisiana was purchased from Napoleon Bonaparte, consul of France, by the United States for the sum of $15,000,000. This event took place before any ceremony had officially made Louisiana French again. It wasn't until November 30, 1803, that the Spanish flag was lowered and the French flag raised in the Place d'Armes, although the transfer of Louisiana from Spain to France had taken place three years earlier, and another transfer had since been arranged. On that same day, (November 30, 1803), Pierre de Laussat, colonial prefect of France, was given the keys to the city and put in possession of the province for France. Although de Laussat's actions were purely symbolic (coming after the sale of Louisiana to the United States), he nonetheless abolished the Spanish Cabildo, appointed the Frenchman Etienne Boré mayor, appointed two adjuncts, and created the first city council of New Orleans, consisting of ten members.

Just twenty days later, on December 20, 1803, the same ceremony was repeated in the Place d'Armes. This time, however, the French flag was lowered and the flag of the United States took its place. William C. C. Claiborne and General James Wilkinson (acting for the president of the United States), and Pierre de Laussat, (representing France), signed the papers making the Louisiana Territory a part of America. Claiborne was to be in charge of civil affairs; Wilkinson in control of the army.

In one year, 1803, New Orleans had been under three flags: first, Spanish, then French, and then American.

Circumstances leading up to and surrounding the purchase are interesting and complex. To begin with, Napoleon, having recently lost the island of Saint Domingue in the Caribbean, felt that his dream of a French empire in America had ended. He feared that it would be impossible to protect·Louisiana financially or militarily if he went back to war with England, and if he couldn't protect Louisiana against the British, he preferred America to have it. Also, badly in need of money for his European wars, he was receptive to entreaties by Livingston,

U.S. Minister to France, who urged him to sell the Isle of Orleans and West Florida to the United States. Napoleon, through his negotiator, Barbé-Marbois, offered to sell *all* of Louisiana, and the price was $15,000,000.

President Jefferson, without consulting Congress, agreed to the purchase, although there was a total of only $10,000,000 in the U.S. treasury at the time. This was an act which came close to causing the president's impeachment.

Further reason for Napoleon's selling Louisiana to the United States is given in his own words: "This accession of territory strengthens forever the power of the United States, and I have just given England a maritime rival that will sooner or later humble her pride."

The irony of it is that the United States had to make loans from British and Dutch banks in order to finance the purchase.

The Louisiana Territory included 827,987 square miles, which would later be divided to form 13 other states, or parts of states, in the nation. The territory extended from Canada to the Gulf of Mexico, and from the Mississippi River to the Rocky Mountains. Boundaries were in dispute, so it was impossible to give an exact size and value to the purchase, but nonetheless, it was the greatest real estate buy in history.

Throughout the territory, colonists had settled the areas along the rivers and bayous: the Mississippi, Red, Atchafalaya and Ouachita Rivers; and the Bayous Teche and Lafourche. There were, at the time of the purchase, approximately 50,000 people in the territory, excluding Indians, most of whom lived in what is presently the state of Louisiana.

In 1804, the territorial government declared all land grants after 1800 null and void, and confiscated all property given the colonists by a Spanish or French king. On March 26, 1804, Congress divided the land that had been included in the Louisiana Purchase into the Louisiana Territory and the Territory of Orleans. The Territory of Orleans consisted of the present state of Louisiana minus the Florida Parishes (which were later annexed) and an area near the Sabine River. The Louisiana Territory included the rest of the purchase.

In 1803, New Orleans was a city of just under 10,000 population, whites in the majority. The population was composed of "fiery Creoles, plain, upstanding Acadians, yellow sirens from Santo Domingo, staid and energetic men from the German Coast speaking perfect French, haughty Castilian soldiers, dirty Indians, Negroes of every shade and hue, and the human trash — ex-galley slaves and adventurers." All in all, it was a great place to live.

Four of the five forts had, by this time, fallen into disrepair. Only Fort Ferdinand remained. The city had four or five general stores, three Scottish banks, a German business firm, eight or ten commission houses opened during the Spanish period by Americans. The largest percentage of the population consisted of French and Spanish Creoles.

New Orleans was a trade center, dealing in the products of the countryside: rice, indigo, sugar, tobacco, and cotton. These were the cash crops grown for sale. Agricultural products were scarce, and vegetables were, as yet, hard to obtain and expensive.

Education in New Orleans in 1803 was poor. Few citizens could read and write. The Ursulines taught fewer than 200 students, including boarders. There were no colleges, bookstores, or libraries. Men worked as apprentices to learn their trades.

The city was devoutly Roman Catholic, but remarkably liberal in its acceptance of the many brothels, saloons, and gambling halls. Also accepted, (or ignored), was the custom of *placage*, by which white men took quadroon girls into more or less permanent concubinage and set them up in a house in the French Quarter, or adjoining the Quarter on Rampart Street.

In *Fabulous New Orleans,* Lyle Saxon wrote: "There seems to be a certain insidious chemical in the atmosphere which tends to destroy Puritanism."

Now into this community came the Americans. They were certainly not all flatboatsmen, as many of the French had formerly believed. There were East coast businessmen, southern planters and farmers, and Yankee clerks as well, very few of whom knew a word of French, and many of whom had "odd names like Smith and Jones." New Orleans was American now, a part of their country, and they had a right to settle in the Crescent City.

WILLIAM C. C. CLAIBORNE

President Jefferson had appointed William Charles Cole Claiborne as governor of the Territory of Orleans (after both the Marquis de Lafayette and James Monroe had declined). Claiborne was 28 years old when he arrived in New Orleans, a Virginian Protestant who did not speak French. He kept on hand a French and Spanish interpreter, and wisely, he did not dispense with the French-speaking Mayor Etienne Boré, though how they conversed on city problems is hard to imagine. Understandably, Boré did not enjoy his role and in six months, he resigned.

For two years, (1803–1805), Claiborne was almost a dictator in the territory. He set about learning French, translating the laws into English, and re-codifying them. In 1804, he lost his young wife, 21 years old, his daughter, his secretary, and many friends in an epidemic of yellow fever. Five years later, his second wife, also 21 at the time, perished of the same disease. He wrote to President Madison about the filth, garbage and refuse thrown into the river, which he could see from his bedroom window.

Claiborne's opinion of the people he found in New Orleans is expressed in the letters he wrote James Madison in 1804, when Madison was still Secretary of State.

January 10, 1804. "The more I become acquainted with the inhabitants of this Province, the more I am convinced of their unfitness for a representative government . . . I have discovered with regret that a strong partiality for the French government still exists . . . in some circles a sentiment is cherished that at the close of the War between England and France, the great Buonaparte will again raise his standard in this country."

January 24, 1804. "The period allowed by the Treaty for the withdrawing of the French and Spanish forces from the ceded Territory expires this day, and still little or no preparation is made for an Embarkation. The Spanish Officers have conducted themselves with great propriety . . . I cannot speak equally favourable of the French forces . . . some of these are mischievous, riotous, disorderly characters . . . added to this (is) the ignorance and credulity of the mass of the people . . . I would think it wise policy in Congress to appropriate one hundred thousand dollars annually for the encouragement of Education in Louisiana."

January 30, 1804. "On my arrival in New Orleans, I found the people very Solicituous to maintain their Public Ball establishment, and to convince them that the American Government felt no disposition to break in upon their amusements, Gen. Wilkinson and myself occasionally attended these assemblies . . . I fear you will suppose that I am wanting in respect in calling your attention to the Balls of New Orleans, but I do assure you, Sir, that they occupy much of the public mind . . ."

Joseph Dubrieul, one of the wealthiest planters in Louisiana, wrote: "It is not unknown here, after reading over Northern public papers, that the ceded territory has been described to Congress as some sort of 'Tower of Babel,' suffering from a confusion of tongues, and Louisianians as men stupefied by depotism or ignorance, and therefore unable to elevate themselves for a long time to the heights of a free constitution."

Dubrieul and others like him considered Claiborne wholly incompetent and entirely dependent on the English-speaking people for this information. He considered the governor a stranger in New Orleans, a stranger as far as the soil was concerned, its local interests, its customs, habits, and even the language of the inhabitants, and therefore without the most absolutely necessary knowledge to govern.

The city government, created by charter in 1805, provided for a mayor, treasurer, recorder, and city council of 14 aldermen. The mayor was to preside over the council and head the police force and fire department, both of which were largely voluntary. The new government did its best to clean up New Orleans. It outlawed cockfights and forbad the dumping of human waste into the river. It reorganized the police force, inspected ships for disease, added street lights and repaired roads and bridges. It purchased more fire-fighting equipment and enacted a building code. In the first decade of the American Era, however, five epidemics of yellow fever raged.

The years 1803 to 1805 constituted a **period of conversion.** The natives of New Orleans had been firmly French or Spanish. By the Louisiana Purchase, they had become American, but they needed time to adjust, to let go of their European ways, and to learn what it meant to be a part of a democracy. It was a **period of confusion.** Most New Orleanians spoke only French; their governor spoke only English. Communication was difficult, and many of the impressions Claiborne first expressed were due to that lack of understanding. Because of the language difference, there had to be an English court and a French court, an English police force and a French police force, and interpreters everywhere.

It was a period of legal confusion and conflict. The American government wished to impose British Common Law upon its new territory, the law which was practiced in England and throughout the rest of America. According to Common Law, once a precedent had been established, any similar case was decided on the basis of that precedent. New Orleanians fought tenaciously to retain their Civil Law, in which each case stood on its own merits. Under Civil Law, the courts interpreted the law and were not bound by previous decisions.

The fight for Civil Law was not just an emotional demand. The welfare of the citizens depended upon it. Their property rights, the rights of illegitimate children, the rights of the free people of color, forced heirship: all of these were protected under the Civil Code existing then in Louisiana; under Common Law, they would all have had to be re-identified.

Slaves in New Orleans could work for hire. Urbanization had made them less deferential to whites and more defiant of the French *Code Noir* which had continued to govern them during the Spanish period. And yet, the *Code Noir* gave more rights to slaves than they enjoyed anywhere else. Slaveowners could be brought to court (by other slaveowners) if they mistreated their slaves. Masters were forced to abide by the *Code Noir*.

About one-third of the Negroes in New Orleans in 1805 were free people of color (f.p.c.) who enjoyed a legal and economic status unparalleled among black people in the American slave states at the time. They had full freedom to enter into business contracts and to own and transfer property, and they had full competence in civil and criminal litigation against blacks and whites alike. If Louisiana would have lost its Civil Code and been forced to accept Common Law, all blacks would have thereafter been treated alike. Rights and privileges would have disappeared, and a revolt like the Saint Domingue uprising, would not have been difficult to imagine.

In Louisiana, unlike the rest of America, illegitimate children also had legal rights. Bastards could be legitimatized by marriage and could inherit as if born during marriage. This is directly opposed to British legal thinking, which was best expressed by Blackstone, when he said "the son of nobody inherits nothing."

The people of Louisiana fought to keep their Civil Law, and in the end, were permitted to do so. Louisiana's Civil Code of 1808 and the Code of Practices (1824) were based on Roman rather than English law. The Napoleonic Code of 1804 provided the framework, but other elements had gone into its development.

Culture shock was another experience felt by both natives and new American immigrants. Most Americans had had few business dealings with free people of color, for one thing. Americans were also not prepared for the French Creoles, who were poorly educated and provincial, but haughty and proud of their heritage. The Creoles considered themselves a breed apart, and far more cultured, with their theater and their opera, than the Americans with whom they were now doing business. They *were* different, and *cultured,* in those areas considered by them to be important. By American standards, they were culturally backwards, but the Creoles were not interested in using American standards, or being measured by them.

The Creoles, like the colony itself, were not money-makers to any great extent. Creoles like **Bernard de Marigny** could have learned much from entrepreneurs like the American **Samuel J. Peters** and the English actor **James H. Caldwell,** who in 1828, offered to buy and develop the Marigny Plantation, to build hotels, theaters, and gas works. The offer was declined. That they had the know-how to carry out such projects was later proved, not in Faubourg Marigny, but in Faubourg St. Marie, on the upriver side of Canal Street.

When the Americans began arriving in large numbers, they settled in Faubourg St. Mary, as *they* called it. They lived along the natural levee, crowding into sugar plantations that had existed for decades. In the first ten years after the Louisiana Purchase, enmity between Creoles in the Vieux Carre and Americans in the Faubourg St. Mary came alive.

CANAL STREET: NEVER A CANAL

Canal Street was laid out, 171 feet wide, 50 feet of which was allowed for a canal. It is shown in the planning stage on some old maps, but it never materialized. The canal was to tie in to the Carondelet Canal (the Old Basin Canal), which ran to Bayou St. John and then to Lake

Pontchartrain. Industrialists envisioned a river-to-lake waterway. They hoped that the lake would become important commercially, but on the New Orleans side, it never did. There *was* a drainage ditch down Canal Street for a time, but that was as close as it ever came to being a canal.

Canal Street, the widest street in the United States, became a kind of boundary line between the feuding Creoles in the Old Town and the Americans in Faubourg St. Mary. The wide median down the center was called the "neutral ground," a sign of a truce that existed, however fragilely, between the hostile residents of the two communities. In time, all medians in New Orleans came to be called "neutral grounds."

In the early territorial period, *fear of war with Spain* was another disturbing element. After the Louisiana Purchase, the Spanish soldiers were still in New Orleans, as we have seen in Claiborne's letters to Madison. They were also in the Spanish cities in and around New Orleans: Baton Rouge, Covington, and Mandeville north of Lake Pontchartrain, and Mobile and Pensacola to the east. The United States must have realized that they could not continue to hold on to New Orleans if they did not have control of West Florida. A main concern was whether or not West Florida was included in the Louisiana Purchase. At one point, the United States insisted that it was, indeed, included. (West Florida consisted of the parishes of St. Helena, the Felicianas, East Baton Rouge, and St. Tammany.) This area was inhabited by many Americans and English, who had migrated down from the thirteen colonies when West Florida was controlled by the British. Spain, however, believed that West Florida was *not* included in the Louisiana Purchase, and to make sure of this, they delayed acknowledging the transfer.

In 1810, the people living in the West Florida parishes revolted against Spain, taking over Fort San Carlos in Baton Rouge in a minor skirmish and declaring their independence from Spain. They established the West Florida Republic. The flag of the new republic was blue with a white star, and its president had the unlikely name of Fulwar Skipwith. Within six weeks, he asked to have his republic united with the Territory of Orleans. Evidently, he was too late, because Claiborne had already received orders from President Madison to take possession of West Florida. He did so, and West Florida was annexed to the Territory. Spain and Great Britain protested the annexation, but in vain.

LOUISIANA BECOMES A STATE

When Claiborne was appointed governor in 1803, the territory he was to govern was the Territory of Orleans, which was later to become part of the state of Louisiana. From the beginning, the people of the Territory of Orleans wanted statehood. They wanted the benefits of American citizenship, and they pressured Congress for help in this effort.

In 1810, the Territory of Orleans had a population of 76,500. Population of 60,000 in a territory was required for statehood. In January, 1811, Julien Poydras, the territory's delegate to Congress, proposed statehood for Louisiana. The next month, Congress authorized the territory to draw up a constitution. Delegates drew up the constitution and on April 8, 1812, Congress ratified it. It did not include the West Florida parishes, however, which had been annexed to the territory since 1810, but were added to the state by an amendment on April 14, 1812.

The Territory of Orleans became the state of Louisiana on April 30, 1812. Louisiana became the 18th star in the flag. A gubernatorial election was held and Claiborne, who had by this time endeared himself to the people of Louisiana, won easily over the Creole, Noel Destrehan. His efforts to overcome his personal losses and to win the respect of the haughty Creoles had been rewarded.

His opinion of the people had also changed. By 1812, he was quick to say that the natives of Louisiana had a natural ability, that they might not have much schooling but they were very bright, intense people who knew how to do things and knew what they were about.

Several major events in the history of the city occurred during this period:

1) Shortly after Louisiana had been retroceded to France, the Ursuline nuns became terrified that since France was now under the emperor Napoleon, the French government might not honor the Catholic Church. So great was their fear that some of the nuns left New Orleans and went to Cuba. Those who stayed, knowing New Orleans was now to become American, wrote to Thomas Jefferson, asking if they were going to be allowed to practice the Catholic religion. Jefferson wrote them a beautiful letter, allaying their fears, enumerating the many services the Ursulines had rendered in the past, and stating his wish that they would continue to serve the territory in the future. Reassured, the nuns remained.

2) The Legislative Council attempted to divide the Territory into *districts*, which they called *counties*. Municipal districts were called counties in the rest of the United States, and it seemed logical to call them that in Louisiana. From the beginning, however, boundaries of church parishes had been used to mark off municipal divisions in Louisiana. (The word parish is from the French *paroisse*, meaning an ecclesiastical division under the charge of a curate. The exact boundaries of the original parishes in New Orleans are not known.)

In 1805, the year the city of New Orleans was incorporated, counties were established in the territory. For a few years, counties and parishes existed side by side, and the courts labored under the confusion that resulted. In 1807, parishes were legalized by the Territorial Government, but not incorporated into the State Constitution until 1845, after which counties were forever abolished in Louisiana.

THE AARON BURR CONSPIRACY

3) Aaron Burr, born in 1765 and elected vice president in 1801, ended his political career when he killed Alexander Hamilton in a duel in 1804. While vice president, Burr had become a candidate in the gubernatorial election in New York in 1804 and was defeated due to Hamilton's efforts. He challenged Hamilton to a duel and killed him. The coroner declared that Hamilton had been wilfully murdered by Burr. Burr fled and began recruiting an army, allegedly conspiring with Gen. James Wilkinson to wrest Louisiana and other Western states from the United States, or a part of Mexico from Spain. Thus he would set up his own country. Burr was tried for treason in 1807 and acquitted. He went to Europe, still attempting to get support for his Mexican scheme. He returned to the United States under an assumed name in 1812, and practiced law in New York until his death.

But in the summer of 1805, Burr met in New Orleans with Edward Livingston, Daniel Clark, and a group of adventurers who wanted to invade Mexico. In 1806, rumors flew about Burr's developing army. Many believed the Spanish in West Florida were working with Burr.

Claiborne accused Daniel Clark, then a United States congressman, of complicity with Burr. Clark challenged Claiborne to a duel and succeeded in wounding Claiborne, adding to the confusion of American conversion.

THE CODE DUELLO

The two duels just mentioned in the Burr story make it clear how widespread the practice of dueling was at the beginning of the 19th century. Duels could result from any accusation or breach of etiquette, real or imagined, serious or slight. Rules for fighting were spelled out in the *Code Duello*. Creoles in New Orleans never fought with fists, like the Kaintocks, but with weapons, and they were trained by weapons-masters whose academies were established on Exchange Alley. The duel was called an affair of honor. It sometimes resulted in death, but more often, the offended party's honor was satisfied by merely wounding his opponent. Under the "Duelling Oaks" at Allard Plantation, now City Park, or in Père Antoine's garden, back of the Cathedral, thousands of duels were fought, using everything from swords and rapiers to rifles and shotguns.

4) The advent of the steamboat had a lasting effect upon the lives of the people who lived along the Mississippi. Of particular interest was the maiden voyage of the steamer *New Orleans,* the first steamboat on the Western territorial waters. It was built in 1811 in Pittsburg, Pennsylvania, by Nicholas Roosevelt, pioneer in steam navigation, former associate of Robert Fulton's, and great grand-uncle of the future President Theodore Roosevelt. Nicholas Roosevelt was on board for the maiden voyage, which was eventful, to say the least. The boat, 116 feet

Figure 18. Code Duello—Rules governing "Affairs of Honor" were spelled out in the Code Duello. Many duels were fought beneath the Dueling Oaks (now City Park).

(Courtesy Leonard V. Huber Collection)

long and 20 feet wide, left Pittsburg in September, 1811, and did not arrive in New Orleans until January, 1812. Anything calamitous or extraordinary that could happen, did.

A baby was born to Mrs. Nicholas Roosevelt (daughter of architect Benjamin Latrobe) in Cincinnati, during a month's layover, while the passengers waited for the water to rise. The Earthquake of 1811, the greatest ever to strike North America, occurred, frightening the Indians and causing them to attack the steamboat. (The Indians thought the smoke-burping ship had caused the earthquake.) In the midst of all this, the ship caught fire. And when the ship landed in New Orleans in January, 1812, the captain wooed and married Mrs. Roosevelt's maid.

Until this time, there were mostly flatboats and keelboats on the river. There were few boats coming up from the mouth of the river. Now that the steamboat was invented, keelboatsmen who sold their boats with their merchandise in New Orleans could travel back upriver by steamboat, if they could afford it, or have their merchandise shipped by steamer. At last, traffic both ways on the same vessel was possible.

THE EMBARGO ACT OF 1807

5) In 1807, war was being fought on the Atlantic Ocean between England and France. Although the United States was a neutral power, its ships had repeatedly been seized by both warring nations. Appeals by President Jefferson had been made and ignored. Therefore, Congress passed the Embargo Act of 1807, prohibiting the shipment of American goods to either England or France.

Port cities like New Orleans suffered greatly because of the Embargo Act. Imports and exports dropped to one-third of their former volume. Businesses closed. Smuggling resulted. By 1812, the injustices of the British in impressing American seamen, blockading American ports, and encouraging Indian attacks on settlers moving westward led to American involvement in the European war. In addition, War Hawks in Congress were convinced that victory over the British would win Canada and Spanish Florida for the United States. New England states were opposed to the United States' entry in a war for which it was ill-prepared. Nevertheless, within days after Louisiana became a state, the United States declared war against England.

THE BATTLE OF NEW ORLEANS

Early in the war, the British enjoyed far more successes than the Americans. The British continued to blockade American ports. They defeated the Americans at Dearborn and Detroit, and they captured and burned Washington, D.C. In spite of Oliver Perry's victory in the Battle of Lake Erie, most Americans began to realize the state of unpreparedness of the new nation and to abandon hopes of owning Canada.

Meanwhile, in Louisiana, Governor Claiborne prepared for a defensive war. Early in 1814, General Andrew Jackson was assigned to march south to put down the Creek Indians who had been encouraged by the British to massacre white settlers on the Alabama River.

Word reached New Orleans in the spring of 1814 that the British would attack the Gulf Coast and New Orleans. In September, 1814, the British ship *Sophia* sailed into Grand Terre, the stronghold of the privateer-smuggler Jean Lafitte. The Captain had been empowered to offer Lafitte the rank of Captain in the British military and other monetary rewards if he would fight with the British against the Americans. Lafitte refused and informed Claiborne of the offer.

Stories are confused at this point. Some historians claim that Claiborne believed the buccaneer and interceded with federal authorities on his behalf. Others say that it was Claiborne, with the Committee of Defense, that sent a force of United States soldiers to bombard Grand Terre and capture Lafitte. Whatever the case, most of the buildings of Lafitte's compound and many of his ships were destroyed. Lafitte and his brother Pierre disappeared into the swamps.

JEAN LAFITTE

Lafitte had been preying on Spanish shipping and on other vessels in the Gulf since 1806 under a "letter of marque" from Latin American countries which, somehow, legalized his piracy. His base was Barataria in the swamps to the south of New Orleans.

A constitutional prohibition against the importation of slaves in 1808 played right into Lafitte's hands. At Barataria, he held slave auctions once a week, at which he sold hundreds of slaves that were then smuggled into the city. Cutting New Orleans merchants in on his profits from all merchandise made them reticent to prosecute him. At his peak, he had a mansion, a fleet of barges and 1,000 men at Grand Terre.

Hundreds of tales of Lafitte, his brother Pierre, and Dominique You, a former gunner for Napoleon Bonaparte, have been fictionalized beyond recognition, but no one doubts that the pirate was one of the most colorful characters in New Orleans history. From his blacksmith shop on Royal Street, he plotted his illegal seizures and the sale of contraband.

As early as 1813, Claiborne had issued a proclamation offering $500 reward for Jean Lafitte's capture. The brazen pirate issued his own proclamation offering $1,500 for the capture of Governor Claiborne. Pierre Lafitte was imprisoned, but Jean organized a jailbreak to free his brother.

Somewhere along the line, Jean Lafitte turned patriot. It was at this point that he passed the information on to Claiborne that the British had approached him.

Figure 19. Lafitte's Blacksmith Shop.

General Jackson was incensed that Lafitte's stronghold had been bombarded by the Americans. He was afraid that, now, the pirate would turn against the United States.

In September, 1814, Gen. Jackson defeated the British in Mobile and in October, he turned them back in Pensacola. He received letters from Claiborne explaining his poor defenses, the prevalence of spies, and other problems.

When Jackson received word in November, 1814, that British troops were gathering in Jamaica for an invasion of Louisiana, he left for New Orleans on November 22, just days ahead of the British, arriving in the city on December 2. He began at once to set up his defenses. Batteries and earthworks were erected at the Rigolets Pass, the Chef Menteur Road and the two forts below the city, one on each side of the river, thus protecting the approaches to the city by water. He then ordered troops to stand by in Mobile, Natchez, and Baton Rouge in case the British attacked by land.

He recruited every man who could bear arms. He accepted the help of the "free black" military units who were to distinguish themselves in battle. And then, he invited Lafitte and his pirates to join him in fighting the British, promising full pardons in return for their service. Lafitte and his pirates arrived with flint, muskets and other arms and ammunition.

71

Figure 20. The Battle of New Orleans, colored lithograph by John Landis, 1840.

On December 22, British forces began moving across Lake Borgne to Bayou Bienvenu and set up camp on the Villere Plantation. On the night of December 23, Jackson made a surprise attack on the weary British army. It was brilliant strategy, and the Villere Plantation was captured.

In the last week of December, the British brought in fresh troops and supplies. Jackson had recruited every available man, and put them to work building a line across Chalmette between the river and the swamp, marked off by a wall of cotton bales. Everyone came to help: Choctaw Indians, pirates, free blacks, and Creoles. By the time the British under General Sir Edward Packenham had regrouped, Jackson's line was finished. With a reinforcement of 2,000 Kentuckians, Jackson had about 6,000 men, 3,000 of whom were at Chalmette.

Packenham's first advance on December 28 met with heavy artillery fire and was stopped. Then early on the morning of January 8, 1815, when the fog lifted, the Americans, crouched behind their cotton bales, could see neat lines of brightly clad soldiers advancing in their direction, with drummers and bagpipes, weapons and ladders to scale the earthworks.

Jackson gave the order to fire, and his Kentuckians with their long rifles fired, reloaded, and fired again. The British line crumbled, Packenham reassembled his men and charged again but for the second time, the British troops were mowed down, and Packenham himself was killed. His Major General John Keane took up the leadership of the British, driving them back into battle, and once again, they were decimated, including General Keane. The British broke and ran.

When the battle ended, 2,000 British had been killed, and the American army had lost seven men. It was an unexpected and staggering victory. Shallow graves were dug for the British dead, and their wounded were treated in New Orleans hospitals and homes. On January 27, the British left New Orleans, never to return as enemies.

The Battle of New Orleans was unique in American history. It brought together people of many ethnic backgrounds of every social stratum, to fight in a common cause, the defeat of the British. Acadians from the bayous, Germans from the German Coast, slaves and free blacks, Creoles, Kentuckians, and Tennessians, and buccaneers from Barataria all manned guns under the oaks at Chalmette. It was there that they amalgamated to become the American Army in New Orleans, and proved themselves a force to be reckoned with.

Andrew Jackson, hero of the Battle of New Orleans, later became president of the United States, and led the nation into a new era of "Jacksonian democracy."

The British troops then fought against Napoleon, defeating him at Waterloo. Governor Claiborne died two years later at the age of 42. No one knows exactly what happened to Lafitte. Some say he went to South

America and fought with Simon Bolivar and others say he continued his privateering from a base in the Yucatan. It is said that he died at the age of 47 of the fever.

When news reached New Orleans that Napoleon had escaped from the island of Elba, where he had been exiled, Mayor Nicholas Girod offered sanctuary to the deposed ruler. Napoleon, however, got his army together again, was defeated again, and this time, was exiled to St. Helena. Once more, it was announced that Napoleon would be made welcome in the city. The Napoleon House on Chartres and St. Louis Streets was supposed to have been prepared for his stay, while he recruited and planned his next move. The Baratarians, including Dominique You, his former gunner, were to rescue him in a ship purchased by a wealthy group of New Orleanians, but just days before their departure, Napoleon died.

We often read that the Battle of New Orleans was the battle that was fought after the war was over, since the Treaty of Ghent, Belgium, had been signed December 24, 1814, ending the war with England. A delay in communications prevented Packenham's receiving the news, and so, his army attacked at Chalmette. The treaty, however, specified that the fighting was to continue until the treaty had been ratified and exchanged, and it was not ratified until a month after the Battle of New Orleans. Jackson declared that he would remain in New Orleans, that martial law would continue, and that the militia would be kept on the alert until official word came from Washington. On March 13, 1815, word reached New Orleans. Jackson then returned home to Nashville and the British troops left the area.

It was the Battle of New Orleans that broke America away from Europe and denied Britain's hopes for colonial possessions in the New World. The Battle of New Orleans ended an era in the city's history. Survival was no longer the city's main objective. She *had* survived. No longer a "tool of strategy" or a "pawn of empire," New Orleans was a valued port city in a growing country, willing and able to contribute to the growth and strength of the United States of America.

Progress In A Period of Peace — 1820–1860

The Medical College of Louisiana on Common Street, established in 1834, became a part of the University of Louisiana in 1847, when a law school was added. Closed during the Civil War, it later received occasional State appropriations until 1883 when it was the recipient of a huge bequest from Paul Tulane. In 1884, it became Tulane University of Louisiana. In 1894, it moved to St. Charles Ave.

(Courtesy UNO Library)

Figure 21. Canal Street in 1850, from Chambers' History of Louisiana, *1925.*

(Courtesy Leonard V. Huber Collection)

CHAPTER VI

Progress In A Period of Peace — 1820–1860

From 1810 until the Civil War, New Orleans was the largest city west of the Appalachians. Its population tripled in the first seven years that it was an American city (1803–1810). In the next 50 years, the city enjoyed a period of growth, expansion, prosperity and change. New Orleans became a boom town in a period of peace, reaching for the fulfillment of its destiny.

All favorable circumstances came together between 1820 and 1860 to make the city grow and prosper. The invention of the cotton gin in 1793 and the granulation of sugar in 1795 had made these two products inexpensive and available to all. Their production increased a hundred fold, creating a plantation aristocracy in the South. By 1860, 2,000,000 bales of cotton were crossing New Orleans wharves annually. The coming of the steamboat presaged a whole new era of transportation and trade. The river became a highway for steamboats laden with cotton and sugar and other cash crops on their way to Europe and South America, and with manufactured goods on their way back.

People of all nationalities and colors crowded the levees and markets, enjoying the new availability of flour, meat, lard, grain, agricultural products, game and seafood of all kinds. Ships arrived with building materials, lumber, pipes, and lead. The wharves were lined for miles with steamers, schooners and flatboats.

STEAMBOATS

For a brief time, the inventor of the steamboat, Robert Fulton, and his partner, Robert Livingston, (the American negotiator for the Louisiana Purchase) enjoyed a complete monopoly of steamboat commerce on the waters of the West, a privilege they had wrested from the territorial government. In 1814, however, the monopoly was put to the test. Captain Henry Shreve arrived in New Orleans in his own steamer, the *Enterprise*, and the ship was seized by court order. General Jackson was in New Orleans at the time, preparing to defend the city

Figure 22. Keelboats, flatboats and steamboats carried merchandise to New Orleans for decades following the American Revolution.

against the British. He sent Captain Shreve and the *Enterprise* upriver for supplies, thereby temporarily averting a showdown. Later, however, in April, 1817, by a court order, the Livingston-Fulton monopoly was ended forever.

THE STEAMBOAT ERA

The Golden Age of Steamboating on the Mississippi lasted only 50 years, from 1820 to 1870. But in those years, steamboats won a unique and revered place in American folklore. Authors, poets, and songwriters have made them the settings of their works, and with good reason. They were as ornate as wedding cakes. They rivaled the finest hotels of the times, boasting bars, barber shops, orchestras, lounges, restaurants with gasoliers and the finest china, carpeting and even their own newspapers. The tall, stately vessels gleamed white in the sun, churning through the muddy Mississippi with their twin paddlewheelers and their double smokestacks.

Rooms on steamboats were called staterooms because they were named for states that existed in the period.

The captain ruled his boat like a king; the pilot knew every snag and shoal place in the ever-changing river; and the engineer was able to keep the engines churning in spite of all kinds of difficulties. When the steamboat whistle sounded, townspeople rushed to the riverbanks to watch, as goods and passengers embarked and disembarked.

78

Some steamers were of prodigious size. The *Henry Frank* deposited its cargo of 9,226 bales of cotton at the New Orleans levee on April 2, 1881, a record never broken. Hundreds of draymen readied their teams and their "floats," or drays, to haul away the flood of merchandise brought downriver on the steamers. Levees were lively with peddlers, women vendors, beggars, and machine pitchmen. According to J. Dallas, *The Levee—Third Municipality in 1854,* "the busy hum of labor, voices of every tongue . . . boxes and bundles, pork and bananas, mules and beautiful women, Yankees and ruffians, Indians and Dutchmen, Negroes and molasses, all huddled together in Babel-like confusion, presenting a picture of life and abundance no where else to be seen in the world."

The list of riverboat passengers included businessmen, vacationers, and the inevitable gamblers, who made or lost a fortune at the felt card tables of the salons.

Sidewheelers gave way to sternwheelers, which were sturdier, simpler, and more economical to operate, even if they *were* less beautiful. Steamers that served regular routes were called packets.

During the Civil War, steamboats were replaced by gunboats, and after a brief resurgence following the war, were replaced almost entirely by the faster, more functional railroads.

Showboats were floating theaters, offering "clean" shows for the whole family. There were songs, dances, and dramatic scenes enacted. The first showboats were keelboats and flatboats that drifted downriver with troupes of players. Every showboat had a calliope that called river dwellers to the docks, where the actors gave a "sample" of the treats in store for those who had the price of admission.

Eugene Robinson's Floating Palace of the 1890s consisted of a museum, a menagerie, an aquarium, and an opera. Actors often dropped a line to "fish" between performances, and more than once, a player missed his cue while landing a catfish.

The Showboat operator usually sent an advance man to announce the ship's coming. Although the movie, *Showboat,* depicted a self-propelled vehicle, showboats were usually towed into port.

BANKING INSTITUTIONS

The growing business activity in the port city caused a growth in the number of banking houses, insurance companies, commission houses, and cotton and sugar factories. As early as 1811, the Bank of New Orleans and the Louisiana Planters Bank were established. By 1827, there were five banks in the city, one a branch of the United States Bank. They were financed by banking institutions in England and in the Northeast.

FAUBOURG STE. MARIE

After the two disastrous fires in the Vieux Carre, Don Beltram (Bertrand) Gravier decided to subdivide his plantation upriver of Canal Street and sell it for residential lots. Gravier named the suburb Faubourg Ste. Marie, after his wife's patron saint, and it was the first suburb in New Orleans. (Today's Central Business District). Since Americans populated this suburb, it also became known as the American Sector.

The Americans had come to New Orleans for one reason: to make money. They were enterprising and determined to succeed. They circumvented morality and avoided the penalties of the law, focusing their energies on becoming rich. The Creoles, who enjoyed the leisure of aristocracy, and were lethargic both by heredity and environment, scorned their American competitors on the "uptown" side of Canal Street.

FAUBOURG MARIGNY

On the downriver, or "downtown" side of the Vieux Carre, the plantation of the millionaire playboy, Bernard de Marigny, was subdivided in the early 19th century, and began developing into a suburb in the 1820s and 1830s.

Bernard de Marigny was the son of Pierre Philippe de Marigny, who had accumulated a fortune in the service of Spain, and the grandson of Antoine Philippe de Marigny. He is called in his obituary, the "last of the Creole Aristocracy, one who knows how to dispose of a great fortune with contemptuous indifference." In 1803, when he was 15 years old, he inherited seven million dollars, but he squandered much of it away gambling, entertaining, and enjoying life. He was a raconteur and an incessant gambler, who brought the game of "hazards" to the city, naming it "le crapaud," meaning toad, or frog, because of the position the players assumed while playing it.

He subdivided his beautiful Faubourg Marigny and even named one of the streets "Craps," because of his passion for the game. Later, however, the street name was changed to Burgundy, to relieve a source of embarrassment in the delivery of mail to four churches on the street. Bernard de Marigny died at the age of 83, in a two-room apartment with only one servant.

FRENCH CREOLE PLANTATION CULTURE

The stories of two other colorful Americans of French descent are classic examples of the extravagant, wealthy characters who were part of this Creole plantation culture.

Gabriel Valcour Aime lived from 1798 to 1867. In the 1830s he rebuilt a plantation in St. James Parish left him by his father, which dated back to the 1790s. Aime was a scientist, planter, philosopher and financier, with an income of well over $100,000 annually. He could serve a ten-course meal, with everything ranging from fish to coffee, wine and cigars, all from his own plantation. He led the way in scientific experimentation with sugar cane culture. He also operated a private steamboat from New Orleans for the use of his guests. He became a recluse after his son's death from yellow fever, and he died of pneumonia in 1867.

His estate, which was of Louisiana Classic design, was set in the heart of a 9,000-acre plantation. Facing it from a distance, one could see a series of lagoons with stone bridges, gardens where peacocks preened, and wooded areas with rabbits, deer and kangaroos. The first floor of his home was set out in a diamond design of black and white marble. The second floor was made of stone. There were three great stairways of marble, and secret stairways inside the walls. His mansion was called Petit Versailles, an appropriate title for the property of a gentleman referred to as the Louis XIV of New Orleans. The home burned down in the 1920s.

Charles J. Durande was a Creole whose displays of opulence, as well as his life itself, border on the fictitious. And yet, they are so oft-related and so akin to the outlandish deeds of Marigny and Aime as to make us willing to suspend our disbelief.

Arriving in St. Martinville from France in 1820, already an enormously wealthy man, Durande became the owner of thousands of acres of plantation land, which was to be even more valuable later on when it was planted to sugar cane. He built a magnificent home on Bayou Teche and an allée of pine and oak trees that extended from the bayou to his mansion, which he called Pine Alley.

After the death of his first wife, who had borne him 12 children, he became inconsolable. He visited her grave each day, swore never to marry again, and even had an iron statue of himself, kneeling, placed before her tomb. Within a year, however, Durande had remarried and, by his second wife, he fathered another dozen children.

In 1850, as the story goes, when two of his daughters were to be married on the same day, he had imported from China many huge spiders, which he set loose along the allée of trees a few days before the wedding, so that they might spin cloudlike webs across the canopy of the natural arcade, clouds which Durande then had sprinkled with gold and silver dust by a number of young slaves armed with bellows.

Now the 2,000 guests arrived, their gilt-decorated carriages rolling on Persian rugs spread beneath the cathedral nave of sparkling webs that floated above them in the breeze.

During the Civil War, Pine Alley was devastated. The slaves ran away, the Union army stripped the mansion and ruined the crops. The family scattered, and the house began to deteriorate. Some years ago, it was completely demolished. Of the three-mile alley, only a mile remains, leading back from Louisiana Highway 86. Still beneath a cathedral nave, the effect enhanced by the narrowness of the alley and the height of the trees, the road leads to nothing.

LAFAYETTE'S VISIT

In 1825, the Marquis de Lafayette visited New Orleans, an event that would long be remembered in the city. The legislature appropriated $15,000 to furnish an apartment in the Cabildo for the use of the Revolutionary War hero. He arrived on the steamboat *Natchez* from Mobile. The militia passed in review before him, and he was feted in Caldwell's American Theater and the Théâtre d'Orleans.

CREOLES vs AMERICANS

Between 1825 and 1830, the number of merchants doing business in the city spiraled from 60 to 272. The number of taverns increased over 70%, a good sign of the prosperity and ebullient spirits of the times. The most impressive gains were made in the Faubourg St. Mary.

Within a few years after the Americans began to settle in the area, the value of the property equaled that of the Vieux Carre. The Vieux Carre was the retailing center of the city, but importers, exporters and brokers proliferated in the American Sector.

Competition between the Creoles and the Americans manifested itself in many ways. The Creoles objected to the use of English as the official language in the city and to the courts showing favoritism to the Americans in their decisions. The Americans, on the other hand, complained that all civic improvements were being made in the Vieux Carre and none in the suburbs.

Each sector had its own public square: The Place d'Armes (later, Jackson Square) in the Vieux Carre; Lafayette Square in the American Sector. Each had its opulent residential avenue: Esplanade in the Vieux Carre; St. Charles Avenue in the American Sector. Between 1830 and 1850, magnificent structures rose to change the skyline of the city: In the American Sector, the St. Charles Hotel, two blocks above Canal Street; City Hall (now Gallier Hall) on St. Charles Avenue; the University of Louisiana on Common Street; St. Patrick's Church on Camp Street; and the new Custom House at the foot of Canal Street. In the Vieux Carre, the opulence was matched by the St. Louis Hotel on St. Louis Street; the United States Mint at Esplanade Avenue and the river; the Pontalba Buildings, flanking the Place d'Armes; and the St. Louis Cathedral, rebuilt in 1850.

Figures 23 and 24. The Old French Opera House, built on the corner of Bourbon and Toulouse in 1859, burned down in 1919 (upper). The Second Municipality Building (later the City Hall; today, Gallier Hall) was built on Lafayette Square, also by Gallier in 1845.

19TH CENTURY ARCHITECTS

The Irish architect James Gallier, Sr. was responsible for many of the magnificent edifices mentioned above, which are still revered today. He designed the *St. Charles Hotel* to outdo any other hotel in the world in size and extravagance. It was completed in 1837 at a cost of $600,000. With its white dome, its cupola and flagstaff aloft at 203 feet, it was a commanding landmark, visible for miles upriver and down. Under its rotunda, slave auctions were held regularly.

The Second Municipality Hall, later City Hall (today, *Gallier Hall*) was also designed by Gallier, in 1845. This building was the seat of government in 1852. Its Ionic portico and Greek details can be matched only by temple-type buildings and churches in the Northeast.

The Custom House, an A. T. Wood design, with its colossal columns, is said to have the finest Greek Revival interior in America. Work was begun in 1848, but it was not completed until 1881.

St. Patrick's Church at 724 Camp Street was built by the architect James H. Dakin, for $115,000. It was built on the site of the small wooden church, which it replaced in 1838. It far surpassed every attempt at Gothic architecture on this side of the Atlantic.

The Dakin brothers, James Gallier, Sr., and Henry Howard were primarily responsible for the spread of the Greek Revival style of architecture in America. New Orleans Greek Revival architecture is comparable in quality to that found anywhere in the United States.[7]

THE BEGINNINGS OF THEATER IN NEW ORLEANS

Contrary to popular belief, the first theater in New Orleans was started in 1792 by two brothers from Paris, Jean-Louis Henry and Louis-Alexandre Henry. Their theater was the only theater in New Orleans for 15 years.[8] Louis, a carpenter, built the theater at a site approximately where 732 St. Peter Street is today, and acted in the cast for several years. Jean supplied the capital for the venture and became the business manager.

According to New Orleans archives, notarial acts were signed in June, 1791, transferring a piece of property measuring 64 feet × 128 feet from Louis McCarty to Louis Henry. Henry then sold half the lot, retaining a piece 32 ft. × 128 ft. on which he built the theater.

Some interesting regulations for conduct in the theater were issued. By Order of the Government, ... "the performance shall never be interrupted by shouting, whistling, or in any other manner that might tend to force an actor to be silent . . . It is further forbidden to force the

[7]Christovich and Toledano, *New Orleans Architecture — The American Sector,* p. 95
[8]LeGardeur, Rene J., Jr., *The First New Orleans Theater 1792–1803,* p.47

actors to repeat their lines . . . No one shall stand during the performance, nor put on his hat . . . .[9]

In 1793, a certain Mme. Durosier was directing the troupe; she had
engaged quadroon actresses and was acting in the cast herself. A
possibility exists that they all could have been refugees from the riots in
Port-au-Prince, Saint Domingue, in 1791.[10] In New Orleans, in 1794,
there was also in the theater a Denis-Richard Desessarts (godfather of
Jean Henry's son), another actor formerly connected with the Saint
Domingue theater.

On May 22, 1796 the one-act comic opera, *Silvain,* was performed,
the first recorded performance of an opera in the city.

The theater was closed late in 1803 because of insufficient revenues. When it reopened in 1804, under the American regime, the cast
was made up largely of refugees from Saint Domingue. The continuous
history of drama and opera in New Orleans dates from that year.

Louis-Blaise Tabary has long been credited with beginning the
theater in New Orleans. This he did not do, according to historian René
LeGardeur, Jr., who has made an extensive study of records of the
period. Tabary's name first appears in city records in 1806, when he
published a prospectus for a new theater to be built on Orleans Street
between Royal and Bourbon. The first brick was laid by Governor
Claiborne in October, 1806, but Tabary had to abandon the project for
lack of funds and it was taken over by others. This was the Théâtre
d'Orléans, the first of two by the same name on the same site. Tabary
was, however, a pioneer in this effort, and he gave 26 years of service to
the development of theater in New Orleans, an accomplishment which,
in itself, is worthy of notice. The second Théâtre d'Orléans opened in
1819 with the performance of *Jean de Paris.*

For 18 years, beginning in 1819, John Davis, who operated the
Théâtre d'Orléans, staged ballets, concerts, operas and plays in that
theater. Davis gave up his control of the opera in 1837.

Meanwhile, in 1835, in the American Sector, James Caldwell had
built the St. Charles Theater on St. Charles Avenue near Poydras.

Charles Boudousquié was the impressario of the French Opera
House which was built in 1859. He brought a troupe including Julia
Calvé to the city during that period. The French Opera House, on the
corner of Bourbon and Toulouse, built by James Gallier, burned to the
ground in 1919.

PUBLIC TRANSPORTATION

By the 1830s, one could ride "in omnibus" with a dozen other

---

[9]LeGardeur, Rene J., Jr., *The First New Orleans Theatre 1792–1803,* p.4
[10]Ibid, p. 10

passengers for one "bit" (half a quarter). Such a vehicle ran along Tchoupitoulas Street from New Orleans to Lafayette City, a distance of three miles. The driver, perched high in front, blew a bugle as a signal to start. Passengers could sit inside the carriage or on top.

Banquettes were made of flatboat gunwale in the 1830s. By the 1850s, some were of broad slabs of slate. Streets were of mud or dust, kept in fair condition by chain gangs of convicts. *Banquette* is a French word, used to refer to a banked-up area used for walking, the sidewalk (*banquette,* Fr. a low bench).

Sanitary conditions in New Orleans, until the Civil War, were deplorable. Women vendors in open markets, cleaning foul or fish, dropped the entrails onto the earthen floor, where they were trodden underfoot, as they had been for a hundred years. In areas like Connaught Yard, a collection of boarding houses on Girod and Julia at the river, refuse of every discription and "night filth" were thrown daily into the streets from upstairs windows, with a prayer that the rain would wash them away. Such areas were pest-holes for disease.

This section became a refuge for Irish immigrants who had been imported to dig the New Basin Canal in the 1830s. Other areas where they congregated were on the banks of the Canal itself and in a colony on Tchoupitoulas near Canal Street.

James Caldwell introduced *street lighting* in the American Sector, in the form of gas lanterns, suspended on ropes or chains, hung diagonally across intersections from poles. His imported English gas-making machine, which he had used to light his American Theater on Camp Street in 1824, enabled him to begin a gas company that provided street and household lighting to the city.

RAILROADS AND CANALS

In 1831, the Pontchartrain Railroad, the first railroad west of the Alleghenies, began running from the lower end of the French Market, along Elysian Fields Avenue all the way from the river to the lake. Businessmen in Faubourg Marigny hoped to develop a port on the lake, but this never materialized. The railroad connected the city with Milneburg, a small community on the south shore of the lake. The train, affectionately called the Smoky Mary, chugged and snorted along at the great rate of ten miles an hour, scattering cinders and dust, and transporting picnickers to a wharf at the lake's edge. There, several two-room camps, which could be rented by the day, had been built out over the lake on stilts. This railroad was part of the Louisville and Nashville Railroad.

In 1835, the *New Orleans and Carrollton Railroad* connected the town of Carrollton to New Orleans. It operates today as the St. Charles Streetcar, the oldest continuously operating car line in America. (See Streetcars, Chapter VII.)

THE NEW BASIN CANAL

Perhaps the greatest engineering feat accomplished in the Faubourg St. Mary, and certainly the one which would do most for its economy was the building of the New Basin Canal, which was opened for traffic in 1838. Two New Orleans entrepreneurs, Maunsel White and Beverly Chew, are credited with organizing the New Orleans Canal and Banking Company, which was chartered by the Louisiana legislature in 1831 (when the capital of Louisiana was in Donaldsonville). The company was to build a canal six miles long, 60 feet wide and six feet deep, at a point "above Gravier Street" to Lake Pontchartrain. There was to be a turning basin at the city end, allowing ships to return to the lake, bow first.

The need for the canal had been growing as the American Sector grew. In 1828, there was not a paving stone in the Faubourg St. Mary. The site of the future St. Charles Hotel was a pool of stagnant water. There was not a wharf in the suburb. Drayage fees from the wharves on the riverfront in the Vieux Carre and from the Carondelet Canal were enormous. The Carondelet Canal gave the Creoles access to Bayou St. John and thus to Lake Pontchartrain. It allowed them to control trade with the coastal cities of Biloxi, Mobile, and Pensacola, and with those north of Lake Pontchartrain: Mandeville, Madisonville, and Covington.

The population of Faubourg St. Mary continued to expand upriver and farther away from the old canal. It became increasingly difficult for the Americans to make use of that waterway. A new canal in the American sector would allow them direct access to Lake Pontchartrain and competition in the Gulf Coast trade.

Work was begun in 1832. The canal took six years to build. It cost $1,119,000, exclusive of land, and it took the lives of 8,000 Irish and German immigrants, who died of yellow fever and cholera digging in the mosquito-infested swamps. It was a project of relatively greater difficulty than the Panama Canal, given the differences in technology and equipment. Altogether, it was an awesome task.

There were no dredges in those days, so the digging had to be done with hand shovels. Mud was shoveled into wheelbarrows, which were rolled up inclined planks to the banks of the canal. The most primitive pumps were constantly in use to keep the ditch free of water. Ancient roots of giant, water-soaked cypresses had to be hacked through with hand-axes, since dynamite had not yet been invented. Pilings for wharves were forced into the gumbo soil by tons of stone loaded onto their tops.

Laborers, mostly Irish and German immigrants, earned $20 a month, plus room and board, and whiskey money, $6.25 monthly. They worked through the heat and humidity of six interminable New Orleans summers in the swamps of Metairie Ridge.

When the canal was opened in 1838, there was a turning basin

Figure 25. The Old Basin Canal (Carondelet Canal), circa 1900, ran along Lafitte Street from Basin Street to Bayou St. John. The canal existed from 1795 to the 1930's.

(Courtesy Leonard V. Huber Collection)

Figure 26. The New Basin Canal, circa 1929, had its turning basin at S. Rampart Street between Howard Avenue and Julia Street. It ran from S. Rampart to the lake, 1838 to 1961.

(Courtesy Leonard V. Huber Collection)

where the Greyhound Bus Station and the Union Passenger Terminal are today. The landing was two blocks wide on Circus Ave. (now Rampart Street), between Julia Street and Triton Walk (now Howard Ave).

From the beginning, the New Basin Canal flourished. Howard Avenue, in the 1850s, stretching from the turning basin of the new canal to the river, was lined with business houses of traders, speculators, agents and merchants dealing in manufactured goods from everywhere in the United States. Merchants ran back and forth between the river and the basin as ships arrived and departed. Itinerant merchants joined their ranks, staying at the Washington Hall or the Piney Woods Hotel, rushing out to buy and sell "on the levee", where fortunes were made and lost.

Not only businessmen derived benefit from the New Basin Canal. Pleasure seekers took the ride on mule-drawn barges from the city to New Lake End, where there was little more than Dan Hickock's Hotel, at the site of the present day Southern Yacht Club. The flag-bedecked boats consisted of a cabin and a covered upper deck. Bands played for the entertainment of the passengers. Tolls were collected from pedestrians on the Old Shell Road and from boats on the water: 6½ cents for a man on horseback; 12½ cents for a bicycle rider; 37½ cents a ton on the waterway.

In 1946, a century later, the order came to fill in the canal to make way for the Pontchartrain Expressway. The work was completed in 1961. A wide, green expanse, 20 blocks long, still exists on the route of the canal, between Veterans Highway and Robert E. Lee Boulevard, the only reminder that a canal once ran there.

THE THREE MUNICIPALITIES

In anticipation of the New Basin Canal's completion, businessmen of Faubourg St. Mary requested a charter in 1836 for an independent city, such as had been granted in 1832 to the City of Lafayette. Alternatives were discussed, but the differences between the Creoles and the Americans had only sharpened into hostility in the past several years. In 1836, the municipal government of the city of New Orleans ceased to exist. The city split into three autonomous municipalities, each with its own recorder, (who was the chief executive in his own municipality), and its own council. Each handled its own affairs, improvements, and taxes. Once a year, the general council, composed of aldermen from the three municipalities, met with the Mayor in City Hall (the Cabildo), to deal with matters having to do with the city as a whole (parish prison, old debts, revenues having to do with licenses, etc.)

The Vieux Carre was the First Municipality, Faubourg St. Mary was the Second, and Faubourg Marigny, the Third. Faubourg Marigny was less affluent than the other two. There was less rivalry between

Faubourg Marigny and the Vieux Carre, since many of the residents of Faubourg Marigny were displaced Creoles.

By 1852, it was clear that such an arrangement was both inefficient and expensive. All jobs and efforts had to be duplicated. Tension between the communities had relaxed somewhat, so the municipalities reunited, by a charter of the legislature. The Vieux Carre became the Second District of the City of New Orleans; Faubourg St. Mary, the First; and Faubourg Marigny, the Third. At the same time, the City of Lafayette was annexed, and became the Fourth District.

The new government was bi-cameral, with two chambers, one of aldermen, elected by the districts; the other of assistant aldermen, elected by the wards. This system continued until 1870, although suspended in 1862, when the Union took control of the city. The American Sector, with its steamboat traffic on the New Basin Canal and its thriving commercial enterprises, had sufficient clout in 1852 to have the seat of government moved from the Cabildo in the Vieux Carre to the Second Municipality Hall on St. Charles Avenue (thereafter called City Hall, today Gallier Hall).

THE IMMIGRANTS

The two largest groups of immigrants to settle in New Orleans in the two decades before the Civil War were the Irish and the Germans.

THE IRISH

The Irish, before 1820, are hard to trace in population figures, since ports in the New World lumped British, Irish, and Scottish all together. From 1846 to 1856, because of the famines in Ireland, one-third of the immigrants entering America were from that country. By 1860, there were 25,000 Irish living in New Orleans.

The Irish vied with the blacks for jobs digging ditches, collecting refuse, or stevedoring on the riverfront. As a group, they were viewed with disdain, not only because of the work they did, but because they were rowdy, boisterous, and clannish, hot-tempered, hard-drinking, and eager for a fight. Their intemperate dispositions had, no doubt, been honed on the razor edge of hunger.

Besides the Irish colonies already mentioned, on Tchoupitoulas, Julia and Girod Streets near the riverfront, many of the Irish settled in an area now referred to as the **Irish Channel,** which is in the lower Garden District, and may roughly be bounded by Magazine Street, the river, Jackson Avenue, and Felicity Street. Some say the boundaries extend as far as Louisiana Avenue, in which case, it takes in no less than 100 city squares.

Actually, the Irish Channel was originally only one street, Adele

Street, which ran only two blocks, from St. Thomas to Tchoupitoulas, and lay between Josephine Street and St. Andrew Street.

One version of how it got its name is the story of Irish seamen coming up the river, who would see the light outside Noud's Ocean Home saloon on Adele Street, and cry out, "There's the Irish Channel!" Another is that Adele Street was often flooded after a rain. The truth is, it was probably called the Irish Channel because so many Irish lived there.

In 1850, an Irishman could earn $5 a day as a "screwman" on the riverfront, "screwing" or packing cotton into the ship's hold. Their reputation as fighters often made the difference in their obtaining these coveted jobs. The fact is that many claimed to be Irish, although they weren't, so as to be thought handy with their fists.

The Irish lived simply in small cottages. Often, when Creoles abandoned their big homes on the riverfront to build finer mansions on St. Charles Avenue, the Irish moved into these riverfront homes. In time, they became known as "lace-curtain" Irish.

Irish families were large, and food was coarse but wholesome: corned beef and cabbage, Irish stew, potato pancakes, red beans and rice. The neighborhood itself was respectable. It was the riverfront saloons that gave it a bad reputation: Mike Noud's Ocean Home, the Bull's Head Tavern, the Isle of Man. Today, Parasol's Bar on Constance Street represents that green channel still present to entice Irishmen to celebrate their heritage.

One field in which the Irish excelled was fighting.

The first official prize fight in New Orleans was between **James Burke,** (alias Deaf) and **Sam O'Rourke,** on May 6, 1836. Burke operated a club, the Boxiana, in which he taught the manly art of self-defense.

John L. Sullivan trained at the Carrollton Gardens. New Orleans was host to a fight between Sullivan and Jim Corbett in 1892 in the Olympic Club on Royal Street. Corbett won. They fought with gloves, since bare-knuckled boxing had been outlawed.

In 1889, in Richburg, Mississippi, Sullivan fought an illegal fight of 75 rounds with Jack Kilrain. Most of the fans had come from New Orleans. The referree was **John Fitzpatrick,** who later became mayor of New Orleans.

Sir Henry Morton Stanley (1841–1904), the reporter who discovered Dr. David Livingstone in Africa November 10, 1871, had a home on the site of the orange groves of the Jesuit Plantation on Orange Street. Born in Denbigh, Wales, and christened John Rowlands, he was early orphaned and at 18, he sailed to New Orleans where he was adopted by Henry Morton Stanley, who gave him his name.

The statue of **Margaret Gaffney Haughery** (1813–1882), (the first woman anywhere in the United States to be treated as a celebrity) can be found in a triangular park bounded by Camp, Prytania and Clio Streets. It is the seated image of a woman, sculpted in Carrara marble. The woman, in calico dress and shawl, looks down on a child leaning against her chair. It bears the simple inscription, "Margaret."

Figure 27. Statue of Margaret Haughery—Friend of the Orphans, sitting on the same old chair and dressed in the familiar calico gown with her little shawl over her shoulders.

After the death of her husband and child, Margaret Haughery devoted herself to doing good works and helping orphaned children. She established a dairy and bakery, both of which brought in unexpected profits. She gave most of her earnings to the poor. Although she signed her name with an X, never having learned to read or write, at her death, she left $30,000 to charity. With this bequest, St. Theresa's Orphanage on Camp Street was begun.

THE GERMANS

In the 1840s, the largest number of Germans arrived in New Orleans. By 1860, there were almost 20,000 Germans living in the city. The first German immigrants had come to Louisiana in colonial days in response to John Law's circulars. We have seen that they settled in what came to be known as the German Coast, which ran from what is now Norco to Reserve, partly in St. John the Baptist Parish, and partly in St. Charles Parish, on both sides of the Mississippi River. These Germans knew how to make use of the lushness of the land and farm it successfully.

Many spread at an early time into neighboring districts: St. James Parish, and the Parishes of Assumption, Ascension, and Iberville. They spread into Donaldsonville and settled on Bayou Lafourche, marrying into Acadian families. In the course of time, great changes occurred among these descendants of the early Germans. They spoke French fluently, and were confused about their ancestry, trying to trace their origin as "Cajuns," and discovering their German background. Over the generations, the name Foltz became Folse. Herbert became Hebert.

One of the reasons is believed to be that after the Thirty Years War, Germans who inhabited the Palatinate lived in such abject misery for the next 50 years, that it is unlikely that there were any schools. German immigrants to the New World could probably not write their names, and may not even have pronounced them correctly, but according to the dialect of the area. French and Spanish immigration officials wrote them as they heard them. Thus, Chaigne became Schoen. A German named Zweig might point to a limb of a tree to tell the meaning of his name, and a French official might write LaBranche, christening Zweig forevermore with a new French name.

In 1848, many waves of German immigrants came to America to escape political turmoil and revolution in Germany. Many were professionals and were very intelligent. Many were redemptioners, immigrants who worked off their passage in New Orleans as metal workers, draymen, brewmasters, carpenters, and bricklayers.

Germans were the largest group of foreign-speaking people in New Orleans from 1848 to 1900. They lived in Carrollton, Lafayette City, the 9th Ward, and Mechanicsville, Gretna.

Because of the large German population, beermaking became an important business. One beer garden named "Tivoli" was described as having "a large yard shaded by trees . . . little rustic tables and benches . . . beer men . . . with beer jugs . . . an orchestra . . . five cents is paid by each male partner for the privilege of a waltz . . . the 'frauen' pay nothing, heaven bless them!"

Between 1850 and 1855, 126,000 Germans came through the port city. Most of them did not stay in New Orleans, but moved on to towns where land was cheaper and there was no annual threat of yellow fever. Competition with slave labor (slaves in New Orleans were often leased by their owners) was discouraging to newcomers. Many Germans moved on to Texas, Arkansas, Central America, and other points south and west.

In the years between 1876 and 1880, **Fritz Jahncke** gave us our first paved streets (Canal Street and others had heretofore been paved with Belgian block, cobblestones or flatboat wood.) He also brought about the formation of the Sewerage and Water Board and developed the New Basin Canal, bringing sand and shells from the lake.

Other famous Germans to come to New Orleans were **Philip Werlein** (in 1853), who published Dan Emmet's composition, "Dixie,"; **Peter Laurence Fabacher,** (in 1891), a brewer; **Jacob Schoen,** a mortician; and **Ashton Frey,** a butcher in the French Market. All of these men were on the board of the Jackson Brewery, which thrived in the city from 1891 until the 1970s.

THE LAND OF "DIXIE"

Mention of the song "Dixie" should not be dismissed without a word about the derivation of the word "Dixie." It was a nickname for New Orleans, originally, a variation of the word "Dix," as people called the ten-dollar bill printed in the 1800s for use in New Orleans. One side of the bill indicated the denomination in English: TEN; the other side, in French: DIX (pronounced "Dees" by the French, but Dix by the Americans). Since New Orleans was the only place the Dix was used, it was New Orleans, in the beginning, that was referred to as "Dixie."

Louis Moreau Gottschalk, (1829–1869), a Creole of German and French descent, was considered the leading pianist-composer of his day. He gave concerts throughout the world. "The Dying Poet" and "The Lost Hope" are probably his most famous works. He also wrote "La Bamboula" from memories of the music and dancing of the slaves in the Congo Square.

THE YUGOSLAVS

The **Yugoslavs** of New Orleans and Plaquemines Parish have prospered as a result of their cultivation of the Louisiana oyster. They came from Yugoslavia to New Orleans, San Francisco, and New York about the middle of the 19th century, seeking freedom from oppression and better economic conditions. After living near the French Market for a time, they found in the Plaquemines area a brackish water, with the right mixture of fresh and salt water to produce good oysters, and developed techniques of improving their quality. For over 100 years, they have been oystermen on the boundaries of our state—the Atchafalaya River, the Sabine River, and the Pearl River. They settled in Plaquemines Parish toward the mouth of the river, and cultivated the Louisiana oyster in Bayou Cook, Bayou Chutte, and Grand Bayou.

SLAVERY

Negroes have always been a large part of the population of the city. They came here first with Bienville, as slaves for his colony, to join forces with the Indians, the earliest slaves in New Orleans.

Slaves came to New Orleans and Louisiana from West Africa, Haiti, Belize, Virginia, and South Carolina. They arrived at Algiers Point, across the river from New Orleans.

Algiers Point, on the West bank of the river, had been granted to the city-founder Bienville in 1719 when a slave corral was housed on the Point, and African slaves were sold from it to the colonists. The point was also the site of the French colony's slaughterhouse, and was sometimes called Slaughterhouse Point during the colonial period. Powder Street in Algiers Point is evidence that the colonists also had their powder magazine there. It probably was named for the original Algiers, from which pirates terrorized the Mediterranean Sea. General O'Reilly had led an expedition against pirates in the Mediterranean before becoming Spanish Governor of Louisiana in 1769. A ferry route between Algiers and New Orleans was established in 1827, and Algiers began to develop and by 1870, was the Fifth District of New Orleans.

The slaves in New Orleans and their white masters exchanged cultural modes of expression and began a process of amalgamation early in the city's history, although this process was delayed in other parts of the South. The paternalistic French and Spanish rulers encouraged the African culture among their slaves, allowing West African dancing, music, cooking, and architecture to survive without interference. Also, New Orleans Negroes, living as they did in such close proximity to their white masters, in a city of limited size surrounded by water, experienced a greater knowledge of the whites than the plantation Negro, and in the city, the two cultures overlapped.

In New Orleans, slavery was viewed with a unique attitude. A slave was bought for his brawn, which enabled him to work, but he was also enjoyed for his cuisine, his humor, and his many cultural aptitudes.

The term "Blacks of Louisiana" does not accurately describe the Negroes of our state or city, in the beginning or now. After the Haitian insurrection in 1791, incoming people of color (*gens de couleur*) ranged in hue from yellow to coffee to black. There were mulattoes (half-black), quadroons, (one-quarter black), octoroons (one-eighth black), and lighter Negroes in whom the black heritage was all but lost. The term "cafe au lait" was used to describe these people, meaning coffee with cream, or black with white.

A slave coming to New Orleans did not necessarily remain a slave. Occasionally, he was manumitted by his master to enter free society as an indentured servant. On rare occasions, he could work off his slavery as a redemptioner.

In New Orleans, both black people and white people owned slaves. Slaves were called "Blacks"; free persons of color were called "Colored." Africans, who appeared to the white citizens as brutes upon arrival in the city could, within one generation, become transformed into dutiful Christians and skilled laborers.

Slaves were identified as Africans and Creoles. The former had been born in Africa and transported to America. The latter were children of Africans, who had been born in Louisiana. Also, if a slave was from Louisiana, he was referred to as a "Creole" slave, meaning simply "a native of Louisiana." (Sometimes the term got confused and was thought to refer strictly to a black person.)

In the city, there were many free Negroes with slaves of their own. Between 1804 and 1809, many free persons of color came to Louisiana from their homeland in Saint Domingue to escape hostile action by the island's ex-slaves, following the bloody slave insurrection of 1791. This more than doubled Louisiana's free Negro population. These rebellions made slaveholders in America fearful and, in most cases, more liberal and generous in the treatment of their own slaves.

"The slaves of New Orleans were perhaps the most sophisticated group of bondsmen since the days of ancient Rome."[11] Many were tradesmen who were working off their slavery, and could foresee a free future for themselves and their families. Among other oddities, there was a "Slave for a Day" rental service for country patrons who did not wish to bring their slaves with them to the city.

The invention of the cotton gin in 1793 by Eli Whitney fastened slavery onto the South. An institution that would have died out because its cost was insupportable now became a feasible investment. The free labor of slaves, together with a machine that could clean cotton as fast as fifty men working by hand, was to make cotton king of the South and create a southern aristocracy of planters.

---

[11] Taylor, Joe Gray, *Louisiana: A Narrative History*, p.60

By 1860, approximately 25,000 blacks lived in New Orleans. Of these, 11,000 were slaves, owned by whites or free blacks. Some were awaiting sale on the auction blocks at the Cabildo, the St. Charles or St. Louis Hotel, or at Maspero's Exchange on Chartres Street. To make them appear more attractive, slave dealers sometimes dressed the men in top hats and evening clothes, and the women in long dresses and tignons.

Slaves brought into Eastern ports were frequently "sold down the river" to New Orleans. The expression had ominous overtones. Many discovered on arrival, however, that for a slave, it was a better place to live than most other southern cities. They enjoyed the mixture of people, the excitement, the places of amusement (even for *them,* like the Place Congo, where they danced on Sunday afternoons). They liked shopping for their masters in the colorful markets and shops. They enjoyed the looseness of the reins that held them in captivity, and the hope that they could buy or earn their freedom.

JOHN McDONOGH

The Scotsman born in Baltimore, John McDonogh, was one of the city's outstanding philanthropists. He was one of the founders of the American Colonization Society which assisted 300 slaves in the city in obtaining their freedom. Freedom could be purchased, worked for, or simply granted. In some cases, the State Legislature granted freedom to slaves for some particular service.

John McDonogh owned a plantation in Algiers. He bought slaves, but unlike other slaveowners, he did not sell them. Instead, he educated them in a craft and then freed them. He helped many freed slaves leave Louisiana. Almost two decades before the Civil War, he helped 80 of his liberated slaves make their departure for Africa. He saw to it that they had money, clothes, household goods and farm tools, to establish themselves there as free men. Others worked for him, as free men, on his sugar plantation, under the supervision of other blacks. He treated them all like human beings, and for this he was called a radical. When he died in 1850, his estate was valued at $3,000,000. He left $1,500,000 to the cities of New Orleans and Baltimore for schools for the poor.

FREE MEN OF COLOR

From the time of the Spanish period on, free men of color enjoyed both economical and educational advantages in New Orleans. They had full freedom to conduct business and to enter into contracts. Free Negroes even had their own schools. They added substantially to the literate sector of Louisiana. By 1803, there were 1,355 in a population of 10,000. Some of the men were tailors, mechanics, carpenters, or were engaged in small businesses. Some opened schools or performed in theaters. They were sober, law-abiding and industrious. In 1860, the holdings of free men of color in New Orleans was between 13 and 15 million dollars. There were, at this time, 13,000 Negroes and free persons of color in a population of 168,000 in New Orleans.

Free women of color were among the most beautiful women in New Orleans. Some of them lived as concubines with white men. In 1792, an ordinance was passed forcing them to become more recognizable as "women of color" by wearing a headdress known as a *tignon*. It became a mark of distinction, instead of the branding it was intended to be. Surviving portraits of free women of color picture them in black dresses with white lace shawls and tignons.

Concubinage between black women and white men, a custom called *placage* (from the French verb *placer,* meaning to put or place) was the style of the times. It was an understanding whereby a white man and a mulatto woman, the *placée,* lived together more or less permanently. Arrangements were made between the mother of the eligible black woman and the white man (usually, but not always, a Frenchman), to set up the daughter in a house, sometimes with slaves, carriages, all the accouterments of the wealthy, to be the young man's mistress, usually until the gentleman got married, at which time, the house and all its contents belonged to the mulattress for life. Faubourg Marigny and the French Quarter itself including Rampart Street, were the sites for these houses.

The Orleans Ballroom, some historians say, (as well as other locations in the French Quarter), regularly held the famous Quadroon Balls, which were frequented by gentlemen seeking such arrangements. All was handled very discreetly, with care taken to protect both parties as to laws and obligations.

Many of the progeny of these relationships moved on to live in Mexico, Haiti, or Paris, "passing" as whites. From these alliances came many remarkable people.

Norbert Rillieux, a free man of color, born 1806, son of a wealthy French engineer and a slave. While a student in Paris (1830–32), he discovered the multiple evaporation process of making sugar.

Eugene Warburg, the eldest son of Daniel Warburg, a German Jew, and Marie Rosa, a slave of Santiago, Cuba, (whom Daniel Warburg freed), was a noted sculptor. His most famous work is the bust of the U.S. Minister of France, John Young Mason, 1855.

Julien Hudson, a free man of color, was a portrait painter before the Civil War.

Henriette Delille (1813–1862), a beautiful free woman of color, was the founder of the order of the Sisters of the Holy Family. The nuns lived at the site of the former quadroon balls in a building donated to the order by a free man of color, **Thomy Lafon.** (Today, at that same location, is the Bourbon-Orleans Hotel.) **Thomy Lafon** is the only free man of color of whom a bust was made because of his generosity to his fellow men. A public school is also named in his honor.

James Durham, physician, had been sold as a slave to a New Orleans physician who taught him medicine and set him free to become a physician to both blacks and whites in 1788.

THE VOODOO CULT

Voodoo was a dominant force among the black population of New Orleans in the second half of the 19th century. It had come to the colony originally from Western Africa, with the first Negroes brought here as slaves. The practice spread and intensified when the black immigrants from Haiti arrived at the beginning of the 19th century. These Haitians, whose ancestors were also originally from Africa, believed strongly in voodoo and practiced it as a religion. They were allowed much freedom of personal expression by paternalistic rulers and lethargic owners.

The Haitians, when living in Saint Domingue, had believed in voodoo gods and zombies (soulless human corpses taken from the grave and transformed by the voodoos into living creatures). In New Orleans, the voodoos had to make changes in the rituals to appeal to the local populace.

MARIE LAVEAU

Marie Laveau, the most famous of all New Orleans voodooiennes, lived in the same cottage at 1020 St. Ann Street for fifty years, conducting rituals in her yard, in which she danced with a snake, which she called Zombi. After her sensuous exhibition, her performers, young men and women, danced practically in the nude, consuming large quantities of rum *taffia,* drinking blood from the broken necks of roosters, swooning, trembling, and at last, indulging in sexual intimacies.

Once a year, on St. John's Eve, June 23, a more elaborate version of the same ceremony took place near the old Spanish Fort, at a point where Bayou St. John flowed into Lake Pontchartrain. It was a mixture of Christianity and barbarity, and most citizens considered it a blasphemy, but it attracted hundreds of viewers, as well as members of the police and the press.

Marie Laveau's fame spread as a fortune teller, a mind reader, and a dispenser of love charms and satanic potions, and she was sought out by rich and poor, by blacks and whites for advice on personal matters and political concerns, local and national.

She was a free mulatto born in New Orleans in 1794. She was married to Jacques Paris in 1819 by Père Antoine. Both she and Jacques were recorded as free persons of color. Many accounts indicate that her father had been a wealthy white planter, her mother a mulatto with a

Figure 28. In Voodoo ceremony in New Orleans, slaves dance the Bamboula, the dance which inspired song by famous New Orleans composer, Louis Moreau Gottschalk.

strain of Indian blood. Yet, her life is shrouded in mystery. Although she earned great sums of money, she never lived as a woman of means. Her husband died three years after their marriage. On her tomb in St. Louis Cemetery No. 1 is the inscription "Veuve (widow) Paris."

She began the practice of voodoo around 1826, changing the cult to a profitable business, selling charms, favors, and prophecies, but retaining the showmanship necessary to keep the faith of her followers. To the hedonistic exhibitions, she added statues of saints, incense and holy water, for the benefit of the Catholic Negroes in her flock.

She later formed a liaison with Christophe Glapion, a union which produced 15 children. Glapion stayed "behind the scenes," possibly acting as her bookkeeper. She is said to have died at the age of 87.

Voodoo charms can be found at the Voodoo Museum at 724 Dumaine Street. Love powders, boss-fixing powders, money-drawing incense and come-to-me powders can be purchased there, as well as effigies, lotions, and charms. The museum is purported to be the only one of its kind in the country.

THE JEWS IN NEW ORLEANS

Although the Black Code, the *Code Noir* of 1724, governed the treatment of Negro slaves, its first article decreed that Jews be expelled from the colony. It was a strange article, not only because it appeared in the Black Code, but because there was no evidence that Jews *were* in the colony. Jews were too clever at merchandising to be attracted to a floundering trading post, when they could stay in the Caribbean, where they were doing a great business.

The question of why Jews were banned at all comes to mind. In Bienville's words, it was "out of missionary concern for the souls of the slaves." Also, it is said that the French admitted a fear of their aggressive business practices.

In 1758, there is recorded an argument between Governor Kerlerec and his Intendant, Rochemore, concerning the admittance of a ship, the *Texel,* whose captain was a Jew named Diaz. Rochemore declared that it was illegal for the ship to dock. Kerlerec wanted the goods on board. Kerlerec prevailed, and a Jew was in the colony.

In 1801, a remarkable Jewish gentleman arrived in the colony—**Judah Touro** (1775–1854). His business was wholesale consignment; he was an ice importer. In 1838, he was the owner and operator of two ice houses. A man generous to the community throughout his lifetime, he remained a bachelor, living with two other bachelors at #35 Conde Street, an extension of Chartres Street. Some of his fellow boarders were **Jean Baptiste Olivier,** chaplain of the Ursulines; and **Alexander Milne,** who started the community of Milneburg on the lakefront and left funds with which the Milne Boys Home was built.

Judah Touro's total estate at the time of his death was $928,774. His beneficiaries were in Boston, Newport, and New Orleans, and included Christians and Jews alike. In his lifetime, he purchased many slaves for the purpose of freeing them. He gave liberally to numerous charities including the Touro-Shakespeare Home, Touro Infirmary, and Touro Synagogue.

Other notable Jewish citizens were:

Samuel Hermann — builder of the Hermann-Grima House on St. Louis Street.

Judah P. Benjamin — (1811–1880) Confederate Secretary of War and State, who, after having been exiled, lived in England and gained international fame as a lawyer.

Martin Behrman, born in New York in 1864, and elected mayor of New Orleans in 1904, a post he held for 17 years, not consecutively. This was a record never surpassed.

BARONESS PONTALBA AND THE PONTALBA APARTMENTS

Micaela Almonester was born in 1795, when her father, Don Andrès Almonester, was 70 years old. Almonester, a widower, had married a French Creole, 29-year-old Louise de la Ronde, in 1787. Two years after Micaela's birth, her sister Andrea was born. Andrea died at the age of four, leaving Micaela the only heiress to her father's vast estate.

Since Micaela's name and fame have survived so many generations because of the apartment buildings she constructed, flanking the Place d'Armes, it would be well here to trace the history of that property. In the century and a quarter after de La Tour, the French military engineer, sketched the first plans for officers' lodgings on the Pontalba site (1721), buildings rose and fell in that location. When they were destroyed by fire, rains, or hurricanes, they were quickly replaced by others: first, a barracks, used as a place of worship until the first parish church was constructed; then, a warehouse; after that, quarters for the employees of the Government House; a residence for the governor; and then, barracks for French soldiers and sailors. After the Spanish flag was raised over the Place d'Armes, the residence of Don Andrès Almonester was built on the site. Before his death in 1798, when Micaela was three, he had acquired all the land on both sides of the square. It was the choicest real estate in the city, and its use would be determined by his widow and his daughter, the indomitable Micaela.

In 1804, Almonester's widow married Jean Baptiste Castillon, the French consul at New Orleans, who died five years later in 1809. Madame Castillon was now a wealthy woman, controlling the estates of both her former husbands by community property law, and also properties they had given her or she had acquired.

On October 23, 1811, when Micaela was 16, she was married to Joseph Xavier Celestin Delfau de Pontalba, her 20-year-old cousin. He was the son of Baron Joseph Xavier Delfau de Pontalba of Mont L'Eveque, France. Celestin, or "Tin-Tin," as he was called, came over from France for the wedding and had never seen the bride before. Both Celestin and Micaela were heirs to enormous fortunes, as well as to a barony, and nothing else mattered. The wedding had been arranged by the parents.

The young couple went to Europe on their honeymoon, accompanied by both mothers. If ever a couple was suited to such an arrangement, it was Micaela and Tin-Tin. Micaela had been educated by the Ursuline nuns, and was therefore sheltered. Never "pretty," she was strongwilled and intelligent. At the time of her wedding, she was childish in her dress and habits. She wore her hair in pigtails until the day she married, and played with dolls on her wedding day. Celestin was her exact opposite. He was handsome (prettier than the bride, some said) but a weakling, who had been spoiled by his mother and ruled with an iron hand by his father. Now, again, in marriage, he was to be dominated by a determined, headstrong personality, Micaela.

Celestin's father had been born in Louisiana and educated in France. Like Almonester, he was a real estate genius who had accumulated a fortune in rental property.

Micaela loved the activity and gaiety of Paris far better than the quiet of Chateau Mont l'Eveque, which Celestin's father had built and

Figure 29. Micaela Almonester Pontalba built the apartments flanking Jackson Square, leaving an historical monument to the city.

considered the family home. During the early years of their marriage, Micaela had three sons: Celestin, Alfred, and Gaston. When she was pregnant for her first son, her husband requested that she sign a contract,

Figure 30. The Pontalba Apartments.

a "project of testament," (prepared, no doubt, by his father) which put claims on her fortune in case she died in childbirth. She would not sign it. Arguments followed. This was the beginning of the end of the young Pontalbas' marriage. Money and property had always kept the two families wary of each other.

Twice Celestin left Micaela. In 1831, she sailed to Louisiana without him, and wrote that she was beginning proceedings for a divorce. Later, she returned to France, and her son, Celestin, now 17, ran away from military school to live with his mother. Hearing this, the Baron, his grandfather, now 81, dropped the boy from his will. In an attempt at reconciliation, Micaela drove to Mont l'Eveque on October 18, 1834. She lodged in a "little chateau reserved for the use of visitors."

The day after she arrived, the Baron waited until she was alone, went into the chateau, walked upstairs and into her room and locked the door. Immediately, he shot three balls into her chest; then, two more, which missed. While he was priming the pistol, Micaela found the strength to open the door and run to the floor below, where she collapsed.

The Baron, thinking her dead, closed himself in the room once again and fired two shots into his heart, which proved fatal.

The scandal rocked Paris and New Orleans. Micaela, now Baroness Pontalba, having inherited the title, had received four chest wounds, two of which were serious, and she had lost two fingers of her left hand trying to protect herself; yet, this incredible woman lived to the age of 78 and was yet to accomplish her most memorable undertaking. In 1848, she returned to New Orleans to begin work on her buildings.

The buildings were designed by James Gallier. But Gallier and the Baroness disagreed, and in 1849, she turned over the contract to a builder named Samuel Stewart. The architect, Henry Howard, also played a part. The Baroness, Howard said, not altogether satisified with his drawings, called at his office to ask him to make a complete set of plans for the buildings. He asked for $500. She refused. He finally agreed to a fee of $120, without specifications.

The buildings were constructed of dark red brick with cast iron-decorated balconies, probably the first in New Orleans. The design for the iron work was done by Waldemar Talen, who had also done the iron work for Nottaway Plantation on the River Road.

The contract for the buildings called for 16 houses fronting on the Place d'Armes on St. Peter Street for a price of $156,000 using Howard's plans with Gallier's specifications. Micaela designed the AP monogram that can be seen in the cast-iron railings (Almonester-Pontalba). In this, she was assisted by Talen, who made the drawings. When the uptown side was finished, in the fall of 1850, the Baroness and her two sons moved into the the third house from Decatur Street. In 1851, the downtown side was finished at a cost of $146,000. She had talked the builders into accepting $10,000 less on this second contract.

Now, the city undertook the renovation of the Place d'Armes, contracting for an iron fence, which still surrounds the square.

When the St. Ann Street apartments were complete, there were 16 buildings on each side of the Square, with party walls between them, built to be used as stores downstairs and handsome residences above, as they still are today. Each house had an entrance on the street leading to an inside staircase and to a courtyard and service area in the rear. The stores were generally rented to different tenants than the houses and had their own entrances. The second floor consisted of a *salon* with guillotine windows opening onto a balcony overlooking the Square, and a dining room. The third floor was for family bedrooms, the attic for servants' rooms.

To the Baroness's great good fortune, Jenny Lind visited the city just when the buildings were being completed in 1851. P. T. Barnum, the circus impresario, was her sponsor; he had arranged for her to do 13 concerts in New Orleans. She arrived in New Orleans from Cuba on the steamer *Falcon*, and as her ship approached the wharf, cheering crowds estimated at 10,000 people gathered to see the famous singer. One of the Pontalba houses had been reserved for her use, complete with the silver name-plate on the door. Thither they went in carriages, as the crowds pressed in around them. Jenny Lind was delighted with her apartment, and she received applause every time she stepped out onto the balcony. After Miss Lind departed, Mme. Pontalba had the furniture from her apartment sold at auction, bringing in a total of $3,060.50.

JACKSON SQUARE

While the second set of row houses was still under construction, improvements were begun on the Place d'Armes. In 1851, the name of the Square was changed to Jackson Square in honor of the hero of the Battle of New Orleans. In 1840, Jackson had visited New Orleans and laid a cornerstone where a monument to him was to be erected. Now, a decade later, spurred on by improvements all around the Square, the Jackson Monument Association renewed its efforts and the legislature appropriated $10,000 toward the project. In 1856, Clark Mills' equestrian statue of Jackson was unveiled.

Until the Baroness Pontalba's apartments were built, the Cabildo and the Presbytère had only two floors. The old Spanish roofs leaked and needed repairs in any case, so the City Council decided to add third stories to the two buildings with Mansard roof and dormers. Flatboat wood was used and can still be seen in this construction. This addition gave the entire Square a more balanced effect.

In March, 1852, the Baroness and her two sons left New Orleans for France, never to return. She died in Paris in 1874. Her former husband outlived her by four years. They are both buried at Chateau Mont l'Eveque near Senlis, France.

In 1921, the Pontalba heirs, 17 in number, sold the building on St. Ann Street for $68,000 to William Ratcliff Irby, who willed it to the Louisiana State Museum. In 1920, the St. Peter Street building was sold to Danziger, Dreyfous and Runkel for $66,000. They sold it in 1930 to the Pontalba Building Museum Association for $200,000. The Association turned it over to the City.

The Pontalba Apartments are often called "the first apartment houses in the United States." There is no proof of this claim. They are, however, beautifully designed and planned, an outstanding work of architecture, and one of the nation's foremost historic monuments.

THE GARDEN DISTRICT

The land grant given Bienville when he was governor was an enormous territory bounded by the river and what is now Claiborne Avenue, Canal Street and the Nine Mile Point (the Nine Mile Point was a bend in the river beyond Carrollton in what is today Jefferson Parish).

Shortly after the Company of the Indies had made the grant, however, Bienville was notified that such grants were no longer to be made to governors except if the land was used as a "vegetable garden." Bienville immediately had a portion of the concession planted with vegetables (Common Street to Felicity Street, which became the reduced size of his plantation; his house was near the present intersection of Magazine and Common).

Later, when Bienville left the colony for France, as we have seen, he gave his property to the Jesuit priests, who raised sugar cane there, in the area where the Jesuit Church is today on Baronne Street. In 1763, when the Jesuits were expelled, their property was confiscated and sold at auction in parcels. This is how the piece of land we today call the Central Business District came to be owned by Don Beltram (Bertrand) Gravier, at the time the fire devastated the Vieux Carre in 1788. His subdivision of the property at that time created the city's first formally developed suburb. Originally Ville Gravier, it was later named Faubourg Ste. Marie, and still later, Faubourg St. Mary.

German families had been settled to farm the rest of Bienville's original claim, but many left in the wakes of floods and fevers, headed for healthier cities. By 1740, many segments of this land had been sold in tracts, which became riverfront plantations belonging to the families d'Hauterive, Broutin, Darby, Carriere, and Livaudais. These plantations became, in time, three small communities called Nuns, Lafayette, and Livaudais. In 1832, the three communities were incorporated by an act of the state legislature into the City of Lafayette. Eleven years later, the City of Lafayette took in a small settlement on its upper edges, the Faubourg de Lassaiz, extending its boundaries as far as Toledano Street. Finally, in 1852, Lafayette ceased to exist as a municipality and became the Fourth District of the City of New Orleans. The City of Lafayette, in its brief life span, became a gracious area of ante-bellum homes, as well as a hard-working, commercial riverfront territory.

In 1816, there was a crevasse in the river at the McCarty Plantation several miles upriver from the Livaudais property in the City of Lafayette. Most of the plantations were flooded from the site of the crevasse to the city of New Orleans, including the property of Francois de Livaudais. Livaudais had married Celeste Marigny, daughter of Philippe de Marigny, wealthiest man in Louisiana, and one of the wealthiest in America. The Livaudais-Marigny wedding represented the merger of two great fortunes. After their marriage, the young couple began the construction of a castle (on the site that would later be St. Thomas between Sixth and Washington), resembling those of their French ancestors. By 1825, however, they had separated, and Madame Livaudais had moved to Paris, where she was feted by King Louis Philippe and his court.

In the settlement with Livaudais, she had received the Livaudais plantation, which she sold to a group of entrepreneurs for $500,000. At once, the plantation was laid out into streets and lots. (This land extends from First to Ninth [now Harmony St.] and from the river to St. George [now LaSalle].) All she kept was the tract with her mansion on it, which was one block wide, from Washington Avenue to Sixth Street, and from the river to LaSalle. Since her mansion was so enormous, the blocks of the tract were cut wider all the way from the river to LaSalle, in order to conform to the width of that house on that one block.

Over a period of time, this unfinished "castle" was used as a residence for members of her family, as a ballroom, a plaster factory, and a refuge for two old female hermits. It was called the "Haunted House" of Lafayette. In 1863, it was finally demolished.

The lots of the newly dissected Livaudais plantation provided Lafayette City with river frontage, good residential sites, and silt-enriched soil, where anything would grow. Flowers bloomed year round, attracting wealthy Americans and even a few daring Creoles in the second quarter of the 19th century. The area soon became known as the Garden District. It is a quadrangle bounded by Jackson and Louisiana Avenues, and by Magazine Street and St. Charles Avenue. Originally, Apollo (Carondelet) and Josephine Street were included.

During the period of Spanish domination, after 1763, when the embargo existed against all but Spanish vessels trading with New Orleans merchants, British "floating warehouses" sailed up the river on the pretext of going up to trade with British colonies at Manchac, Baton Rouge, and Natchez. Instead, they docked at Lafayette City, where they carried on a brisk commerce in cutlery, cloth, farming utensils, and even slaves with New Orleanians. The Spanish turned their heads, pretending not to notice, until the American Revolution made anti-British sentiment a necesity. In 1777, Governor Galvez seized the British ships and stopped the illegal trade. But it was the British trade that had established Lafayette City as a commercial center on the riverfront.

The Texas cattle trails ended at Gretna, across the river from

Lafayette. Cattle boats then transported the stock across the river to slaughterhouses, where they were unloaded in a noisy, odiferous, earth-shaking herd. The riverfront was lined with the establishments of tallow renderers, soap boilers, hide tanners and merchants, bone grinders, and other "spin-off" industries.

Cotton was brought to the docks by steamboats, which competed for wharf space with flatboats lining the riverfront in the 1840s. It was said that one could walk a mile on the tops of flatboats on the riverfront. By 1850, however, twenty piers had been specially constructed of thick planks to accommodate the steamers.

The earliest homes in Lafayette City were built close to the river. Gradually, however, there was a greater demand for lots "in the back part of the city," where the wealthy built mansions a good distance from the sounds and smells of the slaughterhouses.

In 1852, the population of Lafayette City was 12,651, plus 1,539 slaves. Greek Revival mansions rose along Nayades Street (St. Charles Avenue) and in the Magazine Street area in the 1840s and 1850s.

A conflict arose between those who demanded the removal of slaughterhouses and tanneries from the Lafayette City riverfront (because of the offensive odors and noises) and those who claimed that the city would lose as much as 1½ million dollars a year in trade by such an act. The City Council finally passed measures which removed the cattle landing.

THE YELLOW FEVER EPIDEMIC OF 1853

The events of the terrible yellow fever epidemic of 1853 in New Orleans are so horrible that we read them with disbelief, equating them with the Black Plague in Europe in the Middle Ages. In the 1990s, it is difficult to imagine the reality of death on such a grand scale. It has been called the worst single epidemic ever to hit an American city.

We know today that yellow fever is a virus which damages the liver, preventing if from functioning. Yellow bile pigments gather in the skin. The victim's eyes look yellow and his skin has a yellow tone. His temperature rises rapidly, his bones ache, and he vomits black matter, which consists of partly digested blood, after hemorrhages have occurred in the stomach. Some victims go into a coma. Many die. Those who live have lifetime immunity to the disease.

We know now that the disease is transmitted by the *Aëdes aegypti* mosquito, which carries it from one victim to another. Both the disease and the mosquito almost certainly came from the Old World, probably Africa, and probably on slave ships. The warm, humid climate and heavy rainfall of New Orleans made it susceptible to yellow fever. Open cisterns were perfect breeding grounds for the mosquito, whose eggs must first dry a bit, then hatch when moistened. New Orleans was an ideal host to such a cycle.

110

Epidemics began with the hot weather and ended with the frosts, which killed the mosquitoes. In the 1800s the fever was believed to be caused by poisonous vapors in the atmosphere, water contagion, or droplet infection.

The first epidemic of yellow fever in New Orleans occurred in 1793, the last in 1905, and in the interval, 20 major epidemics struck (although the fever came every summer, to some degree). From 1793 to 1853, the epidemics grew increasingly worse and more numerous, (the high point coming in 1853). This has been attributed to a growing population of impoverished immigrants in a below-sea-level, unhealthy city that had lots of rain. From 1853 to 1905, the epidemics decreased in severity and number. The decline began during the Civil War, when General Benjamin Butler put the unemployed of New Orleans to work scouring the city from top to bottom.

On the morning of May 28, 1853, a New Orleans newspaper editorialized about the glorious future of a disease-free city. There had not been a yellow fever epidemic in six years. That evening, an Irish laborer, recently landed on an emigrant vessel, was admitted to Charity Hospital, suffering from the black vomit. He died within a few hours. The doctor hesitated to diagnose the disease so early in the season. Doctors of the period had a difficult time distinguishing between hemorrhagic malaria, yellow fever, and other diseases, especially when no epidemic was raging. Municipal officers and newspapers hushed rumors of the fever, so as not to discourage tourists and businessmen.

After a second death occurred, the doctor traced the origin of the disease to the ship *Augusta,* which had arrived from Bremen May 17 with 230 European immigrants aboard. The *Augusta* had been in close contact with another ship, the *Camboden Castle,* on which several crew members had died of yellow fever while in Jamaica.

The public was, at that time, preoccupied with a sensational murder trial in the news. In June, rumors of a slave rebellion (which never materialized) swept through the city. No one was concerned that on June 1, an item in a New York newspaper told of a yellow fever epidemic in Jamaica, and warned that the disease was being carried by sailors and dock workers to distant ports. (Jamaica was a long way away.) (Today we know that the *Aëdes aegypti* mosquitoes swarmed thickly in the holds and cabins of ships and bred in their water barrels.)

On June 22, the editor of *The Daily Crescent* commiserated with members of the "Can't-Get-Away-Club," merchants and tradesmen whose business required their presence in the city. New Orleans was a six-months-a-year town because of the heat and the disease. Those who could afford to, had already left the city. Those who remained settled down to the unusual heat and the swarms of mosquitoes, "a barbarous horde of great, ugly, long-billed, long-legged creatures . . . ."

New Orleans was a city of 150,000 people. All told, 50,000 left the city that summer. Of the 100,000 that remained, one out of every ten would die.

Gutters were filled with garbage, human waste, and refuse, which rains would turn into lakes of filth, spreading cholera and malaria. No one would drink the river water, choosing instead to use cistern water, which was a breeding ground for the yellow-fever carrier mosquito. The heat, floods, and surrounding swamps all contributed to the unhealthful conditions. Mayor A. D. Crossman urged health measures, and the City Council agreed to end private street-cleaning contracts and establish a municipal sanitation department, but more immediate measures were needed.

On July 2, it was at last announced that 25 people had died of yellow fever. The following week, 204 more deaths occurred. By the middle of July, the total was 429. A second exodus of New Orleans natives from the city was underway, spreading disease all along the Gulf Coast.

As the death toll mounted, hearses rolled incessantly into the cemeteries. Streets were deserted except for the carriages of physicians. Every evening, artillery was fired to "clear the atmosphere." Flames and smoke from hundreds of tar barrels scattered throughout the city sent dense clouds up above the city and lit up the streets with an eerie glow. (This worked, accidentally, because it killed and repelled mosquitoes.)

Doctors tried the time-honored cures: bleeding and purging. Vomiting did not have to be induced. But without knowledge of the cause, they could not cure the disease.

The worst day of the epidemic was August 20, when 269 people died. At this point, 200 a day were dying in the city. The private and public hospitals were overflowing. Every home in the city was a hospital. In some homes, whole families died within the hour, and there was no one to mourn or make funeral arrangements.

Open wagons passed daily, the drivers calling: "Bring out your dead." Hearses, carriages and wagons massed near the cemeteries. Inside the cemeteries, the rotting corpses "were piled by the fifties, exposed to the heat of the sun, swollen with corruption , bursting their coffin lids . . ." (*The Daily Crescent,* August 11, 1853).

The dead were buried in shallow graves in the cemetery ground, covered with no more than 14 inches of mud. When the rains came, the soil was washed away, revealing grotesque decaying bodies.

In desperation the mayor offered $5 an hour for gravediggers in order to remove such sights from public view:

The New Orleans Bee, August 9, 1853:

"Upon inquiry yesterday, we ascertained that the festering and decaying of bodies which had been deposited in the Lafayette

Cemetery had at last been consigned to mother earth. The eyes will no longer be pained and the nostrils offended by the further continuance of the horrible neglect. The Mayor . . . secured the labor of the chain gang, and set them immediately to work."

The epidemic took the lives of 10,000 people in the summer of 1853.

Figure 31. Our Lady of Guadalupe was originally a mortuary chapel where all Catholic funerals were held (near St. Louis Cemetery No. 1) from 1827 to 1860.

Through the little mortuary chapel on Rampart and Conti Streets passed the bodies of thousands of Catholics who had died of the fever. Funerals in the St. Louis Cathedral had been banned since 1827 for fear that disease would spread. The wardens of the Cathedral had ordered the erection of the chapel near St. Louis Cemetery No. 1, so that Catholics might be properly (though speedily) blessed before burial during yellow fever epidemics. After the Civil War, the ban on Cathedral funerals was lifted, and the mortuary chapel became a parish church, called Our Lady of Guadalupe.

It was another half century before the cause of yellow fever was discovered. In 1900, in Cuba, Walter Reed, of the United States Yellow Fever Board, identified the germ and demonstrated the carrier role of the mosquito. Control measures followed, eliminating the disease as a menace in the Panama Canal Zone. In 1964, the United States began a million dollar program to eliminate the *Aëdes aegypti* mosquito.

It is astounding to relate that in the fall of 1853, the tragedy that had struck New Orleans just weeks before seemed to be forgotten. Trade and commerce was as brisk as ever on the Mississippi, filling warehouses and boardinghouses. Immigrants crowded into customs houses. Newcomers replaced those that had been lost, and the city carried on with the booming prosperity of the 1850s.

THE EMERGENCE OF POLITICAL PARTIES

Soon after the Louisiana Purchase, it became evident that the population of New Orleans was divided into three distinct groups, and it was within these divisions that they would organize politically: 1) the *ancienne population*, 2) the new French, and 3) the Anglo-Americans. In the period between 1820 and 1850, the *ancienne population* and the New French usually joined the Whig Party. Throughout the nation, Whigs were generally wealthy aristocrats. In the South, they were also slayeowners. Anglo-Americans in New Orleans were almost all Democrats. The Democratic Party represented the rise of the common man, since the election of Andrew Jackson in 1828 and 1832. The hero of the Battle of New Orleans was popular in the city.

New Orleans voters operated on many levels. A presidential candidate would be supported as a Democrat or a Whig, according to Party allegiance. A gubernatorial, legislative, or mayoral candidate would win votes as a spokesman for either the Creole or the American faction.

The influx of Irish and German immigrants in the 1830s and 1840s complicated things. The Irish were clannish, but they were quick to be naturalized and they loved involvement in politics. Since the Irish were in such great numbers in the city as early as 1830 (when they tipped the scales for mayoral candidate Denis Prieur), both political parties began to work hard to win the Irish vote.

From 1828 until the coming of the Irish famine refugees in 1846, the arguments between the "Nativists" and the "foreigners" dragged on. The Nativists complained that the immigrants followed their party leaders blindly; that they organized into bands of foreign soldiery, armed and equipped and bearing a foreign name; that they celebrated feast days of their own country's patron saints; and that they were "Europe's most degraded population, men without knowledge, without principle, without patriotism."

Since the Irish, and immigrants in general, had anti-slavery propensities, they were the political targets for the prominent, wealthy, slave-owning Whigs. Although a hostility existed between the Irish and the Negroes (due mostly to competition for jobs), the Irish had been oppressed too long by the British to support an institution that fostered oppression. Paradoxically, many old established Irish business leaders, who had married Creole wives, were not only Whigs but slaveowners. This was also true of some well established Anglo-Americans.

The Democratic Party dominated national politics from 1801 to 1860. During this period, the opposition party had been called, at different times, Federalists, National-Republicans, and finally, Whigs.

As we have seen, the city split into three municipalities in 1836 and reunited in 1852. When they reunited, the Creoles wanted a common council which, in alliance with the Third District immigrants, they could control. The Americans wanted consolidation and annexation of the City of Lafayette, which would support them on basic issues. This latter plan was accepted.

To obtain the support of the Third District immigrants, many of the Creoles in the Vieux Carre joined the Democratic Party. Now the Americans in Faubourg St. Mary, both by choice and necessity, joined the Whig Party.

Just before the Civil War, the national Democratic Party split into the Northern Democrats and the Southern Democrats; the Whigs, divided over the same issue, began to disintegrate. The nation saw the emergence of a new political party, the Republican Party, in 1854–56. With their candidate, Abraham Lincoln, the Republicans won the presidential election of 1860.

In New Orleans, the Whigs ceased to exist, because of their anti-slavery sentiments. Those who had been Whigs and wished to retain their anti-Democratic identity, joined the Know Nothings, rabid "Nativists," whose main objective was to break the power of the immigrants in politics. It was easy to make the change from Whig to Know Nothing. Whigs were wealthy and powerful. The Nativist doctrine of the Know Nothings, which oppressed the immigrants, suited their purposes.

Throughout the summer of 1854, reckless remarks by Know Nothings convinced the Irish that the Americans were going to burn down St. Patrick's Church and slaughter Irish immigrants as they slept.

For ten days in September, armed gangs of Irish and Americans marched endlessly, causing needless destruction. Americans shot up Irish coffeehouses, calling them "headquarters of the enemy." On the evening of September 11, the Americans had gathered at Lafayette Square, the Irish at St. Mary's Market. A fight ensued on Camp Street. Two were killed, many wounded. Hostile feelings flared.

Just before the mayoralty election of 1858, the Know Nothings in New Orleans split. The Independents nominated Major P.G.T. Beauregard, and went after the old Whig vote; the American Party nominated Gerard Stith, a printer, and went after the labor vote. Two days before the election, the Creole-immigrant group formed a vigilante committee to "guarantee a peaceful election." They recruited 500 men, mostly Irish, who occupied the arsenal and the municipal buildings at Jackson Square. The Americans formed an organization which camped at Lafayette Square. Peace was achieved by means of a compromise, and without violence.

From 1860 to 1864, during the War Between the States, political parties had no purpose. Municipal government, as we shall see, gave way to military rule. Then, during Reconstruction, only two political parties remained, the Republicans (the members of the Federal army of occupation, and the blacks) and the Democrats (the defeated Southern whites). For more than half a century, the South was referred to as the Solid South, because of the total and predictable adherence of the whites to the Democratic Party and its policies.

Customs, Carnival, and Cemeteries

Father Douglas Doussan blesses the altar at St. Joseph the Worker Church in Marrero.   *(Courtesy Ethelyn Orso)*

Figure 32. A little girl receives "lagniappe" after her purchase.

CHAPTER VII

Customs, Carnival, and Cemeteries

CUSTOMS

When New Orleans became American in 1803, the port city became a refuge for the world. Down the Mississippi and from across the Atlantic came immigrants, bringing with them customs and traditions, which were to be their lifeline to a world they had left behind.

In a city that was predominately Catholic and known for its love of festivity, it is not strange that as many as twenty-five Holy Days a year, besides Sundays, came to have their own special celebrations.

On **Christmas Eve,** a peculiarity of the area is the lighting of bonfires all along the levee of the Mississippi. It is a very old tradition, supposedly begun by the Acadians, who were "so far from home that they had to guide 'Père Noel,' so he could find them." For weeks in advance of Christmas, river dwellers begin erecting pyramids of logs in graduated sizes, in preparation for the fires. The sight of the line of bonfires, from the opposite side of the river on Christmas Eve, is one of the most memorable spectacles the area has to offer.

Twelfth Night is King's Day, another religious holiday, when the three wise men of the Bible are said to have visited the Christ Child. It is the twelfth night after Christmas. It is celebrated in New Orleans by the baking and eating of "king cakes," circular rings of "coffee cake" dough sprinkled with colored granulated sugar. Inside the cake, a tiny doll or bean or ring is hidden. The guest who "gets" the doll gives the next party, and so it goes on weekly until Mardi Gras.

A forerunner in New Orleans of this charming party custom was the "Bal de Bouquet," which originated early in the 19th century. It was given by a bachelor chosen at the beginning of the season at the home of a lady whom he had designated his queen by crowning her with a wreath of flowers. After a few *quadrilles* at the party, the king (the bachelor) led the queen to the center of the floor, where she crowned a new king with a wreath of flowers. The ritual was repeated weekly until Mardi Gras. (The similarity to today's King Cake parties can easily be seen.)

Mardi Gras is so special in New Orleans and has such a history of its own that it will be treated in a separate section of this chapter.

St. Patrick's Day, March 17, is celebrated by the wearing of the green, as well as by parades, and by dances and banquets given by the Hibernians and other Irish-American organizations.

St. Joseph's Day, March 19, is observed by the building of St. Joseph Altars in the homes of Italians, in thanksgiving to the saint for favors granted. The altars originated in Sicily during the Middle Ages, when famine threatened the island. The people prayed to St. Joseph. One crop, the fava bean, survived to save them, and in thanksgiving, they prepared cooked food and laid it out on an altar for the needy. Orleanians of Sicilian descent still commemorate the day in the same way.

Figure 33. Visitors admire the artistry of the altar at Joseph the Worker Church.   *(Courtesty Ethelyn Orso)*

Throughout the year, many Italians make vows that if a prayer for help is answered, they will build an altar to St. Joseph in their homes each year on his feast day.

Today, the altars are elaborately decorated with bread baked in the shape of wreaths, crosses and hearts. Italian cakes and cookies are decorated with praying hands and Bibles. Baskets of fava beans and St. Joseph medals are placed on the altar to be distributed to visitors (as they did in the old days to ward off famine in the coming year). No meat is placed on the altar in keeping with Lenten penance, but there are dishes of fish, stuffed lobsters and crabs, eggplants and artichokes, as well as vegetables, fruits and pasta of many kinds.

On St. Joseph's Day, children dressed as Mary and Joseph take part in a little ceremony commemorating their search for shelter in Bethlehem. The Italians invite them in to share the wealth of their altars. Then the food is shared with friends and neighbors, or it is donated to a needy organization.

On St. Joseph Night, the Italian community gives a parade through the French Quarter, with floats, horses, bands, and marchers.

An interesting sidelight of this St. Joseph feast is the tradition of members of the black community parading as the Mardi Gras Indians. Only twice a year, on Mardi Gras Day and St. Joseph's Night do they appear in their colorful, elaborate costumes, with the ornate beadwork and the enormous feather headdresses. Tribes like the Wild Magnolias, the Black Eagles, the Yellow Pocahontas or the Wild Squatoolas compete in a colorful display of costumes. It is believed that their appearance on this particular feast day dates back to their veneration of St. Joseph in their voodoo rituals of the late 19th century.

Easter Sunday is a movable feast celebrated on the first Sunday following the first full moon after the spring equinox. This, of course, is a world-wide holiday. But in New Orleans, until her recent death, Germaine Cazenave Wells, descendent of Count Arnaud (founder of Arnaud's Restaurant) arrived at St. Louis Cathederal on Easter Sunday for several decades in an extravagant *chapeau*, after leading an Easter parade through the French Quarter. Today, the Germaine Wells parade continues but is followed by another at noon led by French Quarter entertainer Chris Owens.

The Spring Fiesta is a natural acknowledgement of the beautiful season of spring, conceived to pay tribute to the cultural heritage of Louisiana. Begun in 1947, the Spring Fiesta is a tourist-oriented celebration. For 19 days, beginning on the first Friday after Easter, young ladies of New Orleans, dressed in ante-bellum costumes, escort groups of tourists through the French Quarter ("Patios by candlelight"), and the beautiful old homes of the Garden District. Plantations along Bayou Teche, River Road, Bayou Lafourche, and Feliciana offer similar tours of private homes at this time.

All Saints Day, November 1, has a very special meaning to Orleanians. Since the water table of the city made above-ground burials a necessity, residents took the "opportunity" to erect elaborate tombs and mini-mausoleums to house their dead. The upkeep of these properties was a way of life and a year-round occupation. But special pains were taken in preparation for All Saints Day, which included whitewashing tombs, pulling weeds, sweeping sidewalks, and bringing vases to the burial site. In the olden days, tombs and headstones were draped with flags or with black "crepes." Ground plots were edged with painted shells, China dogs and pig banks. And on the day itself, thousands thronged to the cemetery (and they still do today) to bring flowers and pray for their loved ones in these "cities of the dead."

The first All Saints Day activity celebrated the re-opening of St. Peter's Cemetery in 1742, and the completion of the fence surrounding it. The work had been paid for by the rich, with labor the gift of the poor.

STREET VENDORS

Almost from the very beginning of New Orleans history, there were street vendors, singing their cadences as they advertised their wares to the housewives of the city. In colonial days, slave owners sent older slaves, who could no longer work in the fields, out to sell the surplus products of the plantation. The owners had to buy licenses for their slaves, but thereby increased their annual income by thousands of dollars.

Vendors endured well into the 1960s, and even today, an occasional truckload of fresh vegetables or fruit may still be seen in one of the residential areas of town. At the turn of the century, the housewife depended almost entirely on street vendors, and went to market only if it was in walking distance and if she was in need of meat, an item which did not appear daily on the supper table.

The sight of the mule-drawn vegetable wagon was a welcome one for it was a break in the day's routine, and the sound of the vendor's melodious "Water-melon! Red to the rind!" or "Ah got Ba-na-na, Lay-dee!" was music to the ear of the housewife. The rendition of the vendor's songs and chants was limited only by his imagination and talent. "Black-ber-reees! Ah got black ber-reees!" might be warbled into the morning air with all the pathos of a tenor in the Metropolitan Opera House.

Many vendors walked, carrying baskets filled with a variety of vegetables on their heads. Their prices were low, their produce fresh, and the cost of any item was subject to discussion. Each season saw the appearance of its own specialties. In early summer, there were strawberries, followed later on by watermelons, and in the fall by wild ducks. During Lent, there were always fish and oysters. There were

Figure 34. New Orleanians decorate the tombs of their dead for All Saints' Day.

milk vendors, ice-cream vendors, bread and cake vendors, singing the familiar "Calas! Tout chauds!". There was the Corn Meal Man, the Hot Pie Man, the Waffle Man, the Candy Man, the Broom Man, the Clothespole Man, the Chimney Sweep, the Bottle Man, the Knife Sharpener, the Umbrella Man, Zozo La Brique, who sold brick dust to scrub stoops and walks in certain sections. And then there were spasm bands of small Negro boys who did a slapfoot dance with makeshift instruments, hoping for a handout from passing pedestrians.

At the French Market, Choctaw Indians sold sassafras and other roots and herbs. Negresses in *tignons* sold rice cakes, molasses, and pralines. In the markets, which were spread all over town, everything was available from chickens to fish to oysters to live canaries in cages. Even women in search of "day's work" were singing out their trades, waving their washboards above their heads.

SUPERSTITION

Due to the constituency of the people, superstition ran rampant throughout the city. The Irish had brought over their own superstitions, most of which were considered comic, or at least, not taken too seriously. The blacks, because they so long adhered to the voodoo cult, feared *gris-gris* signs as evil omens (ritual objects such as crossed sticks, circles of salt, roosters' heads). Gamblers, with which the city abounded, were naturals for superstition. Many played the lottery, consulting their "dream books" for the numbers they should play on the lottery if they had dreamed of fire or death or rain or even of red beans.

The Creoles, gamblers or not, all believed that dreams had meanings:

> A dream of pulling a tooth meant death was coming.
> Dreaming of trees presaged joy and profit.

They also feared the following omens:

> Rain or tears at a wedding meant bad luck.
> Flowers out of season brought bad luck.
> The transplanting of a weeping willow will bring about violent death.
> Never spit in the fire: it will draw your lungs up.
> Never sleep with the moon in your face. It will draw your mouth to one side and make it crooked.
> The Creole Mirror superstition: If three men look in a mirror at one time, the youngest will die. If three girls look in a mirror at one time, the eldest will marry within a year.

There were literally hundreds of such omens and superstitious beliefs.

JAZZ

New Orleans is the birthplace of jazz, which is its only original contribution to the arts. Jazz first gained attention around the turn of the century, although its beginnings reach far back into history. When slaves were first brought to America, they carried with them a memory of the music they had learned in West Africa or acquired in the Caribbean Islands. The slaves chanted as they worked, and their songs spoke of love, anger, longing, joy and despair. In New Orleans, under the liberal French and Spanish rulers, slaves were allowed the freedom to sing and dance together, which black people did not always enjoy in other parts of the United States. They made their own musical instruments—banjos, from gourds; reeds, to blow or pluck—and played music to accompany their dancing in the Congo Square, and at the many picnics, parades, and other celebrations in or around the city. Many musicians were needed in a city of so many festivities.

Free men of color often had an entirely different culture from the slaves. Some were even sent by their white fathers to European schools, where they studied classical music. People considered the outbreak of jazz (or ragtime, as it was originally called), around 1887, to be nothing more than European music played badly. Innovations in music, such as syncopation, staccatoes, and timbres, later called "revolutionary," were considered by these trained musicians, to be "mistakes." Variations on a theme, as performed in European music, became improvisations, which were called "jazzing it up." The raw-talent jazz musician would take a melody which consisted of just a few notes, like "When the Saints Go Marchin' In," and play it every possible way for variation. By the standards of European-trained musicians, these jazz musicians either *could not* or *would not* play music as it was written. Nice young ladies were not encouraged to play jazz. It was considered disorderly music, "closet music," rebellious and untraditional. *The Times Picayune,* in 1917, called an attraction to jazz a "low streak in man's taste."

Jazz was not born in Storyville, but grew up and came of age there (1897–1917). The product sold in the bordellos was *not* music. Music was an accessory, paid for by the tips given musicians. With its many dance halls and bars, Storyville gave employment to many jazz musicians. There were also "spasm bands" in the 1890s, playing homemade instruments on street corners, like Emile "Stalebread Charley" Lacombe, who got his start that way and became one of the jazz greats.

The audience at the bordellos was generally mellow and agreeable to whatever was played, which allowed the musicians ample opportunity to experiment and improvise.

Storyville proved to be the melting pot in which the perfect ingredients for jazz were blended: the technical training and know-how of the downtown black Creole musicians and the raw-talent improvisa-

Figure 35. Olympia Brass Band of New Orleans.   *(Photo by Johnny Donnels)*

tions of the uptown black American musicians. Here, the two were forced to mix. Their disparate heritages were wed and soon gave birth to jazz. Alan Lomax, in his *Biography of Jelly Roll Morton,* expressed it this way:

"Creoles (downtown Negroes) who played in Storyville were compelled to accept blacks (uptown Negroes) as equals, and this was bitter medicine."

Paul Dominguez, a black Creole violinist, explained in the same biography:

"See, us downtown people, we didn't think so much of this rough uptown jazz, until we couldn't make a living otherwise. That's how they made a fiddler out of a violinist—me, I'm talking about. A *fiddler* is *not* a violinist, but a *violinist can be a fiddler.*" As to his feelings about black American pure talent:

"I don't know how they do it, but they do it. They can't tell you what's on the paper. But you just play it. Then *they* play the Hell out of it."

This forced cooperation was especially important in building understanding between blacks and whites who played together when jazz was just beginning after the Civil War. Jazz played more than a minor role in the building of mutual respect and admiration between the races. "Piano keys opened doors to many white homes for black musicians," according to Al Rose, *Storyville*.

Many New Orleans-born musicians, like "King" Oliver, Louis Armstrong, and Jelly Roll Morton, achieved fame in Chicago, New York, or on the West Coast after starting in Storyville.

Jazz funerals are still held, though now almost exclusively for deceased jazz musicians. In these processions, the musicians play sad, slow music on the way to the cemetery, but after they have "turned him loose," as they say, referring to burying their dead, they lead the mourners away to the beat of a gay and lively tune, like "When the Saints Go Marchin' In," for they are celebrating the jubilation of a soul gone to its reward. They strut and twirl umbrellas, picking up "second-liners" (bystanders who join in the singing and marching).

Not much has changed in jazz since it beginnings. Emile "Stalebread Charley" Lacombe called his band the "Razzy Dazzy Spasm Band." Today, the Hyatt advertises Le Club as a place where you can swing into everything that's "jazzy, snazzy, and ritzy" in New Orleans. Jazz is alive and well and struttin' in New Orleans!

STREETCARS

Streetcars have become associated with New Orleans, not because this was the only city in which streetcars ran, but because, while streetcars were being replaced by buses in other towns, they remained the mode of public transportation in New Orleans for many decades. New Orleans has a way of lagging behind in such matters, as it did with horse-and-buggies well into the automobile era, and with gaslight when other big cities were long electrified. This lack of desire for change stems not only from lethargy, which might be blamed on a debilitating climate, but from a habit of clinging to the old ways, the gracious passing lifestyle.

The streetcars of New Orleans were successors of its original railroad lines. The early railroads were extremely crude. They were nothing more than iron bars nailed to wooden beams laid lengthwise across ties about five feet apart. The rails often worked loose and penetrated the floors of the coaches. Boilers exploded, flying cinders set fire to nearby crops, floods washed out bridges, and cars jumped the rails.

The earliest railroad in New Orleans was the Pontchartrain Railroad, chartered in 1830, which ran on Elysian Fields from the river to Lake Pontchartrain. It ran 5.18 miles, with horse-drawn cars, replaced in 1832 by a steam locomotive, the "Smoky Mary." The line (probably the second to have been built in the United States) ran for 101 years until 1932.

The St. Charles Streetcar Line, whose predecessor was the New Orleans and Carrollton Railroad, is the oldest continuously operating street railway in the world. The line was incorporated as the New Orleans and Carrollton Railroad Company on February 9, 1833 by the Louisiana legislature, and continues to operate today.

It ran from the business district of the city up St. Charles Avenue (then Nayades Street) through the Garden District, on its way to the city of Carrollton. As far back as 1834, a spur route turned off St. Charles and came out Jackson Avenue to the river along the city's most elegant thoroughfare. This had been a mule-car railroad. The rate of travel could not exceed four miles an hour. The N.O. & C.R.R. was later a steam driven railroad, and by 1900, it was all electric.

Originally, the N.O. & C.R.R. terminal was roughly at the end of St. Charles Avenue. In 1846, the town of Carrollton began to extend Carrollton Avenue back through the swamps to a navigation canal known as the New Basin. The roadway was complete in 1862, and an omnibus line was initiated.

After the Civil War, in 1866, General P.G.T. Beauregard and some of his associates leased the N.O. & C.R.R. for twenty-five years. Many new omnibus and street railway companies were formed in the late 1850s and the 1860s. These included the Pontchartrain Railroad.

By 1876, the N.O. City and Lake Rail Road started running steam "dummy" trains along the route of the New Basin Canal from the city to the lake. An amusement park arose, christened West End Park in 1880. (See Chapter IX.) The railway line, electrified in 1898, was a 6½-mile ride from New Orleans on West End trains which consisted of a motor car pulling several opensided trailers, a thrill enjoyed by thousands.

In 1909, the New Orleans Railway and Light Company acquired a site known as Spanish Fort. The fort had been in existence as a resort long before West End Park, and the two parks on the lakefront were long to be competitors for the business of lake enthusiasts. Electric cars ran out to the resort in 1911. The railway company rebuilt and reopened the amusement center, which had been abandoned when railway service was discontinued in 1903. (See Chapter IX.)

By 1953, only two streetcar lines, the St. Charles and the Canal, remained in operation in New Orleans. Ten years later, the New Orleans Public Service removed the Canal Line and replaced it with buses, not without loud and vehement protestations.

On May 31, 1964, the St. Charles Streetcar became the last streetcar line in New Orleans. The electric streetcars now operating on the route (which provide visitors with a tour of the New Orleans business district, the mansions of the Garden District, the University area, Audubon Park, and the Carrollton area) are typical of the streetcars in use in the early part of the century.

The car in use was designed and built by the Perley A. Thomas Car Company, High Point, North Carolina, in 1923–4. It is known in New Orleans as a streetcar, not a trolley, and it is treasured by the city. Over the years, modifications have included replacement of the mahogany sash and canvas roof with metal. Recently, exact change fareboxes and metal automatic doors were installed to facilitate one-man operation. The most nostalgic features are the exposed ceiling lightbulbs and the rich wooden seats. The seats can be reversed, depending on the streetcar's direction, and have fine brass hand holds on their aisle corners. The historical character of the streetcar is painstakingly maintained. In 1973, the Streetcar Line was placed on the National Register of Historic Places by the Department of the Interior 140 years after it was organized.

Through 1987, free transportation was provided on public transit to the nuns of the city, because the Ursuline nuns prayed so unceasingly for victory in the Battle of New Orleans in 1815, when victory seemed so impossible.

In 1988, seven vintage streetcars painted red with gold trim, became operational. These "Ladies in Red," the first to begin running since 1926, run 1.9 miles, connecting the many new riverfront attractions.

CARNIVAL

Most customs, as we have seen, were based on the celebration of feast days of the Roman Catholic Church, although they were not all religious celebrations. The most famous of these is *Mardi Gras,* also known as **Carnival,** which is the farthest thing from a religous holiday. The words *Mardi Gras* are French for Fat Tuesday, a name that hints at the feasting and partying that goes on throughout the day. **Carnival** is derived from Latin, meaning "farewell to the flesh."

Mardi Gras is celebrated the day before Ash Wednesday, when the 40-day season of Lent officially begins, and Catholics are to fast and do penance. The feast of Mardi Gras was brought to America by Iberville and Bienville, when they christened the bayou they discovered on March 3, 1699, Mardi Gras Bayou. They had found it on Shrove Tuesday, the day before Ash Wednesday.

In the years between 1806 and 1823, after Louisiana was American, laws forbad masking and balls, so private clubs began. In 1827, some students, returning from their studies in Paris, donned costumes and danced in the streets, as they had seen maskers do in Paris. They threw flowers to the crowds watching them. (Later on, they threw flour *on* the crowds.)

The first parade was held in 1837. Because hostility existed between the Irish and the Blacks over jobs, and violence was likely, masks were forbidden. In 1839, the first float, a papier maché creation, appeared. On it, a design called Chanticleer flapped its wings and crowed. On this occasion, it seems, lime was thrown on the crowds instead of flour. Trouble was brewing in the tempestuous heterogeneous population. Activities were becoming dangerous, and the press was calling for an end to Mardi Gras. A small group met soon after to form a secret society that would restore order and dignity to the New Orleans celebration.

In 1857, the **Mystick Krewe of Comus** was born, the organization that was credited with saving the institution of Carnival. Their tableau was an ambitious one, based on *Paradise Lost*.

In 1870, the **Twelfth Night Revelers** emerged, staging a tableau with the nebulous theme of the Tide of English Humor. Quite a sophisticated project for a population reputed to be uneducated!

Rex, the King of Carnival, whose parade takes place on Mardi Gras Day, held his first reign in 1872. *The Bee,* a New Orleans newspaper, referred to the organizers as "Swine-eating Saxons," an insult directed at their English heritage, although there were, undoubtedly, some French Creoles among the organizers. In the same year, the **Knights of Momus** made their debut. Other krewes soon materialized, each with its own special parade and ball date.

Rex had been organized by 40 enterprising men in just a few weeks, to honor the visit of the Grand Duke Alexis Romanoff Alexandrovitch, of pre-revolutionary Russia, who had made an amorous pursuit of Lydia Thompson, a singer, to New Orleans. Miss Thompson had sung a song in a burlesque show, *Bluebeard,* entitled, "If Ever I Cease to Love," which the bands at the Mardi Gras balls obligingly played and which became the theme song of the holiday. Although its lyrics include such nonsense as "If ever I cease to love, If ever I cease to love, May oysters have legs and cows lay eggs, If ever I cease to love," it has nevertheless remained the theme song of Mardi Gras for over a century.

Also introduced by Rex were the Mardi Gras colors: purple for justice, green for faith, and gold for power. The most plausible explanation for their selection is that they were the colors of the king's costume in the production of Richard II, enacted by Lawrence Barrett, which was playing in the city at the time.

On that first day of Rex's reign, the king rode a bay charger. The fatted beef (Boeuf Gras), the symbol of Mardi Gras, was represented by "Old Jeff," a bull from the stockyards. The krewe was masked as playing cards. The following year, there was such a demand for invitations to the Rex Ball that 4,000 were mailed, and the ball had to be held in Exposition Hall. In 1874, Rex arrived in the city by steamboat at the foot of Canal Street on the Monday before Mardi Gras. All the

Figure 36. The "Arrival of Rex" on the Monday before Mardi Gras was inaugurated in 1874. This old print from Frank Leslie's Illustrated Newspaper shows Rex's arrival by the Rob't E. Lee for the 1879 Carnival. (Courtesy Leonard V. Huber Collection)

131

ships in the harbor tooted their whistles in greeting. To this day, there is a river parade. Rex is the only king not masked, since the original Rex was made up to look like Richard II in the play.

The organizations are now so numerous that it takes two full weeks for all parades to roll, frequently several on the same date, and the balls now begin before Christmas, so that all may fit on the social calendar.

Each organization pays for its own parade and ball. The parades are a gift to the people of the city; the balls are private parties for the entertainment of the friends of krewe members.

The most prestigious krewes are those of Comus, Momus, Proteus, and Rex, who hold both parades and balls. The Twelfth Night Revelers, founded in 1870, is the oldest non-parading krewe. Other organizations that date back to the 19th century are: Atlanteans (1890), and the Elves of Oberon (1894), Nereus (1896), and Mithras (1897). In 1871, the Twelfth Night Revelers established two carnival traditions. A queen was introduced for the first time at a carnival ball, and the throwing of trinkets was begun by a member of the organization, dressed as Santa Claus. Both traditions remain to this day in almost all carnival organizations.

Bacchus and Endymion, both begun in 1968, are organizations which have broken with tradition. Instead of selecting their monarchs from the lists of prominent social and civic leaders, they choose internationally famous show business personalities like Danny Kaye, Phil Harris, Bob Hope, Perry Como, and Englebert Humperdinck. Entertainers like Pete Fountain and Doc Severinsen are on hand annually to play for the krewe members and their friends. These organizations are now big business.

In 1982, the total cost of the Bacchus ball and parade was $980,000, according to Bacchus Captain Augie Perez. Bacchus was formed in 1968 by a handful of businessmen who met to study the possibility of changing the whole concept of carnival organizations. Their floats are the largest ever constructed, costing as much as $100,000 for a single float.

The doubloon, which is struck in the image of a particular Mardi Gras organization, is a modern innovation, which was begun by the Rex Krewe in 1960. The 1960 Rex doubloon was designed by H. Alvin Sharpe. Today, more than fifty organizations throw doubloons to the spectators, and many have become collectors' items.

The Rex and Comus jewels (crowns, scepters, necklaces, etc.) are made in Paris each year by an old firm of worldwide renown. They are allowed to be imported duty free, because of the public nature of the celebrations.

On Mardi Gras Day, in the Garden District and on St. Charles Avenue, Mardi Gras flags fly before the homes of former kings of Rex.

No Mardi Gras celebrations were held for two years during World

War I, for four years during World War II, and in the year 1951 (Korean War). In 1951, Mars (War) paraded instead of Rex.

The expansion of Mardi Gras into the suburbs in the 1960s and 70s opened participation to more neighborhoods. Super krewes such as Bacchus and Endymion, helped modernize the festivities.

Parading krewes traditionally admitted new members of their own choice until 1992 when a ruling was passed by the City Council restricting the use of city streets for parading to organizations admitting any and all applicants. Three of the city's oldest krewes—Momus, Comus, and Proteus—discontinued parading, although they continued to hold their Carnival Balls. Others, like Rex and Hermes, complied with the new regulation and continued to parade. Orpheus, a beautiful new parade bagan to roll in 1994, replacing Proteus on its traditional Monday (Lundi Gras) night before Carnival.

CEMETERIES

Some visitors to New Orleans are astonished at the sight of more than 40 cemeteries, where above-ground burial takes place. Such internment reflects French and Spanish burial customs and accommodates the high water table, which is the result of both climate and terrain. Heavy rains are common, and because the city is largely below sea level, coffins would rise to the surface of the ground, unless properly anchored.

Early in the 18th Century, mortuary architects began building six-foot-thick brick walls to keep deadly diseases inside the cemetery. Later, the walls contained casket-sized niches called "ovens," available as year-and-a-day rental tombs. Into these ovens the coffins were slid, inscribed marble (or wooden) slabs closing off the opening. Walls of "ovens" surrounded the first cemeteries and are still found in St. Louis Cemeteries #1, 2, and 3, and in other old cemeteries like Lafayette and St. Roch.

Cemeteries were always built on the outskirts of town. Because of this, we can trace the growth of the city by the dates and locations of its main cemeteries: St. Louis No. 1 on Basin Street in 1789; St. Louis No. 2 on Claiborne Avenue in 1824; St. Louis No. 3 at the end of Esplanade near Bayou St. John in 1854.

The first cemetery in the city was St. Peter's Cemetery, dated 1724. The first Protestant Cemetery was on Girod Street, built in 1822. Many others followed, and by 1860, there were fourteen cemeteries at the end of Canal Street.

The city was growing in population and wealth, and in the thirty years after the opening of St. Louis No. 2 (1824), the new cemeteries began to be filled with private family tombs, many of them elaborate and beautiful. The Avet and Lazzize tomb, and the Pilié tomb in St.

Louis No. 2 are among the most striking examples of iron craftsmanship to be found.

J.N.B. de Pouilly, who came to New Orleans from France in 1830 and designed the St. Louis Exchange Hotel and the present St. Louis Cathedral, brought scale drawings of tombs from the Père Lachaise Cemetery in Paris, the best to be found in Greek Revival design. From these sketches, de Pouilly built such beautiful burial places as the Plauché tomb in St. Louis No. 2, of Greek Revival design. He created a style of mortuary architecture which continues in New Orleans to this day.

Metairie Cemetery was built in 1872 on Metairie Ridge, on the grounds of the Metairie Race Track by a syndicate of New Orleans businessmen. During the Civil War, a portion of the track area had been converted into Camp Miller, an army training camp, for a short time. It became the largest and most elaborate burial ground in the city. There are more than 4,000 above-ground vaults and tombs, and as many ground plots, spread out over 150 acres, with a 1 1/16-mile track as the roadway.

Charles Howard of the Metairie Jockey Club died in 1885 and is buried in an ornate mausoleum on Central Avenue in Metairie Cemetery. A marble figure of a man with his finger to his lips decorates its exterior. The story is told that his exclusion from the Metairie Jockey Club as a non-Creole inspired his decision to turn the track into a cemetery, when he later bought the property. After the Civil War, the South was too poor, in any case, to support a race track.

Josie Arlington, a famous "Storyville" madam, had a tomb in Metairie Cemetery. She bought it in 1914, before her death. Because of a stop light's reflection on her pink marble tomb, it seemed that Josie, even after death, was still in the "red-light" district.

Daniel Moriarty built a magnificent monument to his wife who died in 1887. The tall shaft of the Moriarty Monument stands just to the left of the entrance, graced by the statues of four life-size female figures at its base. The statues are simply stock figures placed on the monument for effect by the builder, but the story is told that the famous humorist, Irving J. Cobb, when visiting the cemetery in the 1920s, asked about the identity of the four females. His cab driver answered: "Faith, Hope, and Charity." Cobb asked: "And the fourth?" to which the cabby replied, "And who else but Mrs. Moriarty?" (In actual fact, the fourth represents Memory, carrying a wreath of immortelles.)

Kemper Williams is buried in an Egyptian temple.

P.B.S. Pinchback, Louisiana's only black governor, was buried in Metairie Cemetery in 1921.

Metairie Cemetery is one of the showplaces of the city, with its beautiful landscaping, paved walks, lagoons and many fine trees. Its main aisle fronted on Bayou Metairie and was the location preferred by prominent citizens. Bayou Metairie is now Metairie Road.

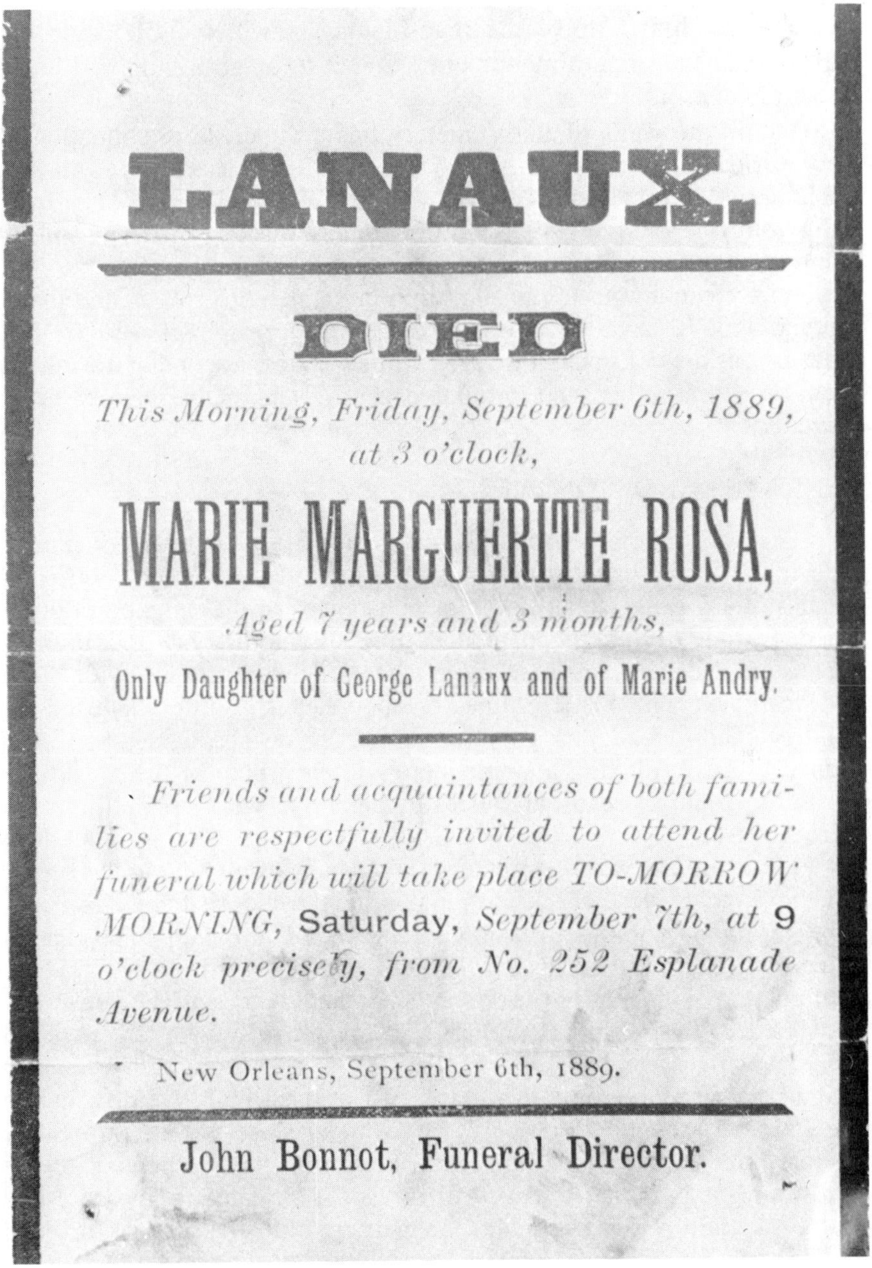

LANAUX.

DIED

This Morning, Friday, September 6th, 1889,
at 3 o'clock,

MARIE MARGUERITE ROSA,

Aged 7 years and 3 months,

Only Daughter of George Lanaux and of Marie Andry.

Friends and acquaintances of both families are respectfully invited to attend her funeral which will take place TO-MORROW MORNING, Saturday, *September 7th, at* 9 *o'clock precisely, from No. 252 Esplanade Avenue.*

New Orleans, September 6th, 1889.

John Bonnot, Funeral Director.

Figure 37. Death notices were tacked to lampposts in 19th and early 20th century to notify neighbors and friends.   (Courtesy Leonard V. Huber Collection)

135

In the center of a large green mound surrounded by palm trees is the handsome granite shaft, the Army of Northern Virginia Monument, commemorating the Confederate general, Stonewall Jackson, and the men of the Louisiana Division of the Army of Northern Virginia who fought under him. Above the mausoleum, in which 2,500 men are buried, rises the granite monument, 32 feet in height. Atop this is the statue of Jackson.

Within the walls of this cemetery lies an interesting collection of New Orleans characters, including seven governors, six mayors (including Martin Behrman, who closed Storyville; he and Josie Arlington, one of its madams, are neighbors in the cemetery) and 49 kings of Carnival.

As a closing note to our narration on cemeteries, let us add that a century ago, because of the abundance of cypress in the area, New Orleans was the coffin capital of the United States, a fact that must have been both reassuring and profitable during the many yellow fever epidemics.

FUNERALS AND MOURNING

The care of these burial sites was a subject of great concern to Orleanians, as were the rules and traditions that governed mourners. Death notices were tacked to poles and fences in the neighborhood of the deceased, giving the date and time of internment, and inviting friends. Horses, pulling black shiny hearses, were draped with black and decorated with black plumes on their heads. White was used for children, and lavender or grey for middle-aged. The horses had been trained to march, taking a single step with each note of the music.

At the hour of death, all clocks in the homes were stopped, mirrors were covered, and a crepe was hung on the front door. The huge "wake" coffee pot was resurrected, since wakes were held in the home. All the women wore black clothing, which could be bought second-hand or rented for the occasion. Undertakers provided a service of redecorating poorly furnished homes and provided chairs for the visitors. A few touches of black crepe here and there, and the house was transformed. "Mourning Hangings and Catafalque" were advertised at moderate prices, or on moderate terms. "Coffin Furniture" was also offered at reasonable prices, and the cast iron furniture we now use in our gardens was first designed for cemetery use, to accommodate visitors. At wakes and funerals, mourning was expected to be unrestrained. Lamentations were revered. To Orleanians, the care one took of the family burial site was the measure of his respect for the dead and the grief he still bore. Creoles, especially, kept an eye on burial sites close to their family tombs, and were quick to comment on the lack of care given this vault or that plot.

136

NEW ORLEANS
YESTERDAY AND TODAY
ILLUSTRATIONS
1857–1994

1857. Parlor of Gallier House, 1134 Royal Street, built by architect James Gallier, Jr., for his home in 1857. A museum property of Tulane University.
(Photo by Susann Gandolfo)

1925. Four rows of Canary Island palms graced Anseman Avenue in City Park. The bare-breasted statues in front of the rows, which came from the Cotton Exchange, caused much outrage and were removed to the Metairie Cemetery. (Courtesy City Park Collection)

1984. At entrance to the Louisiana World Exposition, semi-nude figures reminiscent of the City Park statutes, once again caused a furor in the city; but remained from May to November, 1984, to welcome visitors to the Centennial Plaza.

1929. The lighthouse in Lake Pontchartrain, built in 1838, guarded Milneberg and offered a signal for ships from the lake's north shore. The light was extinguished in 1929 and the lighthouse turned over to the Levee Board. It found itself high and dry in 1935 when WPA money helped pump sand from the lake bottom to create lakefront property. In 1939, Pontchartrain Beach Amusement Park moved to the end of Elysian Fields (now UNO) and the lighthouse wound up in Kiddieland. Pontchartrain Beach closed in 1983.

1928. A "20s" look. A statue of Hebe, the Olympian cup bearer, gazed down Lelong Avenue for sixty-five years. Donated by Commodore Ernest Lee Jahncke.

1922. A "20s" sound. Reverend Edward Cummings, S.J., president of Loyola University, made the first radio broadcast in Louisiana March 31, 1922, the day the license for WWL was granted. The telephone-like apparatus was in Marquette Hall at Loyola. (Courtesy Father Thomas Clancy, S.J. and Loyola University)

1923. *King Oliver's Creole Jazz Band. Sitting, L to R: Baby Dodds, Honore Dutrey, Louis Armstrong, Johnny Dodds, and Lil Hardin (Louis Armstrong's second wife). Standing, L to R: King Oliver and Bill Johnson.* (*Courtesy Hogan Jazz Archives, Tulane University Library*)

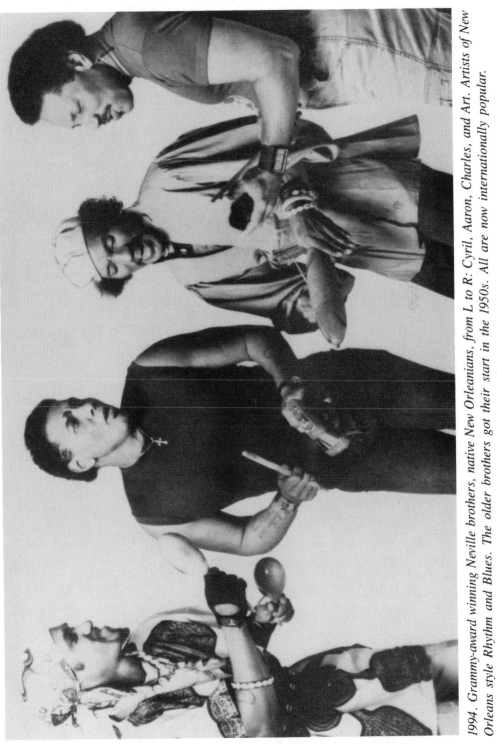

1994. Grammy-award winning Neville brothers, native New Orleanians, from L to R: Cyril, Aaron, Charles, and Art. Artists of New Orleans style Rhythm and Blues. The older brothers got their start in the 1950s. All are now internationally popular.

Photography by: Michael Jang

1929. Canal and Baronne before the Canal Street Beautification Project of 1930–31. On left side of Baronne, note Liggett's Drug Store advertising Jacob's Candies and the Strand Theater. Continuing left, the Exclusive Shop, Miller Brothers, the Godchaux Building. On the lake corner of Baronne, Parlor Stores for rent.

1967. Canal and Baronne on Mardi Gras Day, 1967. Left, Walgreen's Drug Store (where Parlor stores were for rent in picture on facing page), Graff's Men's Store, Cine Royale. Right, behind REX sign, Maison Blanche, then Audubon Bldg., Kress five-and-dime (white facade).

1950s. The river at Canal Street with pedestrian ramp to Algiers Ferry. Note Poydras Street Wharf (lower left); L&N Railroad Shed (to right of ramp).

1994. The river at Canal Street, now flanked by the Hilton and Marriott Hotels. The riverfront, cleared of warehouses, is beautified by the Aquarium (left foreground), raising its circular disk to the sky and a 19th-century design riverboat.   (Courtesy Port of New Orleans)

1920. Grand Stand at the Fair Grounds Race Track.

1993. On December 17, 1993, the historic Fair Grounds Race Track was razed by fire, destroying a century-old landmark on Gentilly Boulevard.

(Photo by Chris E. Mickal. N.O.F.D. Photo Unit)

1960. Civil Rights pickets walk in the rain outside Woolworth's five-and-dime on Canal and Rampart Streets.
(The Marion James Porter Collection. New Orleans Public Library)

1960. Civil Rights sit-in at the lunch counter at Woolworth's. (The Marion James Porter Collection).
(Courtesy New Orleans Public Library)

On May 11, 1988, the Cabildo, where the Louisiana Purchase was signed in 1803, was set afire by a roofer's torch. The third floor and cupola were destroyed. Many artifacts were water damaged.

(Photo by Chris E. Mickal, N.O.F.D. Photo Unit)

On February 27, 1994, the Cabildo reopened after an eight-million-dollar renovation.

1994. Faulkner House, 624 Pirate's Alley, is now the site of a rare bookstore, Faulkner House Books. It is headquarters of The Pirate's Alley Faulkner Society and the literary magazine, The Double Dealer *Redux. The store is located in the room where William Faulkner lived.* (Courtesy Faulkner House)

New Orleans, An Occupied City, 1862–1876

General Benjamin Franklin Butler headed the occupation of New Orleans for seven months during the Civil War. He was loathed by the natives who called him "Beast" Butler and "Spoons" Butler.
(Courtesy Lloyd Huber for the late Leonard V. Huber)

(Courtesy Leonard V. Huber Collection)

Figure 38. Federal Fleet passing Forts Jackson and St. Philip. Fort Jackson is at the left.

CHAPTER VIII

New Orleans, An Occupied City, 1862–1876

A picture of New Orleans in the decade before the Civil War is pre-requisite to an understanding of why certain events took place *here* rather than somewhere else. In 1860, New Orleans was the largest city in the South, and the largest cotton market in the world, handling in that one year, two million bales of cotton. Thirty-five hundred steamboats docked at its wharves, and its total trade amounted to $324,000,000. It was a trans-shipment center for all exports coming down the Mississippi, and the port held a virtual monopoly on trade in the interior of the country. New Orleans was slow in building railroads, however, having built only 80 miles of rails when the war began. And although the steamboat had made its first voyage early in the century, there were still impediments to shipping, like snags and low water points, especially at the mouth of the river. The service of bar pilots was unsatisfactory, and the rates for towing were prohibitive.

New Orleans, with a population of 168,000, was sixth in size among urban cities in the nation. An urban aristocracy existed by the middle of the 19th century, to which one belonged by virtue of birth or property. Citizens whose ancestors had been in the city several generations called themselves "Creoles," a term whose definition is still much in dispute. According to *Jewell's Crescent Illustrated,* the local directory of 1873, it meant simply "born here." If this is so, in 1860, there were Creole French, Creole Irish, Creole Germans, Creole Jews, and even Creole Negroes.

The middle class consisted of businessmen, skilled workers, clerks, and grocers. The proletariat consisted mainly of Germans and Irish, who had arrived too recently in the city to have earned places among the upper classes, and were considered a laboring class on the lowest level. In the fourth social class were the blacks, who enjoyed considerable freedom in New Orleans in the twenty years before the Civil War. Many were skilled workers or house servants. If they were slaves, they were sometimes hired out by their masters; if they were free, they could easily get work. Free Negroes included small businessmen and skilled artisans, many of whom were well-to-do. As the slavery issue grew more tense, the state legislature put more restrictions on free persons of color, finally forbidding manumission in 1857, causing some free Negroes to emigrate to Haiti, and all Negroes who remained to welcome the Federals when they arrived in 1862.

In 1853, as we have seen, the worst yellow fever epidemic ever to hit New Orleans took the lives of 10,000 people. But yellow fever was not the only "sickness" from which the city suffered. Drinking was widespread, prostitution was accepted and even advertised, and gambling was a way of life. Political corruption and illegal voting, especially among immigrants, was tolerated.

And yet, it was a city of contrasts. The architecture in the richer parts of town was beautiful, the homes of the wealthy exquisitely furnished, the cuisine superb. Pleasures abounded during Mardi Gras season. There was a regular opera season, and, at any time of the year, there were plays at the Théâtre d'Orléans. Concerts were staged featuring well-known artists. There was horse-racing at the Metairie Track, and hunting and fishing within easy reach of the city. Even the Negroes had their enjoyment on Sunday afternoons, when they danced uninhibitedly in the Congo Square (in front of the present Municipal Auditorium.)

Most citizens were Catholic. Others were Episcopalian, Methodist, or Jewish. Fraternal organizations had already been formed to assist the immigrants in coping with their problems.

New Orleans' citizens were opposed to secession. This was not because they opposed slavery. On the contrary, they defended it vehemently. But they were afraid that secession would destroy the city's trade with the upper Mississippi Valley, which was paramount to its prosperity.

To New Orleanians, secession did not seem to be necessary to protect the institution of slavery. When Lincoln was elected, however, sentiments changed rapidly. Lincoln had said that he favored non-extension of slavery. The handwriting was on the wall: eventually, he would see to it that it was wiped out altogether. In 1861, Louisiana had to decide whether to follow the other southern states and make a final break with the union, or attend a convention of southern states to make one last attempt at compromise. Louisiana voted on secession.

The problems of the Confederacy were numerous. There was no organized government at the time of the outbreak of the war. A Confederate cabinet had to be appointed, agencies set up for coordination, and decisions made for strategy. There was a minimum of ships and war materials, and no factories to produce more. President Jefferson Davis decided, for this reason, to fight a defensive war.

BATTLE OF THE FORTS

A major episode of the War between the States was the Battle of the Forts at the mouth of the river and the fall of New Orleans in April, 1862. Not until Vicksburg fell in July, 1863, was the conquest of the Mississippi River really complete, but the events of the intervening 15 months were disastrous to the people of New Orleans.

There was no area in the country so exposed to attack as the Mississippi Valley, where there were no mountains; but the mouth of the river was thought to be well protected by forts that had existed for a long time. There were shallow areas in the river that were hard to navigate and swamp lands that would be difficult to penetrate. New Orleanians felt that their defenses were impregnable.

Even when the flotilla of **Flag Officer David G. Farragut** had crossed the bar at the mouth of the river in 1862, the *Picayune* newspaper announced that "Forts Jackson and St. Philip had 170 guns . . . that the navigation of the river was stopped by a dam about a quarter of a mile from the forts . . . that no flotilla on earth could force that dam in less than two hours, during which time it would be within cross range of 170 guns of the highest calibre."

Many New Orleanians were not in the city, but fighting in Virginia, since no one had expected an invasion from the "well-protected" mouth of the river. Able-bodied men built breastworks around the city, giving special attention to the Chalmette Battlefield. They sunk obstructions in the bayous leading into the city, and prayed their defenses would hold.

But disasters were to befall the city. When Farragut's flotilla came to the area of the forts, the guns were discovered to be too small, and their shells fell short. The dam, or "boom" of cypress logs that had been built across the river was broken by the rising water, which was soon to be in flood stage. The fleet simply cut through the rebuilt boom and sailed on toward New Orleans. Also, the ironclads under construction in the South were not finished in time for Farragut's arrival. There were more Union losses than Confederate losses at the Battle of the Forts, but the fleet continued on its way to its destination.

On April 24, the day before the city fell, state officials moved archives by railroad and steamer to other cities. On the levee, citizens burned 15,000 bales of cotton to prevent them from falling into the hands of the Yankees. The drydocks on the Algiers side of the river were sunk by order of General Lovell, and privately owned steamboats were set on fire by their owners to drift downriver. On Canal Street, there was a bonfire of the records of the Custom House. Normal business ceased. Aliens thronged to their consuls' offices to have their valuables stored. The criminal element of the city and the poor looted warehouses on the riverfront of sugar, molasses, and food. That night, the governor and other state officials left the city by steamer and railroad, abandoning the residents.

On the morning of April 25, General Lovell sent his small force to Camp Moore, 70 miles north of the city, to prevent the bombardment of the city. He believed that the fort had fallen, and that it would be absurd to confront a flotilla of forty vessels equipped with more than 100 large calibre guns, with less than 3,000 militia, armed with shotguns.

Mayor Monroe urged storekeepers to open their shops. People gathered on the levee to watch the flotilla sail up to the docks. Farragut disembarked and joined the mayor to make his demands.

After a week of unsuccessful negotiations between Mayor Monroe and Captain Farragut, the U.S. flag had still not been raised before the U.S. mint, the Custom House, or the City Hall. Farragut had no desire to bombard the city. For one thing, he would not have had enough ammunition left for his attacks on Baton Rouge and Vicksburg.

What brought matters to a head were the actions of an irresponsible group of New Orleanians who could not resist showing open defiance to the Yankees. On a Saturday morning, a week after the arrival of the flotilla, the captain of the *Pensacola* took a small party ashore and raised the U.S. flag over the federal mint, which was at the end of Esplanade Avenue near the river. He warned the watching mob that his ship would fire howitzers loaded with grapeshot if the flag were molested. Almost immediately, **William B. Mumford,** a local gambler, went up to the roof and lowered the flag. He and his friends dragged the flag to Lafayette Square, where they tore it to bits and distributed it as souvenirs. Farragut replied with an ultimatum. "It becomes my duty," he said, "to order you to remove the women and children from the city within 48 hours."

The city council protested that bombardment was inhuman, and that it was impossible to evacuate in so short a time, Now, Farragut received word that the forts had fallen. Actually, the forts had never surrendered, but seeing wreckage floating downriver from New Orleans, the officers at the forts thought that New Orleans had fallen. Their own provisions were running low, so the Jackson garrison mutinied and left in small boats. Fort St. Philip had no choice but to do the same. Now, it was possible for General Butler's troops to come up an undefended river and take command of the city.

Mayor Monroe now agreed to the raising of the American flag at City Hall, and the military occupation of New Orleans began. It was to last fourteen years, longer than any other American city was ever occupied by a hostile power. Loss of control of the Mississippi River and of the largest city in the South was a major blow to the Confederacy. It boosted Northern morale and had a tremendous effect on the attitude of Europe. (England and France might otherwise have eventually recognized the independence of the Confederacy, or even come into the war for economic reasons when a cotton embargo created a shortage of this product.)

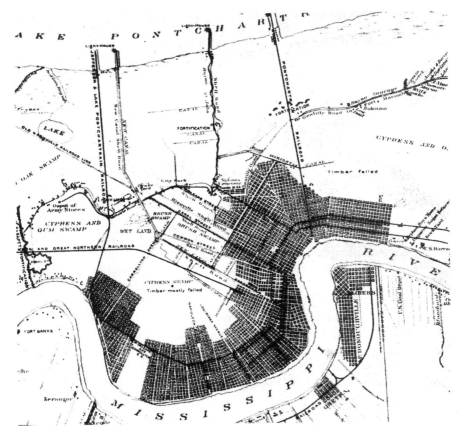

Figure 39. The "Banks Map" of 1863 shows routes into the city to be used by the Union Army for military purposes during the Civil War. Settlement is shown only along the natural levee of the Mississippi and along the small levee of the Bayou Metairie-Gentilly.

GENERAL BENJAMIN BUTLER—COMMANDER OF THE DEPARTMENT OF THE GULF

Of all the traditional villains in Southern history, none are painted blacker than Sherman who marched through Georgia and Butler who served as military commander of New Orleans for seven months in 1862. Since there were no precedents to follow, commanders of occupied territories arbitrarily created policy as they went along, using as a guide legislation passed in Washington, such as the Confiscation Act of 1862 and the Emancipation Act of the same year.

General Benjamin Franklin Butler, 42 years old at the outset of the war, a fat man with a brilliant mind and a driving political ambition, had made a name for himself in Boston fighting for the rights of labor,

143

and then later representing men of great wealth. Energetic, shrewd, and often unscrupulous, he had decided from the beginning that he would employ harsh treatment with the Rebels. He considered them traitors. Butler felt that he had been robbed of the glory he deserved as Occupation Commander of New Orleans, since it was Farragut who had lowered the Confederate flag over City Hall before he left the city. Now, Butler was determined to make his power felt.

He entered the city as Commander of the new Department of the Gulf with 18,000 troops, mostly infantry, but some cavalry and artillery. When urged by McClellan just to occupy Algiers and the city of Carrollton, since the rest of the city had enough Union sentiment to control it, Butler said, "I find the city under the dominion of the mob. They have insulted our flag, torn it down with indignity. This outrage will be punished in such manner as, in my judgment, will caution both the perpetrators and the abettors of the act so that they will feel the stripes if they do not reverence the stars of our banner." On another occasion, he declared, "New Orleans is a conquered city. It has been conquered by the forces of the United States and by the laws of nations, and lies subject to the will of the conquerors."

The municipal government was allowed to continue its many functions, but martial law was to prevail. All persons in arms against the United States were to surrender themselves and their equipment. Those who wished to pledge their Oath of Allegiance to the United States would be protected in person and property. Violation of this oath was punishable by death. Those who refused to take the oath would be treated as enemies. The American flag was to be respected by all. Citizens were to go on about their business as usual. All assemblages, private or public, were forbidden. Only U.S. taxes, and those for sanitation, could be collected. Fire companies were to continue to operate. Military courts would try those accused of major crimes or of interference with the laws of the United States. Minor crimes and civil suits would be handled by city authorities. The press was to submit all copy to military censors. The army took over telegraphic communications. Butler stated that he would prefer to administer the government mildly, but if necessary, he could be ruthless.

Mayor Monroe said he would suspend the municipal government at once, but the councilmen objected. There was a division of authority between municipal and military for two weeks, after which the General had the Mayor arrested and forced the councilmen out of office by insisting they sign the Oath of Allegiance. After the municipal government of New Orleans was overthrown, federal officers were appointed to act as mayors, judges, and provost marshals for the duration of the war.

THE WOMAN ORDER

The women of New Orleans had their own way of protesting the military occupation. If they met federal officers on the sidewalk, they would lift their skirts and move out into the streets. If federal officers got into a streetcar or a church pew they were occupying, they would leave at once. They were also insulting. It was after one woman spat in the face of two officers that Butler passed General Order No. 28, on May 15, 1862. It read as follows:

"As the officers and soldiers of the United States have been subject to repeated insults from the women of New Orleans in return for the most scrupulous non-interference and courtesy on our part, it is ordered that hereafter, when any female shall, by word, gesture, or movement, insult or show contempt for any officer or soldier of the United States, she shall be regarded and held liable to be treated as a woman of the town plying her avocation."

Southerners considered it an open invitation for Yankee soldiers to ravage women of all ranks, and Butler's Chief of Staff warned him that his own officers might take the same meaning. Butler referred to the women of New Orleans as "she-adders." The women responded to the order by restraining themselves, but continued to express dedication to the Confederacy by singing the "Bonnie Blue Flag" at every opportunity. It is said that prostitutes in the city put Bulter's picture in the bottom of their "tinkle pots."

THE HANGING OF MUMFORD

Three weeks after the **Woman Order,** on June 7, 1862, **Mumford,** who had torn down the flag at the U.S. Mint, was hanged at the scene of his crime. One week earlier, a military commission had pronounced his execution. Immediately thereafter, criminal elements had threatened to assassinate Butler if he went through with the execution. But Butler had refused all pleas, including that of the prisoner's wife. Butler was thenceforth called the "Beast."

By comparison with other southern cities, New Orleans was not treated as badly as many of its residents thought. The city was never bombarded. It was governed efficiently, and the physical comfort of the citizens was better during the federal administration than it had been under the Confederacy. Mayor Monroe and the city council, by *not* cleaning the streets, had hoped to hasten the coming of a yellow fever epidemic, which they believed would kill off many of the federal army, while the Southerners, who were immune, would survive. By *not* providing food for the poor, they forced Butler to do so. By *not* restraining crime, they forced him to keep more troops in the city. For the safety of his own men, as well as the city, Butler suppressed the criminal element. He allowed food to be brought into the city from Mobile. He allowed the sale of some army provisions to civilians. He relieved the destitute, using federal government funds for a time, and forced the city to hire 2,000 unemployed to clean the streets. His preventive measures kept the city free of yellow fever during the war and for some time thereafter. He collected "donations" of $350,000 from individuals and firms, which was spent on public works or given to Charity Hospital.

Another epithet by which the general was known was "Silver Spoons" Butler, referring to the profits he allegedly amassed through confiscation of personal property, under the protection of the Confiscation Act. First, he claimed, in the name of the government, all property belonging to the U.S. government, such as the U.S. Mint and the Custom House. Then, he seized many private homes for the use of the military, usually homes of Confederates off fighting in the war.

The Second Confiscation Act of 1862 provided for the seizure of all property belonging to officers of the Confederacy, and to all Rebels who continued to resist signing the Oath of Allegiance for 60 days after the law was passed. When this grace period had ended, some 3,000 citizens still refused to sign, forfeited their property, and were classified as "irreconcilables," but were allowed to leave the city if they chose. Their homes and personal effects were sold at auction for low prices.

Who is to say if Butler's actions during his brief term of office were legal? A state of war existed, and there were no rules to follow. Laws were made up as the war progressed. They could be enforced only within an occupied territory, and it was always possible that they might be countermanded by the president and his cabinet. The hanging of Mumford (the only New Orleans citizen killed during Butler's administration), inspired fear as well as hatred, perhaps resulting in the saving of many lives and the prevention of many prison sentences.

Many New Orleanians had volunteered for military service early in the war, and had been sent to Virginia, like the Crescent Rifles, the Louisiana Guards, and the Washington Artillery. They were the aristrocrats. But from the slums and the underworld came the Louisiana Tigers Battalion. The Sixth Louisiana Infantry was composed of Irish laborers and free Negroes, and were used for militia duty only.

New Orleans was the recruiting and debarkation center of the State. Troops on their way somewhere else would stay at Camp Lewis in Carrollton, and Camp Walker on the Metairie Race Track. By the fall of 1861, there were 23,000 men in the military from Louisiana. Many men volunteered for military service in the summer of 1861 because there were no jobs to be found in the city.

No one knew exactly what to do with the Negroes in the occupied territories of the South. These territories were part of the Union, and the

146

Emancipation Proclamation applied to "slave states," not to any part of the Union. Butler pleaded with Lincoln for guidance, but Lincoln told him to "get along" with the problem in the best way he could, trying not to insult either the Northern abolitionists or the Southern conservatives. Lincoln was having his own problems and hoping to win another election in 1864.

New Orleans, in any case, was no commander's dream. There were not only Negro slaves, but free Negroes as well, to say nothing of thousands of blacks who had rushed into the city as soon as it was captured, seeking security under the flag of the United States. Once here, they could not return to their owners: this had been ordered by an act of Congress. And Butler could not let them starve. He put them to work at rough labor or assigned them to work for his officers. By the fall of 1862, he was supporting 10,000 blacks. Fearing an insurrection among the Negroes, he continued the curfew and refused to allow General Phelps to enlist black men in the army and give them weapons. He freed slaves belonging to French and Spanish aliens, and those in jail who had belonged to Confederate soldiers away fighting the war. He allowed them certain civil rights: they could testify in court against white men, and ride in all streetcars. He used them as spies against their masters, and did not allow jailers to whip black prisoners. In the fall of 1862, he used Negroes as free labor on confiscated plantations. It is a matter of record that he handled the Negro problem as wisely as anyone could.

Father James Ignatius Mullon, served the congregation of St. Patrick's Church as pastor from 1834 to 1866. An ardent Confederate, he often locked horns with the chief of military occupation, General Benjamin F. Butler. It was a daily custom for the congregation to unite in prayer after Mass for the success of the Confederate cause. Butler sent word for this to cease. Ostensibly, Father Mullon complied, but he told his parishioners to pray in silence. Once, when accused of having refused to bury a Union soldier, Father Mullon told the General that he stood ready to bury the whole Union army, Butler included, whenever the occasion was offered.

On the evening of December 14, 1862, General Nathaniel P. Banks arrived in New Orleans with papers assigning him as Butler's replacement. Shattered with disappointment, Butler went home to Lowell, Massachusetts.

Banks was a man of a different temperament altogether. He thought he could win over the people of New Orleans with conciliation, but the time was past when such an approach would succeed. If it ever had a chance, it would have been at the beginning of the occupation. By the start of 1863, New Orleanians no longer trusted any moves their federal captors made.

Banks promised fair treatment for all and compensation "for losses by acts of the United States, including slaves." The Episcopal Churches, which had been closed under Butler, were reopened on Christmas Eve of 1862. The sale of confiscated property was suspended, and more than a hundred political prisoners were released. Federal officers were forced to return houses they had seized, and Banks promised to investigate cases of extortion, confiscation, and speculation. He and his wife began holding balls, inviting the élite of the city in the hope that these entertainments would win them over.

Taking this leniency as a sign of weakness, the Rebels responded by showing every manner of disloyalty. The women once again began insulting the federal officers. Teachers sang "Dixie" with their students. Newspapers refused to publish information submitted by federal officers.

In April, 1863, Banks was forced to do an "about face." He issued severe orders, telling registered enemies of the Union to leave the territory within 15 days, requiring the Oath of Allegiance of all who remained, and promising the death penalty to all who gave supplies to the Confederate Army.

From the start of the war, New Orleans was a garrison city. Though it was never attacked, it lay within a combat area. After the fall of Memphis and Baton Rouge, Vicksburg surrendered on July 4, 1863. In April, 1864, Banks's expedition against Shreveport produced the bloodiest fighting in Louisiana, which took place at the battles of Mansfield and Pleasant Hill. From 1862 to the war's end, there were two armies and two civil governments in the state.

It was the Federals who originally blockaded the river, knowing that the Rebels depended for their food and staples on the ships of Europe. By the end of 1862, the port city was on the brink of starvation. In time, however, the Federals saw that they, too, depended on incoming vessels for their survival. They lifted the blockade, after which the Confederates, *themselves,* put up a blockade at Vicksburg, prohibiting free commerce on the river because now, it would have benefited the Union. The Federals depended on cotton and sugar for their economic recovery, and they had not captured enough of the area where those products were raised to bring this recovery about.

When the first blockade was lifted, merchandise coming from New England could be brought up the river from the Gulf, but there was no cotton or sugar to exchange for it. The Red River campaign of 1864 had as its purpose the capture of Shreveport, which would be used as a base for a drive into Texas. There, the Union would acquire enough cotton to help bring about a Northern victory. But the campaign ended in disaster for the Federals, and Banks was removed from his command.

As long as the Confederates were able to keep the city cut off from the river, the progress of the Federals was slow, and the Rebels simply continued with their passive resistance to the Union. But once

Vicksburg had been captured, and the river was open to Federal traffic, economic progress began, and New Orleanians feared that Federal control of the region would become permanent. Then, when Banks was defeated in the Red River campaign, hopes of a Southern victory were revived, and hostility sharpened once again.

In 1864, a free election was held, under the supervision of General Banks, and Michael Hahn was elected governor of Louisiana. Lincoln recognized Hahn as chief executive. At last, Louisiana had a civil government, however limited its powers.

WEAKNESSES OF THE SOUTH

The South's weaknesses during the war were its specialized economy and its dependence on external markets. Cotton, sugar, tobacco, and other staples had, for decades, been sent to Europe and the North in exchange for manufactured goods and food. Cut off from these markets, the South could not long continue to feed its own civilian population, to say nothing of a military force. The blockade hindered the importation of necessary goods, and depression spread. Men who had worked in trade and transportation were now unemployed.

Before the war, New Orleans had been the *most* commercial and the *least* industrial of the large cities of the nation. It had no rice mill, no flour mill, and only one sugar refinery. It had foundries and shipyards but were mainly for repairs, and even *these* were destroyed when Farragut was approaching the city in 1862. During the war, New Orleans was a city without industry.

After the capture of New Orleans, speculators from the North poured into the city, expecting to make quick and easy money. Word of Butler's profits in confiscated property spurred them on, and they came in droves, expecting to be rich within months. Southerners hated them because they took over functions formerly belonging to them. Northerners hated them because they traded with the Rebels, a transaction that could only help their enemies.

Actually, the only way speculators hurt the economy was by keeping prices high, which was inevitable, in any case, in time of war. But speculators were the only businessmen in the community with a supply of capital and the ability to direct business operations. However selfish their motives, they helped New Orleans out of the Depression.

Lincoln had hoped to make Louisiana the model for all the southern states. It was to be the first state to accept his plan for re-entry into the Union. For this reason, he extended leniency whenever possible to the residents of the region, and life for the people of Louisiana was more comfortable than for most residents of occupied territories.

The upper classes suffered most, seeing their securities, their businesses, and their other assets diminish in value. Many suffered shortages of food, the ignominy of defeat, the sorrow of deaths of husbands, sons, and brothers, and the lack of social attractions. Women rarely went out. In 1863, General Banks forbad the observance of Mardi Gras, to the great chagrin of the people.

The Yankees were no happier about being in New Orleans than the citizens were to have them. They were bivouacked in tents at camps outside the city proper where the terrain was difficult and they had to suffer heat, rain, and flooded land, all of which brought on diarrhea and fevers. When in good health, soldiers sought relief from their misery and boredom. Food was scarce in the city, but women never were, and there was much loss of time and services from soldiers with venereal disease.

Heavy drinking was the rule among laborers and soldiers on leave. Dives were still abundant on Gallatin Street, Girod Street, and St. Thomas Street. On St. Charles Avenue, between Canal and Lafayette Streets, 45 places sold liquor within six blocks. In the saloons, if you didn't continue to drink, the proprietor threw you out; if you did, you usually wound up doped and rolled. Gambling was brisk with games of pitching pennies, shooting craps, or playing poker or three-card monte.

On marches from Camp Parapet above the city to Pass Manchac, Yankees saw everything from alligators to mosquitoes to snakes, and back in camp, they were at the mercy of lice. Cheap rooms in the city abounded with bedbugs and cockroaches.

Yankee officers, who were able to live in a better part of town got a better impression of the city with its flowers and trees that flourished even in the winter, its duck hunting, its theater, its French opera, and its beautiful (though rude) young women.

The war ended in 1865, and in November of that year, the ex-Confederates were once again in control of the state. In most of the South, political reconstruction did not begin until the end of the war, but in Louisiana, the issues had been debated and voted on long before Lee's surrender. Early in 1865, the Negroes, the scalawags and carpetbaggers were forming a party which, despite its first defeat, would soon gain control of the state.

According to the Congressional Act of 1867, Louisiana was occupied by Federal troops under General Philip Sheridan, who interpreted the terms of the act so strictly that half of the white citizens could not vote at all, but all adult male Negroes could vote. The Constitution of 1868 enfranchised Negroes and gave them full equality of the races in public schools and on common carriers.

In the state election of 1868, Henry Clay Warmoth of Illinois, a carpetbagger, and his lieutenant governor, P.B.S. Pinchback, a mulatto, were elected.

In 1872, Kellogg and Antoine, (another mulatto), replaced Warmoth and Pinchback as governor and lieutenant governor, respectively.

Jefferson Davis
President of the Confederacy

Gen. Albert Pike   *Father Abram J. Ryan*   *Col. Charles Didier Dreux*
Episcopal Bishop   *Poet-Priest of the Confederacy*   *First Confederate Officer from*
                                                           Louisiana killed in the Civil War

Figure 40. Civil War commemorated on Jefferson Davis Parkway.

President Grant used Federal troops to install them and to put his Republican supporters in control of the legislature. For the next four years, however, Louisiana had two governors and two legislatures. (Grant used troops to support the Republicans).

In the presidential election of 1876, both the Republicans (Rutherford B. Hayes) and the Democrats (Samuel J. Tilden) claimed victory. Four states—Louisiana, South Carolina, Florida, and Oregon had submitted two sets of electoral returns, one by the Democrats and one by the Republicans. The Electoral College gave the disputed votes to Hayes, making him the winner. But the Democrats cried fraud and challenged the decision.

In January, 1877, a 15-man Electoral Commission was appointed by Congress to make the final decision. In a private meeting, representatives from Louisiana, South Carolina and Florida agreed not to oppose the decision of the Electoral Commission (which would be to name Hayes the winner) if in exchange, the states would be permitted to elect their own governors, with no federal interference, and if all Federal troops would be removed. As a result of this meeting, Hayes became president, ex-Confederate Francis T. Nicholls became governor of Louisiana, and the Federal troops were removed. After fourteen years as an occupied city, New Orleans was at last free again.

Rebirth and Resurgence — 1865 to 1930

The Cotton Exchange Building, corner Gravier and Carondelet, built in 1882–83, was ready for the wrecker in 1920. Statues on third floor were moved to City Park for a brief stay. Two on the ground floor, called Caryatids, now stand in 100 block of City Park Avenue.

Figure 41. St. Charles Hotel from Canal Street, the third on the same site, circa 1925. It was demolished in 1974. Today, the site of Place St. Charles.

Figure 42. Opulent lobby of the third St. Charles Hotel, 1925.

CHAPTER IX

Rebirth and Resurgence — 1865 to 1930

The years of Reconstruction were the darkest in the history of New Orleans. It was a time of violence, lawlessness, and corruption. Confederate soldiers, returning from the war, found Unionists in charge of all civic affairs. Negroes, not knowing what to do with their new liberties, crowded in the city under the protective wing of the "Freedmen's Bureau." Carpetbaggers from the North came in droves to take possession of commerce and politics, to whatever extent it was possible.

The Southerners tried hard, in spite of poverty, to regain their position in the city. Unionists feared that the Southerners might return to power, and Carpetbaggers feared that they, themselves, might be thrown out. Their efforts to seat blacks in the legislature brought about the **Massacre of 1866** at Mechanics Institute on Dryades Street (now University Place), when 44 Negroes and 4 white men were killed, and 160 others wounded.

During the administration of Governor Warmoth, control of New Orleans was taken from the Democrats by a new form of city government. The mayor and seven administrators were now to be appointed by the governor. New Orleans was virtually in the grip of a dictator. Warmoth appointed local police, registrars, and a returning board for the city.

Results of any election could be altered by Warmoth's returning board, which had the power to review the results and throw out whatever votes they chose. In fact, voting became dangerous. Fights broke out, and fatalities occurred at every election. Saloons were wide open, gambling thrived, and robbery and violence were the order of the day.

THE BATTLE OF LIBERTY PLACE

The Crescent City White League was formed in 1874 for the defense of the rights of the white citizens against radical State government. On the morning of September 14, 1874, the White Leaguers met at Clay Statue on Canal Street to make plans to take possession of the city and State government, thus breaking the power of the Metropolitan Police. Reassembling at Camp and Poydras in the afternoon, armed for an encounter, they advanced down the levee at four o'clock. The Metropolitan Police had been stationed at several points throughout the city, the main body under General Badger at Canal Street and the river. The General saw the men of the White League coming and opened fire. The White Leaguers had no artillery, but they charged into the police and cleared the street. They drove the police back to Jackson Square, where both armies remained throughout the night. In the morning, the police surrendered the State House, the Arsenal, and Jackson Square. In the fray, a total of 31 had been killed, and 79 wounded.

But victory was short-lived. The White Leaguers installed Lieutenant-Governor Penn in the State House on September 15, 1874, but President Grant immediately sent reinforcements and demanded the reinstatement of Governor Kellogg without delay. And so the city was to remain in the grip of a Republican governor for three more years.

After the compromise in which President Hayes was elected (Chap. VIII), "General" Nicholls, the Confederate patriot, served as Louisiana governor for only two years, from 1878–1880, but was to return in 1888 for a four-year term. He had lost his left arm in combat at Winchester, and his left leg at Chancellorsville. (One cannot help but wonder what he was doing at the Battle of Chancellorsville without an arm.) In placing his name in nomination, Tay Goode of Terrebonne Parish said, "I give you all that is left of Francis Nicholls, because all that is left of him is right."

THE LOUISIANA LOTTERY

In 1868, an institution known as the Louisiana Lottery Company was born in a corrupt era. From the state legislature, its founder, **Charles T. Howard,** managed to obtain a 25-year charter, which enabled the Lottery to keep control of city, state and even national politicians, who were on its payroll. To mask its vice, the Lottery made regular contributions to charitable causes such as the Charity Hospital and the French Opera House, and was always ready with cash in times of hurricanes and floods.

New Orleanians loved the Lottery. For 25¢, they could purchase a ticket and a dream of leisure and luxury. Tickets were sold in denominations as high as $40, for which the prize was $600,000. More than 200 shops dotted the city, and there were branch offices in many other major cities. Drawings were held each day in public, and throngs gathered to watch, as two Confederate heroes, P.G.T. Beauregard and Jubal Early (hired to give respectability to the proceedings) drew the numbers.

The Lottery supported and was supported by many Republicans and Democrats. It was the subject of political debates for 25 years. Its charter was to expire January 1, 1894. The United States Supreme Court spelled out the beginning of the end of the Louisiana Lottery when it affirmed the right of Congress to prohibit the Lottery's use of the mail in advertising. The Company continued in the state until it expired in 1894, but its back had been broken. *The New Orleans Delta* declared, "The Lottery is now like a postage stamp . . . licked and put in a corner." It was out of business by 1895.

New Orleans had reached its lowest depth as a municipality in the early 1880s. It had surrendered all its franchises, duties and privileges to private individuals or corporations. The only thing it still controlled was the police force, which was in the hands of the mayor, who so administered it that it was overrun with politics and filled with corruption. A State Lottery was begun in 1992.

MAYOR JOSEPH A. SHAKSPEARE

Joseph A. Shakspeare served as mayor in the years 1880–1882, and returned again to serve in 1888. Shakspeare, knowing that the blackmail and corruption in the city had grown out of the gambling business, introduced the Shakspeare Plan, which was nothing less than a payoff to his office for police protection for gamblers. The amazing thing was that it succeeded. Gambling had always been rampant in the city. Statutes against it were impossible to enforce and gave the police an opportunity to collect graft. The mayor could not license it, since it was against the state constitution. Therefore, for a small monthly payment, Shakspeare, as Chief of Police, agreed not to allow his officers to molest the gamblers. The money thus collected was used to establish the Shakspeare Almshouse and to support other charities. It was ultimately abused, needless to say, and the Shakspeare fund disappeared from the revenues of the city.

Shakspeare was defeated in 1892 by **John Fitzpatrick,** a candidate of the Regular Democratic Organization. Ever since the 1870s, municipal elections in New Orleans have been battles fought between the Regular Democratic Organization, which held power most of the time, and a reform movement, whose purpose it was to wipe out the RDO or keep its candidate out of office. The first of these "reform" candidates was, surprisingly enough, Shakspeare himself. Another reform mayor, **Walter Flower,** took office in 1896.

THE 17 YEARS OF MAYOR MARTIN BEHRMAN

In between the terms of Shakspeare and Flower, **John Fitzpatrick** of the RDO held office. His protegé was a young man named **Martin Behrman,** who was orphaned at an early age and ended his formal education at St. Philip School, when Warren Easton was still the principal there. Living in Algiers, Behrman had worked in a family grocery store until he was married at the age of 22. Then, he became clerk in the district assessor's office, but lost his job when Shakspeare's "reform" administration replaced all RDO men with "reform" followers. When Fitzpatrick of the RDO defeated Shakspeare, Behrman was appointed clerk to three city council committees, was elected delegate to the Constitutional Convention in 1898, and state auditor in 1904. Later the same year, he was nominated for mayor and won in a landslide.

Behrman was re-elected in 1908, 1912, and 1916. The RDO (or Choctaw Club, as it was called) was the New Orleans version of New York's Tammany Hall, a political machine that was seemingly invincible.

As early as 1907, the Behrman organization was referred to as the "Behrman Ring," and "Ring politics" grew stronger as Behrman won election after election. The "anti-Ring" leaders formed a "Good Government League," nicknamed the Goo-Goos," who supported Luther E. Hall for governor, in the hope that he would replace the New Orleans mayor-and-councilmanic form of government with a commission form, which they thought would reduce Behrman's powers, and eventually, his popularity. Hall was elected and the change of government was made as promised in 1912, but to the great disappointment of the "Goo-Goos," Hall was taken over by the Behrmanites, who adopted the commission council form of government as their own.

John M. Parker, another "reform" candidate, was elected governor in 1920, and he launched a movement to oust Martin Behrman, who had been asked by the Old Regulars to run for mayor for a fifth term. Behrman lost the election to **Andrew McShane** in 1920, but was re-elected in 1925. His supporters changed their campaign rallying cry from "Papa's Coming Home" to "Papa's Back." Behrman died in office a year later, having served as mayor for 17 years, the only man in the city's history to have been elected five times as mayor.

Of this period in the city's political history, T. Harry Williams, in his biography of *Huey P. Long* said, "Louisiana (and hence, New Orleans) politics, was speculative, devious, personal, exuberant, and highly professional. The objective was to win, and in no other state were the devices employed to win—stratagems, deals, and oratory—so studied and admired by the populace." Louisiana's people are accused of having a tolerance of corruption found no place else in the United States. This tolerance is described as "a Latin enclave of immorality set down in a country of Anglo-Saxon righteousness."

But in spite of occasional riots, labor unrest, and corruption in government in the late 19th and early 20th centuries, the people managed to effect a resurgence in the economy. The American Sector became a modern city with burgeoning commerce, and mansions mushroomed all along the main thoroughfares. People had time to turn their minds to a bit of leisure at one of the new amusement parks that were now available for their enjoyment.

RECREATION AND AMUSEMENT

West End Park offered swimming, picnicking, amusement rides and outdoor movies, some of the first movies seen in the city. New Orleanians took the barges along the New Basin Canal to the site of the present Southern Yacht Club, as early as 1838. Then, after 1876, when the New Orleans City and Lake Railroad started running trains to the lake, they traveled by train. At that time, a large wooden platform was constructed over the water, and a hotel, restaurant, and structures to house amusements arose. It was called New Lake End until 1880, when it was re-christened West End Park, and for the next 30 years, it remained a popular lake resort. In 1909, the city constructed a seawall 500 feet out in the lake, and filled in the space between it and the old embankment to form the present 30-acre West End Park.

Another lakefront amusement center popular in the period was **Spanish Fort,** which grew up around the site of an old colonial fort originally built by the French in 1701 at the mouth of Bayou St. John. Because it was rebuilt by the Spanish in 1779, it was called Spanish Fort. The fort never saw warfare, but was used as an observation point in the War of 1812. The area around Spanish Fort was sold in 1823 to Harvey Elkins, who built the Pontchartrain Hotel there. In 1874, the hotel was rebuilt, about the same time that a railroad was constructed to connect the resort to downtown New Orleans. In 1878, Moses Schwartz bought Spanish Fort. He built a casino with a restaurant offering meals for $1, a theater which featured light opera and band concerts. In 1880, Otto Touché opened the "Over-the-Rhine" Bar and Restaurant, which could be reached by a swing footbridge, across the bayou from Spanish Fort.

Spanish Fort became the site of an amusement park in 1883. It was abandoned for a time in 1903 when railroad service to the site was suspended, and its buildings burned down in 1906. The property was acquired in 1909 by the New Orleans Railway and Light Company, who rebuilt and reopened an amusement center, including ferris wheel and other rides, picnic pavillion, restaurant, and bathing facilities. Ownership of the property later reverted to the city. Plans were drawn in 1928 to develop the lakefront from West End to the Airport, writing the final chapter to Spanish Fort as an amusement center.

In 1928, the amusement park was relocated at the lake end of Bayou St. John on land already "filled" and its name was changed to Pontchartrain Beach. Eventually, the Levee Board decided to establish a permanent site for an amusement park several miles farther

Figure 43. West End Amusement Park, a gathering place for pleasure-seekers at the turn of the century.

(*Courtesy Leonard V. Huber Collection*)

Figure 44. The Old Shell Road ran alongside the New Basin Canal to West End Park, a lovely ride at the turn of the century.
(Courtesy Leonard V. Huber Collection)

east and to grant a 20-year lease. The Batt family, (Harry Batt, Sr. president) acquired control in 1934, and in 1939, the new Pontchartrain Beach opened at the end of Elysian Fields Avenue. The Zephyr was the park's symbol. World War II created a boom for the park, bringing servicemen in droves to enjoy the recreation. The park closed in 1983.

Another delightful outing at the turn of the century was a drive on the Old Shell Road, which ran along the Metairie side of the New Basin Canal. The drive went past the New Orleans Country Club on Pontchartrain Boulevard and the new Metairie Cemetery, a trail lined with palms and oleanders and a view of pleasure boats on the water.

THE SECOND RENAISSANCE OF THE VIEUX CARRE — THE VIEUX CARRE COMMISSION

Baroness Pontalba is credited with the *first* rebirth of the Vieux Carre in the mid 19th century, at a time when the trend was to move out of the old part of town and build a mansion on St. Charles Avenue. Her beautiful apartments flanking the Place d'Armes served as a catalyst, stirring up renewed interest in the French Quarter and pride in its history.

In the decades following the Civil War, there was a sharp decline in the commercial importance of the city, and New Orleans remained impoverished. There was no money for expensive renovations, and once again, the French Quarter began to deteriorate. Families who could afford to move migrated to the newer parts of town. Jackson Square, at the turn of the 20th century, was once again seedy. The Pontalba Buildings were derelicts with vagrants for tenants, and the whole neighborhood was fast becoming a slum area.

In the year 1908, an entire block of the finest buildings in the Quarter was destroyed to build the Civil Courts Building. The Old St. Louis Exchange Hotel, with its majestic dome, once the pride of the Vieux Carre and the site of the State Capitol in 1874, was allowed to fall into decay; badly damaged in the 1915 hurricane, it was eventually demolished.

Orleanians who cared about preserving our historic treasures began to take note in the 1920s and 1930s that unless something was done to protect what remained of the Quarter, it would soon disappear and be lost forever. The Vieux Carre Commission was therefore established in 1921, and by state constitutional amendment in 1936, was given the power to regulate architecture through control of building permits. Its purpose was to renovate, restore, and remodel the old buildings and put them to new uses so that they might pay their own way. Thus began the *second* renaissance of the Vieux Carre.

Fortunately (and in another way unfortunately), President

Roosevelt's WPA almost simultaneously moved in with money and talent to recondition parts of the Quarter, giving special attention to the French Market and Jackson Square, the Cathedral, Cabildo, the Presbytère and the Pontalba Buildings. While no one would dispute the fact that a slum area was rehabilitated, and that land values began to rise, it was equally true that "progress," as envisioned by legislators in Washington, had a different definition in New Orleans. WPA "progress" involved the demolition of some of the city's earliest structures.

The WPA's main concern was to put food in the mouths of the hungry (workers on these projects were earning $15 to $20 week), but it began "making improvements" by eradicating some of the French Market's oldest buildings. The Old Red Store (1830) was demolished, and Gallatin Street on the riverfront, that "dark alley of mystery and murder," was wiped out altogether "to relieve the city of an area of human decay." According to Robin Von Breton Derbes, in *New Orleans Magazine,* July, 1976, this act was "the equivalent of demolishing Camp Street to get rid of Skid Row."

None of this was done, however, without a fight. Daily, the powers that be in the WPA and the Vieux Carre Commission locked horns, the WPA arguing that slum clearance was its first concern, the Vieux Carre Commission insisting that the French Quarter retain its Caribbean character. But the WPA plowed forward.

Improvements *were* made, however, and some would argue that they were for the better. Gallatin Street was replaced with the present airy steel sheds of the Farmer's Market. And, since a major restoration in 1975, the historic French Market, its buildings distinguished by graceful arcades and stately columns, offers a glimpse of a scene of activity that has existed in the same place for almost 300 years. The Halle des Boucheries (built in 1813), the Halle des Legumes (1822), the reconstructed Red Store, the renovated Bazaar Building, and the new Halle des Cuisines, are all part of the rebuilt French Market complex that authenticates early French Quarter architecture. One end of the market is tucked into the bend of the river; the other is at Jackson Square.

Flagstoned promenades, sparkling fountains and old-fashioned benches add touches of a by-gone era. At the Jackson Square end is the Cafe du Monde with its inimitable coffee and *beignets* (square hot donuts with powdered sugar) without which no visit to New Orleans is complete.

Just outside the Cafe du Monde, the visitor walks up the steps of the beautifully landscaped "Moonwalk," decorated with fountains, lampposts and benches, and well secured by guards so that the visitor may safely view by night, not only the river, but turning in the opposite direction, the Cathedral, breathtakingly illuminated.

STREET PATTERNS

The circuitous route that the river takes in meandering around the city of New Orleans affected the entire way of life of the people. Only the Vieux Carre, laid out in a grid pattern, had straight streets. Beyond the Vieux Carre, property lines extending back from the river date back to the earliest land grants of more than two centuries ago. Property lines ran perpendicular to the levee in long narrow strips, for good reasons. All landowners needed access to transportation, and transportation *was* the river. Also, the only good land was on the natural levee; its value diminished as it approached the backswamps.

But the river wrapped the city in concave and convex curves. On the land inside the convex curves, the property boundaries fanned out; on the land inside the concave curves, they were squeezed together. Cross streets ran parallel to the river, running in straight lines toward the curve of the river, then shifting slightly in conformity with the curve as they crossed property lines (which later became boulevards: Melpomene, Jackson, Louisiana, Napoleon, Jefferson, Broadway, and S. Carrollton).

St. Charles Avenue (originally Nayades) was the great boulevard running parallel to the river. It was actually the rear boundary line of the original land grants. It was inevitable that such a wide boulevard, situated on a habitable part of the natural levee, halfway between the noisy riverfront and the backswamp, would become the main residential avenue of the American city.

BLACK AND WHITE POPULATION PATTERNS

It was the street patterns that brought about the patterns of black and white population settlement. In early New Orleans, in spite of social segregation, there was no geographical segregation of blacks and whites. Slaves lived in the homes of their owners. Free blacks working for whites lived within walking distance of their employers, usually in small houses in back of the the big houses owned by the whites. When the boulevards were divided into blocks, neighborhoods developed with an affluent white perimeter, enclosing a small nuclear cluster of blacks, which has survived until today. The architecture of these cluster houses was not conspicuously different from that of poor whites. It was, in fact, a far less detrimental type of segregation than that which is found in most Northern cities.

ORIENTALS IN NEW ORLEANS

After the Civil War, when slaves were no longer available for work in the cotton and sugar cane fields, orientals began arriving in Louisiana. Many remained in New Orleans and there developed a

Chinatown, of sorts, near the present Public Library, extending in the direction of the Loew's Theater, opium dens and all, before the beginning of the 20th century.

Since the weather was hot and humid in New Orleans, and since it was the style for businessmen to wear starched linen shirts and suits, Chinese laundries were popular with the male population and sprung up in every neighborhood. The Chinese also dried Louisiana shrimp, prepared in their own villages in the swamps below New Orleans. Many Chinese restaurants emerged, and although some Chinese have become Presbyterians, this is an ethnic group that has retained its own speech, culture, and attitudes more than any other to come to our city.

NEW ORLEANS, A RAILROAD CENTER

After the Civil War, the mode of transportation in the United States changed to railroads. New Orleans, complacent in her leadership on the river, was caught unprepared for the competition. In the decade before the Civil War, New Orleans had only 80 miles of railroads. During and after the war, steam locomotives hauled goods across the continent from the West to the Atlantic, stopping in Chicago and St. Louis, both of which surpassed New Orleans in population by 1865.

Between 1865 and 1945, New Orleans became a railroad center, almost in spite of herself. With her time-honored position at the junction of the Mississippi and the Gulf, she had the advantage of shipping, not only for the agricultural South, but for Latin America as well. The Latin American connection provided two products greatly coveted by Americans: coffee and bananas. New Orleans became a prime port of entry for both.

Bulk cargo continued to travel slowly down the river through New Orleans—products like grain from the Midwest and coal from Illinois and Kentucky. They moved along, sometimes ten on one tow, like great floating islands. By the 1950s, trade on the river from the midcontinent had increased and, in fact, exceeded that of ante-bellum days.

THE EADS JETTIES

Colonel James Buchanan Eads, in 1879, completed a system of jetties at the mouth of the Mississippi River, making possible a deep water channel that would revolutionize navigation on the river.

From the earliest days of settlement, the mouth of the river had always filled up with silt and logs, and engineers had worked unceasingly, dredging it out to allow passage for ships. After the Civil War, larger ships were being built. Often, they were stuck on a sandbar for days, even weeks, holding up the passage of other ships. Clearly, something had to be done.

Eads visited the mouth of the river and declared that the way to open it to commerce was to build parallel dikes, or jetties, at the mouths of the passes, constricting the channel and causing the stream to flow faster. This faster current, he claimed, would scour its own deep-water channel. This provoked a storm of controversy. He took the proposal to Congress, where he struck a bargain with the legislators. He claimed that he was so sure he could produce and maintain a 28-foot channel, that he would ask for $10 million if he succeeded, but nothing if he failed. After much debate, he was given a contract to build a jetty at South Pass for $5,250,000 and a $100,000 maintenance fee for 20 years.

Work began in June, 1875, and four years later, the channel was 30 feet deep and the bar had been swept into the Gulf. Eads had given new life to the river and saved the port of New Orleans, which had fallen from 2nd to 11th place in the nation. He had also, indirectly, written the end to any plans for industrializing Lake Pontchartrain.

THE WORLD'S INDUSTRIAL
AND COTTON CENTENNIAL—1884

The Cotton Centennial was an extravaganza organized by **Major Edward A. Burke,** state treasurer, lottery agent for Louisiana, and editor of the *New Orleans Times Democrat*. He convinced Congress to grant a loan of $1,000,000 to the fair, and to give a gift of $300,000 for government exhibits. The city government donated $100,000, and the rest of the capital was provided by the sale of private stock.

The display covered 249 acres in a rural track between the edge of Uptown and the recently annexed City of Carrollton (later, the site of the fair would be Audubon Park). The site was about two miles long, from the river to the backswamp, with St. Charles Avenue and the Carrollton Railway to Canal Street cutting squarely across its middle.

The Fair boasted an area of 51 acres "under cover" in the five main buildings, and the most dazzling display of electric lights ever seen anywhere. It could be reached from Canal Street by six street railroads or by steamers on the river which left the foot of Canal Street every 30 minutes. An electric railroad three miles long encircled the entire fairground, and one of its cars passed every few minutes. But, in spite of art galleries, industrial displays, restaurants, railroads and rolling chairs, the Fair, built at a cost of $2,700,000, was a financial failure. It lost half a million dollars, and the walkways for tourists became seas of gumbo in the New Orleans rains.

In 1915, the last of the World's Fair buildings was demolished by a hurricane. Now, the only remaining evidence that there ever was a Fair at the site is a huge boulder in the middle of the Audubon Park Golf Course. It resembles a meteorite, but actually is a sample of iron ore from the state of Alabama. The Fair entrance on Exposition Boulevard and

St. Charles Avenue is still in use as a path through the park to the former site of the Exposition.

When the exposition ended, the state turned the fairgrounds on the river side of St. Charles Avenue (the site of the former Foucher and Boré plantations) into **Audubon Park.** It is today a 340-acre park abounding with ancient oaks and lagoons, still enjoyed by golfers and picnickers. On the other side of St. Charles Avenue, the land became the campuses of Tulane and Loyola University. **Loyola University** at 6300 St. Charles Avenue was established in 1912, an outgrowth of Loyola College of 1911. **Tulane University,** financed in 1884 by a bequest from Paul Tulane, was a merger of the Medical College of Louisiana (1834) and the University of Louisiana (1847).

The effects of the Fair, though not a profitable venture, are still very much in evidence in the city. A flourishing late Victorian architectural boom came in the wake of displays at the Fair. The new park and university area was created, around which grew up one of the city's most affluent neighborhoods.

THE REBUILDING OF THE PORT

The Board of Commissioners of the Port of New Orleans, created in 1896, known as the Dock Board, had authority never previously delegated to a body created by the state legislature. It had complete authority over all water frontage in Orleans Parish and considerable portions in River and Canal frontage in adjacent parishes. It could expropriate property, demolish and rebuild structures, operate facilities as it chose, and lease them at will. A landmark law had created this autonomous body, because legislators realized that the port was New Orleans' Number One industry, and the health of the port was the life of the city.

In 1901, the Dock Board began demolishing structures and rebuilding according to the latest standards. Within ten years, most of the port had been totally rebuilt, with cotton warehouses, bulk storage facilities, and one of the biggest grain elevators in the world.

THE ITALIAN MASSACRE

On October 15, 1890, **Police Chief David Hennessy** was shot while walking along Girod Street. He died the next morning. The Chief, appointed as part of Mayor Shakspeare's reform program, had ruthlessly pursued members of the secret Sicilian murder associations in the city.

For some time, a war had been in progress between the Provenzana and Matranga families to control the produce business on the city wharves. Hennessy had met with the families demanding that the violence be stopped. But there was a vendetta against Hennessy that dated back to the beginning of the decade.

In 1881, Hennessy had captured the Sicilian bandit Esposito, who was then in New Orleans, and returned him to New York, from whence he was extradicted to Italy. Indicted for 18 murders and other crimes, Esposito was sentenced to death, but his sentence was later commuted. Vendettas against all who had informed on Esposito had been carried out. Hennessy's part in these events had never been forgotten.

After Hennessy's assassination, 19 Sicilians and Italians were arrested and indicted. Ten were later charged; nine named as accessories. On March 13, 1891, the jury acquitted some of the defendants and declared a mistrial for the rest. The people of the city were incensed.

Just at this time, two ships arrived in port with 1,800 Sicilian immigrants. Stories spread throughout town that the Italians would take over the city. On Friday, March 14, 1891, the morning paper announced that all "good citizens" were to meet at the Henry Clay Statue on Canal Street in order to remedy the failure of justice. The crowd assembled, speeches were made, and a march began to the prison on Treme Street behind Congo Square, (now Armstrong Park).

The sheriff left the prison. His subordinates locked in all the other prisoners, but opened the cells of the Sicilians, telling them to hide wherever they chose. The mob battered down a wooden gate, and found the Sicilians crouching, begging for mercy. The maddened crowd shot the Sicilians one by one, dragging them out and hanging one from a lamppost at Tremé and St. Ann Streets, and another, who had shammed death in a pile of corpses, from a tree in front of the prison on Orleans Street. The affair became an international incident, arousing conflicting opinions across the nation. President Benjamin Harrison called the massacre "deplorable and discreditable," and the United States government paid an indemnity of $25,000 to the Italian government. The people of New Orleans fumed, but the matter was ended.

The incident resulted in the indictment of the entire Italian community in New Orleans, most of which consisted of law-abiding citizens who were as frightened of the Mafia as the rest of the population.

Italians had been immigrating to New Orleans since the French colonial period. Other large migrations had occurred before and after the Civil War. Those who came *during* the Civil War had left Italy after its unification (1860–1870) as exiled refugees, as well as peasant farmers seeking better conditions. Many were uneducated and unskilled. Those who arrived *after* the Civil War had been recruited by Italian merchants and steamship agents (supported by the Italian government) as laborers for the sugar plantations of Louisiana, and for public improvements and railroad construction. This was a profitable endeavor, not only for the agents, who received a commission, but for the plantation owners and construction companies who thus obtained

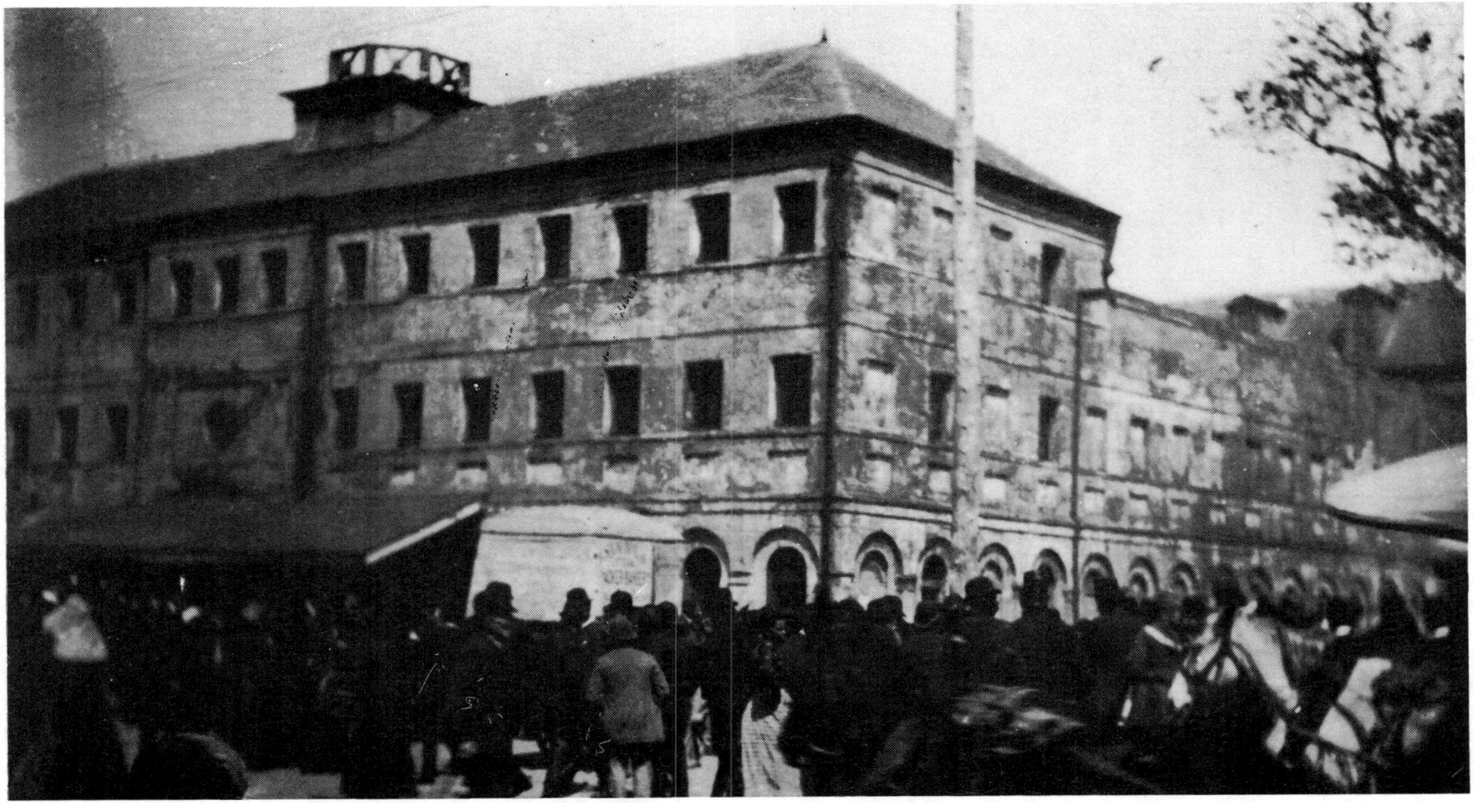

Figure 45. Crowds gather around Parish Prison on Treme Street after mob execution of Italians in 1891.

(Courtesy Leonard V. Huber Collection)

cheap labor. From the plantation sites, many of these Italian laborers found their way to New Orleans, where prejudice and hostility, because of their association with the blacks, relegated them to an inferior position in New Orleans society.

Living in the Vieux Carre, the Italians worked primarily with the importation, distribution and sale of citrus fruit, mostly handled in the French Market. Their business interests later extended to wine, liquor, and truck farming.

After the incident of the Italian Massacre, racial conflicts between Italian and Anglo-ethnic groups grew worse. Italians found refuge in their own benevolent organizations. The *Lega dei Presidente*, formed in 1898, established a school to educate illiterate Italians, and a free medical clinic. It provided financial assistance for a religious orphanage and school. The Italian Hall, on Esplanade Avenue, served as the social and cultural center of Italian activities through the 1950s.

STORYVILLE

Perhaps the best known "reform" during the administration of Mayor Walter C. Flower (1896–1899) was the establishment of Storyville. The ordinance creating Storyville (an area bounded by Basin Street and running down cross streets Iberville, Bienville, Conti, and St. Louis) did not declare it an "area of legalized vice." Instead, it specified the area *outside of which* prostitutes could not live or work.

Prostitution was therefore illegal *outside* of Storyville, but according to the wording of the ordinance, neither legal nor illegal *within* it. But since everyone knew it was there, the city obviously had a right to control it.

Prostitution in New Orleans had existed as far back as Louis XIV and XV. Those monarchs had sent hundreds of prostitutes to the colony. The Mississippi Company of John Law literally kidnapped "women of bad repute" and shipped them to Louisiana as colonists.

After the Louisiana Purchase in 1803, Mississippi River commerce increased enormously, bringing into the city the rough, bawdy keel-boatsmen with their pockets full of money, ready for their whiskey and women. To fill this demand, a stream of prostitutes converged upon New Orleans. Such women were barred from living or working in the city itself (the Vieux Carre), so they moved outside the city to the basin of the Carondelet Canal, where, "with their own hands and the help of levee loungers and General Jackson's forces, they dug a drainage ditch, erected shacks and shanties for themselves, and hung out their red lanterns. 'Basin Street' was open for business" (Al Rose, *Storyville*).

Other tenderloin areas existed in the city, like the "Swamp," on Julia and Girod Streets; and the two-block long Gallatin Street at the river, called the "port of missing men." These areas abounded with cutthroats, dance-house operators, fight promoters, thieves, thugs, and pimps. There were dance halls, brothels, saloons, gambling rooms, cockfighting pits, and rooming houses. Police mortality in these areas was high. "(Gallatin) . . . was the center of narcotics' traffic, as well as the home of dealers in stolen goods . . ." (Al Rose, *Storyville*).

In 1898, **Alderman Sidney Story** introduced the ordinance calling for a "restricted" red-light district, hoping to wipe out all other areas of vice, and control the restricted area. The document was discreetly worded so as to be legally acceptable, and it passed. That the area of brothels bore his name was a dubious honor, and a bitter pill for him to swallow.

Celebrities from all over the country visited Tom Anderson's saloon and bawdy houses like Josie Arlington's, which, in time, became "sporting palaces" with furniture, draperies and chandeliers to equal those in the mansions of St. Charles Avenue. Mardi Gras was a profitable season for the brothels, and the inhabitants of the demi-monde had their celebrations, just as the "society" people did.

Beginning in 1882 (before there was a Storyville) the "Ball of the Two Well-Known Gentlemen" became the focal point of Mardi Gras for all the creatures who frequented the area: the bartenders, prostitutes, musicians, politicians, and policemen. Word spread about these festivities, and nice young women begged their husbands and fiancées to get tickets to the affair, so that they could see with their own eyes (well hidden behind masks) how these brazen creatures carried on. In 1906, Josie Arlington, aware of their curiosity, arranged a police raid in which every lady present would be arrested unless she was carrying a card registering her as a prostitute in good standing. This caused untold embarrassment to a number of high society ladies, who were carted off to the police station, "for *not* being prostitutes."

TOM ANDERSON, THE MAYOR OF STORYVILLE

Tom Anderson, the richest and most powerful "business man" in Storyville, was an Irishman without equal in flair and raw "nerve" in the annals of Old New Orleans. Born in 1858 of a poor Irish Channel family, he sold newspapers in his childhood, became an informer for the police, and added to his earnings by delivering cocaine and opium to two local bagnios. In 1892, he opened a bar and restaurant on Basin Street, which were an immediate success. The well-known brothel owner, Josie Arlington, became his consort, and he rebuilt her "house" and reopened it for business in 1901, renaming it the Arlington Annex.

In time, through friendships made across the bar with policemen and politicians, the blue-eyed, red-haired Anderson boasted two titles, which he juggled admirably. He was "Mayor of Storyville," that

Figure 46. A license for prostitution issued in 1857.

tenderloin of crime and corruption, and "Honorable Tom Anderson," representative in the Louisiana State legislature of a large and important district of New Orleans. From *Collier Magazine,* February, 1908:

> "Tom Anderson overtops the restricted district; he is its lawgiver and its king; one of the names for it is "Anderson County" . . . "saloons with their wide-open poker and crap games; the dives where negroes buy for fifty cents five cents' worth of cocaine" . . . "when a woman of Anderson County commits robbery" (not an uncommon occurrence in the brothels), "and when the victim complains loudly enough that she has to be arrested, Tom Anderson comes down and gets her out. He doesn't even have to give cash bail . . . (she) may be released on the parole of any responsible prominent citizen."

Figure 47: Basin Street in Storyville, looking from Bienville to Canal Street. First house to right is Mahogany Hall (Lulu White's mansion); the Olga Sisters'; Josie Arlington's; Martha Clarke's; Jessie Brown's; Lizette Smith's; Marie Sisters'; Hilma Burt; and Tom Anderson's Annex. (The little house is typical of the pre-Storyville era)

(Courtesy Tulane University Special Collections)

THE SETTLEMENT OF MID CITY — 1890s to 1930s

At the turn of the century, space was running out on the two-mile area of the natural levee of New Orleans. Three options were open if the city was to accommodate more people: expanding toward the lake, expanding farther and farther along the levee, or crowding more people onto the same land.

Lakeward expansion was out of the question, in spite of the New Basin Canal, and the amusement parks at West End and Spanish Fort. The backswamp, which lay midway between the lake and the river was uninhabitable, because of flooding.

Expansion along the river had its limits, too. On the uptown end, at the boundary line between Orleans and Jefferson Parishes, there was a protection levee, running from the river to the lake; on the downtown side, expansion was limited by the simple fact that parts of Faubourg Marigny were regularly "under water" after rains.

What remained, then, was the obvious alternative of packing more people into the same space. New Orleans resisted multi-story residences, through fear of inadequate foundation material.

The homes most typical of New Orleans architecture at the turn of the century were the "shotgun houses," so called because one could fire a shotgun from front to back without hitting an obstruction. The "shotgun" was a string of rooms, lined up one behind the other, usually

Figure 48. Chartres Street in the French Quarter and the St. Louis Cathederal on the site of the first church built in the Mississippi Valley.

without a hallway. It afforded no privacy and little ventilation. It was the cheapest house on the market.

The "bungalow," or double tenement, was as popular as the shotgun. In reality, it *was* a shotgun, or a pair of shotguns, under one roof with party walls. To avoid flooding, builders set them five feet off the ground on piers. Others, like them, had basements, built on the ground floor beneath the residence. (Basements served as cellars, which were never built in New Orleans because of the high water table.) Such houses were called "raised bungalows." None of these houses were invented in New Orleans, but were built to suit the city's needs. However, once they were embellished with New Orleans favorite touches: louvered French doors, floor-lenth windows, Carpenter Gothic cornices and brackets, and gables with stained glass windows, they took on a personality all their own. They were "typical New Orleans."

At last, a gifted engineer in New Orleans by the name of **A. Baldwin Wood** invented a heavy duty pump which could rapidly raise great quantities of water, carry it vertically, and relocate it nearby. With this invention, the city had entered an era of land reclamation that would revolutionize its geography, and nothing would ever be quite the same again. Previously uninhabitable areas would now be open to settlement. But none of this was to happen quickly, or without great difficulty.

Draining the backswamp was a Herculean task, requiring both time and money. A system of drainage canals had to be built to carry the displaced water to Lake Borgne or Lake Pontchartrain. Levees had to be built to secure the newly-drained land. Pumping caused the backswamps to fall considerably below sea level, making flood controls a matter of life and death. The river levees had to be raised and a series of dikes built along the lake to keep out tidal surges. Even then, a line of inner protection levees was needed to connect the levee systems of lake and river. In 1899, Orleans Parish passed legislation to install its first pumping system. Within ten years, much of the middle city had been pumped out, but on the newly drained land, nothing could be built without driving pilings to considerable depths.

DRAINAGE: PUMPING STATIONS

Today, there are 22 pumping stations in the city, the largest drainage system in the country. The city is underlaid with a network of 1,500 miles of drain pipes and more than 240 miles of canals (more than Venice, which has 68 miles of canals). The drainage system has a combined capacity of 36,300 cubic feet per second.

Pumping Station No. 6 on the Metairie Relief Outfall Canal is the largest pumping station in the world.

Since 1899, New Orleans has provided its residents with pure drinking water. The river is the largest supply available in the United

Pitot House   18th Century

Holy Rosary Rectory   19th Century

Shotgun   20th Century

Figure 49. Three centuries on Bayou St. John.

176

Two Victorian Ladies on St. Charles Ave.

1939—Tara—St. Charles Ave.

Camelback on Canal St.

19th Century Victorian elegance.

Figure 50. Architectural styles in New Orleans.

States—309 billion gallons daily, approximately the amount consumed in the entire United States.

THE BUILDING OF THE LAKEFRONT

In spite of the high cost of land, the city moved inexorably lakeward. By the mid 1920s, it became inevitable that something had to be done about the lakefront. The levee, itself, was inadequate, and the old lakefront was seedy and ugly with its fishermen's shanties and its two amusement parks connected to the city by streetcar lines. As early as 1873, **W.H. Bell,** City Surveyor, had suggested a plan for the lakefront combining flood protection with land development. Fifty years later, in 1924, the state legislature asked the Board of Commissioners of the Orleans Lakefront (the Levee Board) to design and carry out such a plan. The Board was to make the lakefront more beautiful with improvements that would pay for themselves. No one denied it was a large order.

But the Levee Board, like the Dock Board, was a powerful body. It had been organized in 1890 and put in charge of 129 miles of levee, 27 miles on the river, and 94 miles of inner-city levees. It could levy taxes, expropriate land, run rights-of-way through property owned by other public bodies, and maintain its own police force.

When the Levee Board at last revealed its plans for the lakefront, the residents of the city were astounded. A stepped concrete seawall, five and a half miles long, was to be built on the floor of Lake Pontchartrain, approximately 3,000 feet out from shore, on which the lake waves could roll up and spend themselves at the top. After this, the enclosure would be filled in with material pumped in from the lake bottom outside the seawall. Behind the seawall, the filled area would be raised five to ten feet above the lake level, making it one of the highest parts of the city. When complete, the city would have not only a new levee but a whole new lakeshore with 2,000 acres of prime land to be disposed of by the Levee Board.

After 200 years of cutting itself off from the river by constructing warehouses, railroads, and docks, the city was now discovering a new waterfront, to be lined with beaches, boulevards and parks, and a new municipal yacht harbor. The Shushan Airport, (now the New Orleans Airport for private planes), constructed on a man-made peninsula at a cost of $4½ million, was completed in 1934. It was one of the biggest and best in the country.

The Depression came, and with it came the Works Progress Administration, which looked upon a public work of this magnitude as manna from heaven, for it offered employment to thousands.

To pay off its bonds, the Levee Board charged rental to the airport and the new Pontchartrain Beach Amusement Park, completed in 1939 just before World War II.

Figure 51. Administration Building Tower, Old Shushan Airport, now New Orleans Airport, built in 1934 on a man-made island at a cost of $4¹/₂ million.
(Courtesy Shushan Collection, Earl K. Long Library, UNO)

Figure 52. Huey P. Long promises "a chicken in every pot" to working men in the early 1930's.
(Courtesy The Deutsch Collection, Earl K. Long Library, UNO)

CHAPTER X

Growth In A Modern City — after 1930

The late twenties and early thirties brought to the city of New Orleans unemployment, soup lines, and deflated bank accounts. Like all other cities in the Unites States, New Orleans was suffering the effects of the Great Depression. The people were without hope, and a hero was needed.

When Huey Pierce Long was elected governor of Louisiana in 1928 and Unites States senator in 1932, Louisianians felt that they had found that hero. In Long, they saw the rise of the most colorful leader since Bernardo de Galvez.

THE KINGFISH

Long had built up one of the most powerful political machines in the United States, and in the face of incredible obstacles, put over his radical program by the sheer exuberance of his personality. His doctrine was one of socialism, a revolution of the poor whites. "Every Man a King" and "A Chicken in Every Pot" were the slogans of his "Share the Wealth" program. He believed and preached that no man should be allowed to earn more than a million dollars a year, and that everything he earned over that should go into a general fund from which the needy would be taken care of. There was a faction that hated him, but his power was such that his endorsement for any political office, state or city, was tantamount to election. His power over the state legislature made it possible for him to pass his entire legislative program.

He was a virtual dictator in Louisiana, and his power was felt most especially in New Orleans. In 1934, he sent the Louisiana National Guard down Lafayette Street to the Orleans Parish Registration Office, across from City Hall, where they broke the lock and took possession of the office. The militia had to be called out by **Mayor T. Semmes Walmsley** to try to prevent the seizure of the office. Militia and police, heavily armed with rifles and machine guns, swarmed around the office and the City Hall. Long was victorious, and the office was reopened under his supervision.

Long abused his right to use the state police during his administration, and the subsequent administration, which he controlled, that of his hand-picked representative, Governor O.K. Allen. Because of this abuse, legislation was passed, between 1936 and 1938, restricting the jurisdiction of the State Police in the city of New Orleans until the late 1970s.

Long was considered a saint and a king to the poor and downtrodden, who heard from his lips the first sound of democracy in action. They had been used to only one kind of government, the aristocratic, one-party kind. If Long wanted to be their dictator, in return for what he promised them, they were willing. He rode into office on their backs.

Long had finished an eight-month law course at Tulane University, passed the bar, and jumped into politics. On his thirtieth birthday, in 1923, he filed for governor and ran third. In preparation for running again, he made use of all the things that had needed attention in Louisiana for a long time: the unpaved roads, the high illiteracy rate, school textbooks, and a Mississippi River Bridge. Promising all of these, he was elected to the office of governor in 1928.

The Kingfish, as he was called, published his own newspaper, the *American Progress*. He wrote a book, *Every Man a King*, in which he outlined his ideas for putting an end to the Depression. Another literary effort, *My First Days in the White House*, was a futuristic exercise in political egomania.

During his term as senator, Long made a history-making, if unsuccessful, filibuster against a bill backed by President Franklin D. Roosevelt. For 15 hours and 35 minutes, he read the Unites States Constitution, the Declaration of Independence, parts of Victor Hugo's "The Laughing Man," chapters of the Bible, a monologue on Greek mythology, and a recipe for fried oysters.

Long made many enemies in Washington. A dozen or more senators would rise and leave the chambers whenever he stood up to speak.

Long was assassinated in the state capital in Baton Rouge on September 8, 1935, allegedly by Dr. Carl A. Weiss, whose father-in-law Long had gerrymandered out of office. Weiss was then riddled with bullets by Long's bodyguards. Suspicion has always lingered that it was his bodyguards, themselves, who may have killed him.

In spite of his Mafia-like tactics, Long was a governor to whom the city is indebted for the Shushan Airport (now the New Orleans Airport), for the extensive lakefront development, the Huey P. Long Bridge, the enlargement of Charity Hospital, the LSU Medical Center, and free school books in the public schools of Louisiana.

MAYOR ROBERT MAESTRI

In 1936, the city was on the verge of bankruptcy when **Robert Maestri** was elected mayor. In less than two years, he put the city on a cash basis. Every morning, he drove around the city with an engineer, checking streets and sidewalks, drainage and public buildings. Every afternoon, he sat at his desk, working to reorganize the archaic fiscal structure of the city and to improve municipal services. In 1942, he was re-elected almost without campaigning, but in his second term, gambling and extra-legal activities increased, which alienated the clergy. Maestri began to spend all his time running the Old Regulars, which he had fused with the Earl Long state-government organization. This alienated the uptown establishment.

A story has always been told that Maestri entertained Franklin D. Roosevelt on his visit to the city by taking him to Antoine's for dinner. There, they dined on Oysters Rockefeller. Proud of the city's seafood, the inarticulate mayor asked the aristocratic president, "How ya like dem ersh-ters?"

SPILLWAYS

In the 1920s and '30s, the Mississippi River threatened once again to divert its path, frightening New Orleanians. One threat of a diversion existed in a weak spot in the natural levee at a place called **Bonnet Carré,** where a crevasse had occurred more than once, carrying flood waters from the Mississippi to Lake Pontchartrain. If it had not been stopped, it might have gone directly on to the Gulf, by way of the Lake, instead of continuing its twisting path for 130 miles southward.

A second potential diversion was above Baton Rouge at a small town called **Morganza** on the west bank. If the river had jumped its course there, it would have poured into the slot between the present Mississippi River levee and the ancient levee of Bayou Teche, a sluggish swampy area 20 miles wide called the Atchafalaya River Basin, which flows slowly toward the Gulf. This was, by far, the most dangerous diversion the river could have taken, for if it would have *strayed* there, it would have *stayed* there, saving itself half the distance to the Gulf.

The crevasses at both Morganza and Bonnet Carré have been repaired, and the Army Corps of Engineers, in 1931, built giant concrete floodgates, which now prevent a breach in either levee, but which can be opened if a flood crest approaches, allowing surplus water to pour into Lake Pontchartrain. The **Bonnet Carré Spillway** has been opened several times since it was built, the **Morganza Spillway** only once, in the record-breaking flood of 1973. New Orleans was saved, but several other settlements were flooded, including Morgan City.

The Bonnet Carré Spillway and the levees make it possible to divert 3 million cubic feet of water per second into Lake Pontchartrain, and eventually, into the Gulf of Mexico.

DURING AND AFTER WORLD WAR II: THE LAKEFRONT

World War II not only brought a shortage of labor and materials and consequently a moratorium on residential building; it cut a striking design into the lakefront area, marking it the fringe of a mobilized city.

From West End to the airport, the lakefront was lined with military installations beginning in 1942. (See map: THE LAKEFRONT DURING WORLD WAR II.) At the western end, near the lighthouse, was the Coast Guard Station. This is the only installation which remains today. Moving eastward, in what are today the West and East Lakeshore subdivisions, were the U.S. Army (Largarde) General Hospital (west of Canal Blvd.) and the U.S. Naval Hospital (east of Canal Blvd.). Continuing eastward, on the lake edge of the Lake Vista subdivision, which had been cut in 1938, was a second Coast Guard Station after 1942. Situated on the eastern bank of Bayou St. John, between Robert E. Lee and Lakeshore Drive, was a building housing the U.S. Maritime Commission.

The Naval Reserve Aviation Base occupied an area on the Lakefront between the London Avenue Canal and Franklin Avenue, Lakeshore Drive and Robert E. Lee. Included in this area were an Aircraft Carrier Training Center and a Rest and Recreation Center, a tent city, where service men on leave were sent to relax. Many of them enjoyed the amusements of Pontchartrain Beach, which was in walking distance on the lakefront.

On Lakeshore Drive, on the western corner of Franklin Avenue, the War Assets Administration condemned a 750-foot tract of land, had it appraised and bought it from the New Orleans Levee Board. Here the Navy Assembly Plant was situated, according to maps of the period in the files of the New Orleans Levee Board. Some of its engineers, however, recall the Consolidated Vultee Aircraft Company, which existed on the spot in the war years, with its ramp which allowed seaplanes to be launched. At that time, there was a fence crossing Lakeshore Drive, and no vehicular traffic was allowed along the Lakefront. After the war, the federal government sold the property to Nash-Kelvinator, and it was later acquired by American Standard. The Levee Board was not able to acquire it. The property now belongs to The New Orleans Levee Board, whose offices are there.

Continuing eastward, between Franklin Avenue and Camp LeRoy Johnson Road, stretched the barracks of Camp LeRoy Johnson. This area is shown on the maps of the period as the U.S. Army Bombing

Squadron. Another interesting feature of this area was the German POW Camp on the far western lakefront corner of this area (Franklin Avenue and the Lake).

Today's New Orleans Airport was Shushan Airport at the time. During the war it was leased by the United States Government, and it housed a National Guard Hangar and a ramp for launching seaplanes. Also, along its western wall was an area occupied by the U.S. Army Bombing Squadron. Pan-American and Delta Airlines used the Administration Building jointly with the government for limited commercial activities; Pan-Am moved to Moisant Airport in 1947.

By the late 1940s, after the war, the face of the lakefront was changing to peacetime construction. Military installations were coming down and work was progressing on the residential areas, which had been earmarked for residential use by the Levee Board. Lots were then sold to help pay off bonds. Plans had been on the drawing board since before World War II for five residential areas.

Once again, starting at the West End of the lakefront and moving eastward (see map on THE LAKEFRONT AFTER 1964), the Coast Guard Station remains to this day at the lighthouse at West End for the protection of boat enthusiasts. The Southern Yacht Club stands on the northernmost peninsula of West End, as it has for over a century. The Orleans Boat Marina has now been built on the west side of the New Basin Canal.

East and West Lakeshore subdivisions, completed in 1953, include 352 residential lots on the sites of the old Army and Navy Hospitals. The Mardi Gras Fountain is situated near the lake in the East Lakeshore subdivision. East and West Lakeshore are bounded by Lakefront and Robert E. Lee Blvd., the New Basin Canal and the Orleans Canal.

The Lake Vista subdivision was completed in 1938, just before World War II. It was laid out in the "City Beautiful" design of Radburn, New Jersey, with a central "common," pedestrian lanes, and cul-de-sacs, providing safe areas for children. Mayor Maestri called it the "poor man's project," but prices of land in this area of premium location and planning would prove the slogan absurd. It was to become one of the wealthiest in the city. Lake Vista is bounded by the Lakefront and Robert E. Lee Blvd., the Orleans Canal and Bayou St. John.

Lake Terrace, completed in 1953, consisted of 440 building sites and 93 acres dedicated to parks for public use. The area is bounded by the Lakefront and Robert E. Lee Blvd., Bayou St. John and the London Avenue Canal.

The next segment of lakefront moving eastward is occupied by the University of New Orleans West campus. Its boundaries are the Lakefront and Leon C. Simon Blvd., the London Avenue Canal and Elysian Fields (195 acres). In 1964, this land was leased to the Louisiana

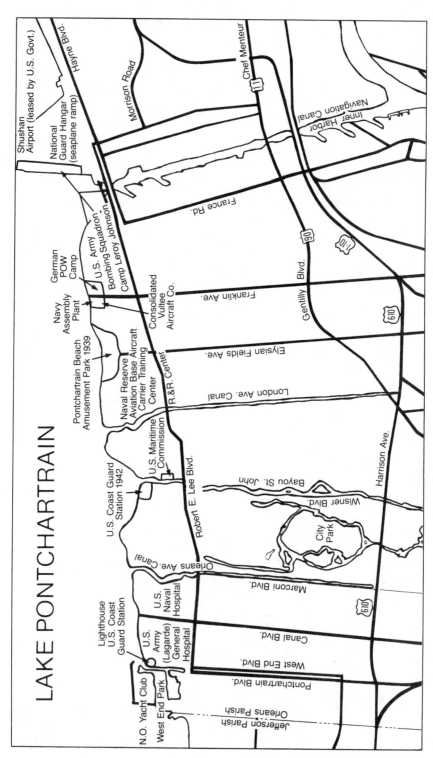

Figure 53. Lakefront during World War II. (Most military installations existed from 1942 to end of 40s.)

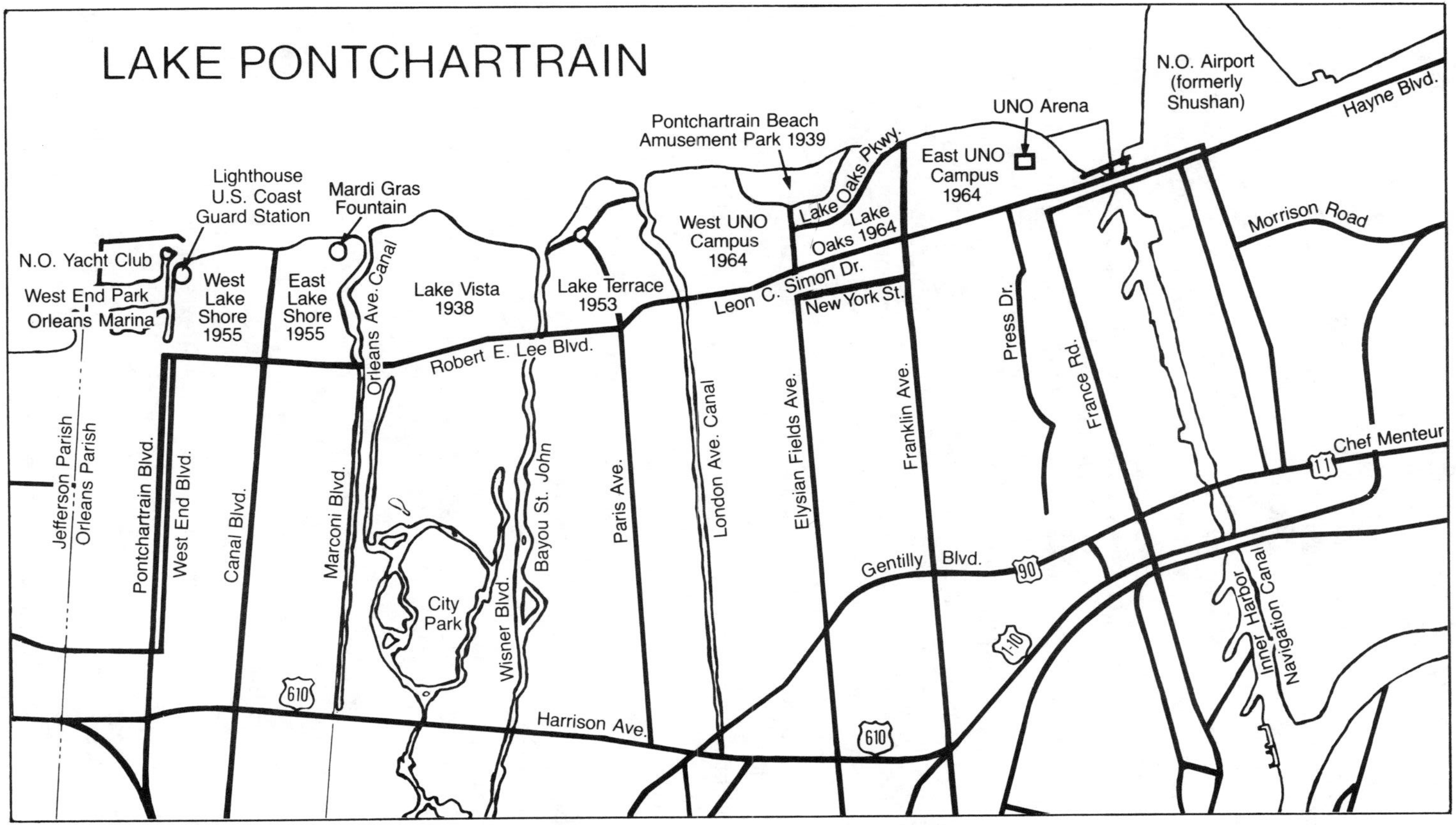

LAKE PONTCHARTRAIN

Figure 54. Lakefront after 1964.

(Map by M.L. Widmer)

State University in New Orleans (it became the University of New Orleans in 1975) for 99 years @ $1 a year.

Coming eastward, Lake Oaks subdivision has boundaries which are slightly out of line with the other lakefront developments. It lies between Lake Oaks Parkway and New York Street, Elysian Fields Avenue and Music Street. Completed in 1964, it consisted of 290 homesites.

Pontchartrain Beach Amusement Park, 1939–1983, was located on a 50-acre site on the lakefront, abutting both West UNO Campus and Lake Oaks subdivision.

To the east of Lake Oaks, an additional 195 acres were leased to the East campus of LSUNO (now UNO) in 1964 for 99 years @ $1 a year. It is bounded by the Lakefront and Leon C. Simon, Franklin Avenue and Press Drive. On that site is a multi-purpose indoor sports arena with a seating capacity of 16,000. On the grounds between the arena and the lakefront, a beautiful altar was erected for the Papal Mass said by Pope John Paul II when he visited New Orleans September 12, 1987.

The New Orleans Airport, formerly Shushan Airport, is today a facility for privately owned planes. All commercial airlines now operate out of New Orleans International Airport in Kenner.

The seawall at Lake Pontchartrain, built at a cost of $2,640,000, is the world's largest grandstand. Along its 5½-mile expanse, there is also a yacht harbor, a boat marina, a university, public recreation areas and an airport.

THE VETERAN CANDIDATE

In 1946, when Mayor Maestri once again threw his hat in the ring, he was to find himself opposed by another "reform" candidate, the handsome, vigorous, 33-year-old **deLesseps "Chep" Morrison,** a product of the silk-stocking crowd, who was just returning from a tour of duty in Europe as a Colonel in the U.S. Army. Before World War II, he had been in private law practice, worked in the labor law section of the NRA, and had become a member of the state legislature at age 28. He had been re-elected to the legislature in 1944 in spite of his absence. Attractive to both women voters and veterans, he was a natural for politics. He agreed to enter the race, although he thought he had no chance whatsoever of victory. No one was more surprised than Morrison when he defeated Maestri in the first primary (with the possible exception of Maestri himself). Maestri had a saying, "I was shaved without soap," which meant that someone had got the best of him. He undoubtedly made that remark the morning after that primary.

Morrison's organization was the Crescent City Democratic Organization. He was re-elected the 2nd, 3rd, and 4th terms, serving all but the last year of his fourth term, when he resigned (in 1961) to accept the post of ambassador to the Organization of the American States, which had been offered him by President Kennedy.

SCHOOL INTEGRATION

In 1954, the U.S. Supreme Court, in its historic decision—**Brown vs. Topeka Board of Education**—ruled unconstitutional the "separate but equal" doctrine as applied to public education. New Orleans, like most Southern cities, had never really implemented this segregationist doctrine, although it professed to do so. The Orleans Parish School Board had for many years maintained a distinctly inferior school system for black children.

The School Board fought the decision with delaying tactics, and the state legislature enacted a number of pro-segregationist statutes, all of which were cut down by the U.S. Supreme Court. Some thought it would be best to close down the public schools completely, as whites had done after the Civil War. Mayor Morrison remained silent, saying that he was "not responsible under state law for the public schools, only for the keeping of law and order."

On November 14, 1960, federal marshals escorted four small black girls as they entered first grade classes at two white schools. Crowds gathered, and some threatened the students and their parents. On November 15, **Judge Leander Perez** of Plaquemines Parish addressed 5,000 Orleanians at Municipal Auditorium, exploiting their prejudices and racial fears, urging them to stop the four black children from attending the white schools.

The following day, thousands rioted in the Central Business District, finally forcing action. The New Orleans Police arrested 250 citizens, after much violence and vandalism, including attacks on blacks.

In time, the turmoil subsided, with the help of Church groups, as well as the academic and business communities. School integration was at last accepted and there was a return to law and order.

Morrison's terms in office signaled the end of a half-century of machine-dominated politics. On May 22, 1964, Morrison was en route to Mexico with his younger son Randy in a chartered plane on a combined business and pleasure trip, when his plane crashed into a mountain, bringing his career to an untimely end.

THE SUBURBAN EXPLOSION

After the Mid-City and Lakefront areas were well settled, the population of the city continued to grow, consuming land like locusts, especially in the aftermath of World War II. By 1950, the internal area of the city from river to lake had been filled in.

Suddenly, in the late 1950s, the population rolled like a wave beyond the Orleans Parish line into the East Bank of Jefferson Parish, following the direction of the Airline Highway (which ran from Baton Rouge to New Orleans, built by Governor Huey P. Long in the early 1930s). Veterans' Highway, which paralleled Airline Highway, now became the "Main Street" of Jefferson Parish. Moisant Airport became New Orleans International Airport. In 1957, the 24-mile long Lake Pontchartrain Causeway spanned the lake between Jefferson Parish and St. Tammany Parish. The world's longest bridge, it offered commuters an opportunity to work in New Orleans and reside in Covington, Mandeville, or Folsom. The second causeway was completed in 1969.

Shopping centers in Jefferson Parish mushroomed: Lakeside Shopping Center, Clearview Mall, and Fat City with its shops and restaurants.

By the 1970s, another vast new suburban area was waiting only for the completion of the Interstate Highway-10 to follow the pattern of Jefferson Parish, but on the opposite extremity of the city. It was New Orleans East, which, in the early '70s, began to feel the trickle of the first wave of population roll-in. As early as the 1960s houses and businesses had already begun to crop up in New Orleans East in an unorganized fashion along the newly-located Chef Menteur Highway, which cut across New Orleans East in much the same way that Airline Highway cut across Jefferson Parish.

Soon, it was evident to land developers that real estate along the route of the new I-10 would be worth its weight in gold. New Orleans East is 50 square miles and will be a community where, eventually, 250,000 people will live, which is equal to one-fourth the total area and population of Greater New Orleans.

Because of the speed with which this expansion took place, and the enormity of the area it covered, New Orleans has become, in the last quarter century, a city within a city. At the center is the old New Orleans. On the outskirts is suburbia. In this respect, it is no better or worse than most big urban communities, and it is following a national pattern.

Sad to say, much of this newly developed land is sinking, and many of the new subdivisions are subject to flood. Unlike neighborhoods that had developed at a snail's pace before World War II, each with its individual architectural personality (Gentilly Terrace in the 1920s showed a preference for Spanish mission-style houses of white stucco and red-tiled roofs), the new suburbs seem boring and homogeneous.

There was one more direction in which the population could move, and it rapidly did so in the early 1980s. That direction is southward from the West Bank of the river in the direction of Bayou Barataria. This may prove to be the largest surge of all.

THE MAYORS: AFTER 1961

When Morrison resigned in 1961, the City Council voted to make **Victor H. Schiro** interim mayor. Schiro was at the time Councilman-at-large on the City Council. Born of an Italian father who had been involved in banking business in Honduras, Schiro had spent much of his boyhood in Honduras, where he learned Spanish, a language that was of great value to him when he was mayor, traveling in Central America.

As a young man, he attended Tulane University and graduated from Santa Clara in California, after which he spent three years in Hollywood, working under Frank Capra in movies. In World War II, he served in the Coast Guard for three years. Returning to New Orleans, he worked as program director and announcer in radio, entered the insurance business for Metropolitan Life Insurance Company, and then opened an insurance company of his own.

His first effort in politics was his vigorous support of a Home Rule Charter for New Orleans. Mayor Morrison endorsed him in his candidacy for City Council, and he was elected in 1950, becoming Commissioner of Public Buildings and Parks. In 1954, he won a seat as Councilman-at-large on the City Council, which had been established as part of the Home Rule Charter in 1954. He was re-elected in 1958 for a four-year term, but was to take over the office of mayor when Morrison resigned in 1961.

MAYOR VICTOR H. SCHIRO —
CHANGES IN RACIAL TOLERANCE

In the summer of 1961, when Schiro assumed office, he was immediately confronted with the problem of school integration, which was, as yet, far from solved. The episode of the previous fall, with the black children breaking the segregation barriers, and the abusive by-standers jeering at them and spitting on them, had brought New Orleans to the attention of the nation, and criticism had been strong. Intent upon preventing such an incident in 1961, Schiro instructed the police to set up barricades to keep die-hard segregationists a good distance away from the school children. In this way, additional demonstrations were avoided, and school integration proceeded more smoothly.

Schiro ended the segregation of rest rooms at City Hall. He appointed the first black executive assistant to the mayor's office and was the first mayor to sanction the appointment of blacks as heads of important boards and commissions since the end of Reconstruction.

These changes in racial tolerance and good-will were no doubt exactly what the city needed to prevent the racial upheavals which occurred elsewhere in the 1960s. New Orleans was one of the few cities with a large black population where violence did not erupt during the period.

During his administration, the Space Program brought thousands of highly skilled technicians, engineers, and administrators to NASA's Michoud Assembly Facility. This meant new households, growth in retail sales, and an expanded tax base. Schiro also sponsored the initial effort to plan the construction of the Domed Stadium (Superdome).

When Hurricane Betsy struck New Orleans September 9, 1965, (the most devastating hurricane to reach mainland United States until that time), Schiro's prompt and effective coordination of relief efforts played a major role in the city's recovery. Schiro was, however, a master of malaprops, and is unfortunately best remembered during that frightening time for his remark on television, (hard hat and all), as the storm gathered force. "Don't be afraid," he said. "Don't believe any false rumors until you hear them from me."

MAYOR MAURICE "MOON" LANDRIEU —
PRINCIPLE BEFORE EXPEDIENCY

Schiro was succeeded in 1970 by **Maurice "Moon" Landrieu,** a lawyer, an army veteran, the father of nine children, and a representative in the state legislature. In the late 1950s, he had become active in the Young CCDA, an organization aligned with the CCDA led by the then-Mayor Morrison. It was with Morrison's endorsement that he had won a seat in the State House of Representatives.

In November, 1960, **Governor Jimmy Davis** convened a special session of the legislature to consider a package of pro-segregationist bills to circumvent the federal court orders integrating New Orleans public schools. The legislature could not nullify the federal judiciary's integrations judgments, but almost the entire legislature chose the path of least resistance, rather than lose segregationists' votes. Landrieu was the only member of the Louisiana House of Representatives to put principle before expediency and vote against the bills. At the time, this was followed by death threats, but in the late '60s and '70s, his support for equal rights proved to be an asset. In 1965, he won a seat on the City Council as Councilman-at-large. In 1969, he was elected mayor.

The new administration strove to deal with the city's fiscal problems on a long-term basis. Landrieu named the first black to head a department of city government. He chose qualified personnel, regardless of race. He was also responsible for the advancement of women in high places in city government. He promoted the growth of tourism by public improvements and renovation projects.

The Moonwalk, named in his honor and built during his adminis-

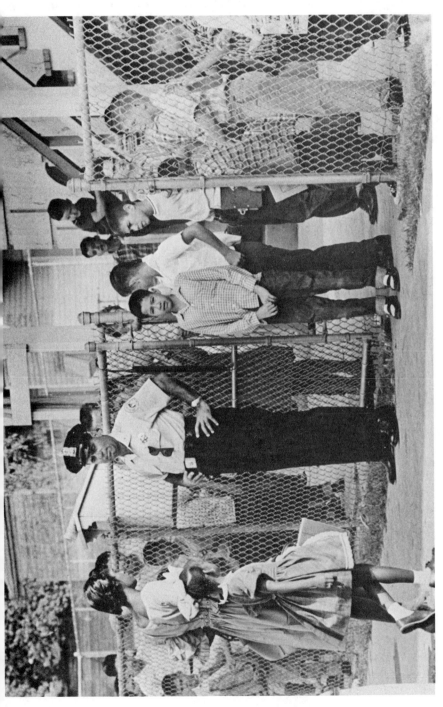

Figure 55. 1961: A Negro girl enters the first grade, integrating McDonogh 11 School in Mid-City New Orleans after an order by Judge J. Skelly Wright in 1960. The Civil Rights Act was later signed by President Lyndon B. Johnson in 1964.

(Courtesy Times-Picayune Publishing Co.)

tration, stretches out atop the levee at Jackson Square, and gives the visitor an unparalleled view of both the river and the Cathedral.

In 1975–76, Landrieu served as president of the U.S. Conference of Mayors, and he was nominated by President Carter as Secretary of Housing and Urban Development September 24, 1979, an office which he held until the end of the Carter administration.

MAYOR ERNEST "DUTCH" MORIAL — TRAIL-BLAZER

Mayor Ernest "Dutch" Morial blazed trails and made history for his race as the first black mayor of New Orleans. In 1965, Morial was made the first black assistant in the U.S. Attorney's office. In 1967, he became the first black in the legislature since Reconstruction. In the 1970s, he became the first black juvenile court judge and the first Black elected to the State's Fourth Circuit Court of Appeals. He served as mayor from 1978 to 1986. Few people can claim such a collection of "firsts."

Morial tried to create more jobs and bring a greater stability to the city's economy. During his administration, major improvements were made in the port's docking facilities. He also attempted to improve existing job training and vocational programs and to create new ones where they were needed.

His efforts to expand tourism included a new $88 million Convention and Exhibition Center (now called the Ernest N. Morial Convention Center) and a World Exposition and Fair in 1984. Morial died on December 24, 1989.

MAYOR SIDNEY BARTHELEMY — MAYORAL LANDSLIDE

Mayor Sidney J. Barthelemy won the race for mayor of New Orleans in 1986 by the largest landslide of a non-incumbent in the city's history. The mayor had served as Director of the City Welfare Department. He was the first black Louisiana State Senator elected since Reconstruction. During his first year in office, he was elected president of the National Association of Regional Councils and was on the board of directors of the U.S. Conference of Mayors.

MARC MORIAL — SWEEPING VICTORY

Marc Morial, at 36 the youngest mayor in our city's history, and the second half of a father-son mayoral team, was elected to office March 5, 1994. In his campaign, he promised a "safe" city and work opportunities for all.

Figure 56. Aerial view, L to R, shows the Civil District Court Building, City Hall, State Office Building, State Supreme Court, and the New Orleans Public Library, 1960.
(Courtesy New Orleans Public Library)

195

Figure 57. This aerial view shows the river, the Central Business District, and the Superdome.

CHAPTER XI

New Orleans Today

Waterways still play an important role in the story of New Orleans. The Mississippi River and the business it brings is vital to the existence of the city. And so, the U.S. Engineers work to keep the river running past our door on its familiar route. The lakes and bayous used by the explorers are still important to commerce as well as recreation. And so, the Lake Pontchartrain Basin Foundation works to keep these waterways free of pollution and inviting to human and wildlife habitation.

The Vieux Carre remains the city's chief attraction. More pedestrians cross Jackson Square and its bounding streets each year than any other area of equal size in the entire United States. What keeps the attraction alive and exciting aside from the beautiful architecture of the Jackson Square area? It is the fact that the French Quarter's buildings, while not a living museum like Williamsburg, have retained that European city look, that ancient Bohemian essence that makes it one of a kind, *sui generis*, in all of North America.

New challenges and needs are being met as the city moves into the 21st century. From the days when cotton was king to the rise of the global economy, the port of New Orleans evolves with the changing face of world trade and remains one of the busiest ports in the United States.

PORT OF NEW ORLEANS

The Port offers shippers modern facilities, the most modern intermodal connections in the country and efficient, experienced labor. Every imaginable cargo crosses the Port's wharves, from sugar and textiles to steel and soybeans. The Port continues to make gains in niche cargoes with increased tonnages in coffee, export forest products and natural rubber imports.

The Port Authority of Greater New Orleans (Dock Board) began in the 1960s a project of rebuilding scheduled to take three decades. This was made necessary by a change in the technology of shipping: the use of container vessels and barge-carrying ships. Container docks require large alongside assembly areas, huge "stuffing" sheds, large yards for the assembly of trucks and railroad cars, and cranes for moving containers from ship to vehicle.

The Dock Board decided to start from scratch in a brand new location, establishing the France Road and Jourdan Road river terminals, which have greatly increased the Port's general cargo and bulk cargo capabilities. By the year 2000, twenty-nine existing wharves in downtown New Orleans will have been retired and development will have increased in New Orleans East. For the first time since Bienville landed 300 years ago, New Orleans will have a riverfront uncluttered by wharves.

THE INTRACOASTAL WATERWAY

Why is it being built in Eastern New Orleans? The answer goes back to the 1920s, when the Dock Board and the city collaborated to build a deep water canal between the Mississippi River and Lake Pontchartrain. Its name is the **Inner Harbor Navigation Canal.** It is referred to by New Orleanians as the **Industrial Canal.** It was later attached to the **Intracoastal Waterway,** which led off eastward to Lake Borgne and the Mississippi Gulf Coast. In 1923, the canal was connected to the river by locks. In 1934, on the West Bank of the river, the Harvey Canal was finished, linking the Mississippi River, Bayou Barataria, western Louisiana, and the Texas Coast. Both the Industrial Canal and the Harvey Canal became links in the newly-finished Intracoastal Waterway, which eventually led from the Rio Grande River to the Florida Coast.

New Orleans is now the **Total Port,** offering every maritime service. It earns the title **Centroport, U.S.A.** It is a part of the greatest port complex in the world (from Baton Rouge to the Gulf), with twice the tonnage of Rotterdam, the world's No. 1 Port.

New Orleans is served by seven major railroads, the U.S. Interstate Highway System, the Mississippi–Gulf Outlet, and 19,000 miles of navigable waterways. More than 100 steamship lines offer regular sailing from New Orleans to all parts of the world.

TOURISM

Tourism continues to be the "rising star" in our economic sky as the first Lake Pontchartrain Casino, "Star," begins business and the first riverboat casino, "Hilton Queen of New Orleans," begins its life on the Mississippi.

Excursion boats allow the same view of the St. Louis Cathedral and Jackson Square enjoyed by steamboat passengers a century ago. The last two overnight paddlewheel steamboats in the United States, the **Delta**

Queen and the **Mississippi River Queen,** still offer from the "old" a view of the "new." The Natchez, the largest sternwheeler built in the United States this century, offers cruises on the river, as do the Creole Queen, the Cotton Blossom, the Mark Twain, and the Commodore, names and designs evoking memories of the steamboat era.

Figure 58. The First Street Wharf on the East Bank has 1275 feet water frontage and 50 feet wide front aprons, Public Belt Railroad front and rear aprons, providing direct discharge to rail or truck.
(Courtesy Port of New Orleans).

CASINOS AND RIVERBOAT GAMBLING

On June 11, 1992, the Louisiana legislature signed the **Louisiana Economic Development and Gaming Corporation Act** into law. This act allows a single land-based casino in New Orleans near the French Quarter. Riverboat gambling was legalized on the Mississippi and other Louisiana waterways in 1991. Other gaming riverboats are to follow, reviving the traditions of the past.

The Golden Age of Steamboating on the Mississippi is recalled as ships, reminiscent of that earlier era, fill the river, dodging containerized freighters, ferries, tows with their strings of barges, cruise ships, ocean liners, oil tankers, all vying for their space in the river. New Orleans keeps the old and just adds the new.

THE CENTRAL BUSINESS DISTRICT AND THE POYDRAS STREET BOOM

The Dock Board's decision to abandon the riverfront wharves and its plans for the building of the Superdome were both responsible for the revival and restoration of the Central Business District. The **Rivergate Project** came first in 1968 with its central 33-story International Trade Mart, now called the World Trade Center.

Hotels followed, like the **Marriott, Hilton, Meridien, Sheraton, Windsor Court, Le Pavilion** and **Westin Canal Place** with its shopping complex. Others are the **Hyatt-Regency Hotel** which includes a shopping mall called the Poydras Plaza. Another development is the **International Rivercenter,** now called the **Riverwalk,** with its shopping malls, restaurants, lounges, and parking facilities. Like the Rivergate Project, all met with success because of their proximity to the French Quarter, the riverfront, and the Superdome.

Much activity was generated by the building of the **Louisiana Superdome** and the presence of the **Louisiana World Exposition** on the riverfront in 1984, opening this area for future development.

The construction of the second span of the **Greater New Orleans Mississippi River Bridge** completed in 1988 (both spans now called the **Crescent City Connection**) required elevated ramps which necessitated changes in the neighborhood. Poydras Street, the center of the area between the bridge ramps and Canal Street, became the new scene of construction and business activity.

POYDRAS STREET A MONUMENT TO THE OIL BOOM OF THE EARLY 1980s

Poydras Street is a monument to the oil boom of 1981, when a record 502 rigs were pumping off the shores of Louisiana. By 1986, only 92 were left. The culprit was OPEC, which reduced the price of oil from $35 a barrel to as low as $10. The impact was devastating. Oil-related jobs disappeared. In 1983, major manufacturers like Kaiser Chalmette Works, formerly one of the world's largest aluminum reduction plants, shut down, causing 2000 workers to become unemployed. It has not reopened. The Port of New Orleans lost business to other ports. People were leaving the city. Houses were for sale. Values fell. Now, by the mid-nineties, prices have come back up and the oil companies say they can survive. Even so, the future may well be with natural gas.

THE SUPERDOME

The **Superdome,** built at a cost of $161 million, was opened with a football game in August, 1975. It is probably the most extravagant building in the world. With a seating capacity of 72,000 for stadium events, the dome has a Texas flavor about it but it outdoes the Houston Astrodome in size (the astrodome could fit inside it with 30 feet above it to spare). With the opening of the Superdome, the city was announcing that it was officially "open for business."

The comfortable armchair seats of the Superdome are set out in alternating colors, which play strange tricks on the eyes and on the TV cameras, giving a "busy" look and not allowing the bleachers to look empty, even when they really are.

The carpet on the exit tunnel is laid out in alternating Mardi Gras colors of purple, gold, and green in horizontal stripes to give the illusion of stairs, in order to slow down the throngs of people exiting and avoid claustrophobia by creating a feeling of space.

The dome, built on 52 acres, rises 27 stories above the site of the old railroad yard and is the most visible building in the city. It is the "world's largest room" unobstructed by posts.

The Superdome is home to the Tulane football team, the New Orleans' Saints NFL team, and the Sugar Bowl game, played traditionally on New Year's Day.

Adding to the sports picture, by 1994, **English Turn** is not just a place anymore. It's a country club development with a Jack Nicklaus–designed championship golf course, where a PGA Golf Classic is held each year.

NEW BUILDINGS IN THE CBD

Since 1970, the list of buildings constructed is indeed impressive. Some of these are: Number One Shell Square, 50-stories high; the Lykes Center, headquarters for Lykes Brothers Steamship Company; the Bank of New Orleans; the Entergy Corporation; the Freeport McMoran Oil and Gas; Place St. Charles; and Pan-American Life Insurance.

INDUSTRY AND NATURAL RESOURCES

The **Avondale Shipyards,** across the river from New Orleans in Avondale, Louisiana, employs 6500 people in the building of ocean-going craft. It is the largest private employer in Louisiana. It has been contracted to build sealift vessels (carriers of military cargo) and Coast Guard polar ice-breakers.

The 832-acre Michoud plant called the **NASA Michoud Assembly Facility** in Eastern New Orleans has been used for fabricating rocket boosters for flights in space. Martin Marietta currently manufactures the Space Shuttle internal fuel tanks under contract to NASA.

Freeport McMoRan, a Fortune 300 natural resource company headquartered in New Orleans, produces sulphur, copper, and gold. Its contributions to the community have been many. In the field of education, the company has contributed to the public schools of Louisiana. It has made enormous contributions to human service organizations, such as the United Way Agencies. In the arts, it has contributed to organizations such as the Metropolitan Arts Fund. And in helping environmental groups, Freeport McMoRan has made huge contributions to the Louisiana Nature and Science Center.

The **Audubon Institute** is a non-profit organization which operates the Audubon Zoo, the Aquarium of the Americas, Audubon Park, Woldenberg Riverfront Park, Freeport McMoRan Audubon Species Survival Center (1993); Audubon Center for Research on Endangered Species (1995); and the Audubon Insectarium (1955). It has an impact on the local economy of $100 million annually. It is in part supported by household and individual memberships. The Institute began as "Friends of the Zoo" in 1974.

GOVERNMENT AND CIVIC CENTER

New Orleans operates on the parish council system. Orleans Parish and the City of New Orleans share boundaries; therefore, the parish and city government are the same. The New Orleans mayor is assisted by a chief administrator and a city council made up of seven members, five from districts and two at large. The **City Hall,** where government administration takes place, is an 11-story building which is part of the **Civic Center** built in 1957. It includes the 8-story **State Office Building; the State Supreme Court Building; the Civil Courts Building; and the Main City Library.** The Civic Center, which covers an area of 11 acres in the CBD, was built at a cost of $19 million.

UNIVERSITIES

New Orleans is home to many universities and colleges: Tulane on St. Charles Avenue (1834); Dillard on Gentilly Boulevard (1869); Loyola of the South on St. Charles Avenue (1912); Xavier on Washington Avenue (1915); Our Lady of the Holy Cross College on Woodland in Algiers (1916); Delgado Community College on City Park Avenue (1921); Southern University of New Orleans on Press Drive (1956); and the University of New Orleans on the Lakefront (1958).

LOUISIANA WORLD EXPOSITION

From May to November, 1984, New Orleans was host to the **Louisiana World Exposition** held on the riverfront between Poydras Street and the Greater New Orleans Mississippi River Bridge. The Fair's theme was "The World of Rivers—Fresh Water as a Source of Life." A 550-seat amphitheater provided a superb view of the proscenium stage, with the magnificent Mississippi River as a backdrop for the international artists who performed there. An open-air aquacade extravaganza further carried out the water theme.

Although the World's Fair lost a great deal of money, it left a valuable legacy to the people of New Orleans in the development of the riverfront, the construction of hotels and parks, and the improvement of roads. The **Riverwalk,** a major shopping mall, attracts millions of tourists annually. The **Ernest N. Morial Convention Center,** which covers 700,000 gross square feet, is now the third largest in the nation. (For the Aquarium of the Americas and Woldenberg Park, see Parks following. For Red Riverfront Streetcars, see Streetcars).

PARKS

CITY PARK is one of the largest municipal parks in the United States, covering 1500 acres of land. The original park was the Allard Plantation, bought at auction by John McDonogh, who willed it to the children of New Orleans. Allard lived on the land till he died and was buried beneath the one remaining Dueling Oak. The park tripled in size in the 1920s.

AUDUBON PARK was once the plantation of Etienne Bore and the site of the World's Industrial and Cotton Centennial Exposition. It now boasts The AUDUBON ZOOLOGICAL GARDEN, the South's largest zoo, located at the juncture of Magazine Street and the Mississippi River. Besides white alligators, swamp exhibits, and the world of primates, it features waterfalls and tropical vegetation that simulate a natural habitat for more than a thousand animals.

ARMSTRONG PARK, on Rampart Street between St. Ann and St. Peter, is a square with an interesting history. Named in honor of the black New Orleans-born jazz musician who was the city's goodwill ambassador to the world, it is home to many festivals and celebrations. The city purchased the square from Claude Tremé in 1810 and subdivided the neighborhood. In this area, many free people of color and skilled black craftsmen lived side by side with white families, who built Italianate and Greek Revival homes.

After the Civil War, the square was renamed Beauregard Square in honor of the Confederate General P.G.T. Beauregard. In 1930, a Municipal Auditorium was constructed to the rear of the square. Now called the **Morris F.X. Jeff Auditorium** in honor of the city official who helped provide recreation and sports activities for African-American children, it continues to provide accommodations for operas, plays, and Carnival balls.

WOLDENBERG RIVERFRONT PARK, which opened in October, 1989, provided the landscaping for the Aquarium which was to open the following year. The park is named for Malcomb and Dorothy Woldenberg, philanthropists who gave tremendous sums to Tulane University and to the Woldenberg Village for the elderly in Algiers. The park consists of thirteen acres of green space featuring oak trees, magnolias, crepe myrtles and a brick promenade along the river. It is graced with a beautiful kinetic sculpture by a New Orleanian, John Scott, who won the commission in a contest sponsored by the Audubon Institute. His work, called "Ocean Song," is sixteen feet tall, made of mirror-finished stainless steel. Its top elements move in the wind.

THE AQUARIUM OF THE AMERICAS, part of the **Audubon Institute,** opened in 1990 on a sixteen-acre site on the riverfront near Canal Street. It offers an up-close view of sea life, showing the aquatic worlds of the Caribbean, Amazon Rainforest, Gulf of Mexico, and Mississippi Delta. The zoo and the aquarium, both on the Mississippi River, can be accessed by the **John James Audubon Riverboat** which connects the Uptown and French Quarter attractions.

THE LOUISIANA NATURE AND SCIENCE CENTER at 11000 Lake Forest Boulevard is a haven for wildlife in the city. It offers special educational programs, a science resource center, forest and wetland nature trails, and a planetarium.

MUSEUMS

In April, 1993, THE NEW ORLEANS MUSEUM OF ART in City Park completed a $20 million renovation, doubling its gallery space, expanding its educational facilities, and adding a restaurant. NOMA's collections include works of art of Western civilization from the pre-

Christian era to the present. Among its collections are the arts of Africa, the Far East, pre-Columbian America, a special Fabergé collection, and a group of works by the impressionist Edgar Degas. It is the city's oldest fine art organization and has a permanent collection of 35,000 objects valued in excess of $200 million.

THE HISTORIC NEW ORLEANS COLLECTION at 533 Royal Street is a private, non-profit organization established in 1966 by Gen. and Mrs. L. Kemper Williams to serve the public as a museum and research center for state and local history.

MUSEE CONTI WAX MUSEUM OF LOUISIANA LEGENDS, at 917 Conti Street, tells the story of three centuries of New Orleans history in costumed wax figures and settings.

Other museums in the city are the CABILDO (see below), the PRESBYTERE, the 1850 HOUSE in the lower Pontalba Apartments, the OLD U.S. MINT, the CONFEDERATE MUSEUM, the PHARMACY MUSEUM, and the CHILDREN'S MUSEUM.

DESTRUCTION AND RENOVATION OF THE CABILDO

On Wednesday, May 11, 1988 at 4 p.m. a fire broke out in the historic Cabildo and raged for 90 minutes, bringing down the cupola and the Mansard roof and damaging a storehouse of historic furniture on the third floor. Artifacts on the lower floors were seriously water-damaged. New Orleanians and tourists watched as the fire department hoses sprayed from all directions and as firemen and volunteers made repeated trips into the building to salvage art works. A possible cause of the fire was a spark from a welder's torch during repairs to the roof gutters. The St. Louis Cathederal next door remained unharmed.

Six years and eight million dollars later, on Sunday, February 27, 1994, New Orleanians got to see the renovated building, improvements, and new exhibits. James F. Sefcik, director of the **Louisiana State Museum,** said that the fire had given them the opportunity to do the comprehensive exhibition on the history of Louisiana that he already had in mind. The renovated building now includes carefully planned exhibits telling the story of Louisiana from the European explorers to 1877, with emphasis on the American Indians, black slaves, and free people of color, not just the Spanish, French, and Anglo-Americans who controlled their politics.

CUISINE

Because of the variety of seafood and vegetables in and around New Orleans, much experimenting has been done with cooking, resulting in such delicacies as stuffed merlitons, eggplants, and artichokes, as well as soups, sauces, stews, gumbos, and étouffés prepared with "Creole" tomatoes, onions, garlic, and green peppers. Red beans and rice is also a mainstay of the New Orleans family.

The colonial French learned from the Choctaw and Chickasaw Indians how to use roots and herbs in their cooking, like sassafras in their gumbos and chicory in their coffee. The Acadians brought with them their one-pot dishes, which started with a "roux," a gravy made with browned flour. In the 1890s, the Italians came with their highly-seasoned dishes.

Some of the oldest French restaurants in the Vieux Carre still in operation today are **Antoine's** (1840), **Galatoire's** (1905), **Arnaud's** (1918), and **Broussards** (1920). Others of equal stature are **Brennan's, Commander's Palace, Delmonico's, Mosca's, Tujague's,** and **Dooky Chase's.**

Reflecting the additions to our population, many ethnic restaurants are operating successfully in New Orleans today, such as Korean, Japanese, Greek, Cuban, Indian, Chinese, Vietnamese, Thai, and Turkish.

THE MUSIC OF NEW ORLEANS

The Crescent City is known for jazz because of pioneers like **Buddy Bolden, King Oliver, Louis Armstrong,** and **Jelly Roll Morton.** Jazz is still nurtured by musicians like Danny Baker, the Humphrey brothers, and Dr. Michael White. It's also being played by brass bands like the Dirty Dozen and Re-Birth. New Orleans boasts modern jazz players like Red Tyler and Clarence Ford.

Ellis Marsalis has come back to New Orleans to a prestigious professional post at UNO. His sons **Wynton, Branford, and Delfeayo** are enjoying well-deserved success on an international scale. The same may be said of multi-talented New Orleans singer-pianist **Harry Connick, Jr.**

Rhythm and blues became an art form in the fifties, when hometown hero **Fats Domino** topped the national charts. Another R&B artist was the late **Professor Longhair (Roeland Byrd),** whose Afro-Cuban rhumba style bore evidence of New Orleans connections to Caribbean culture. An artist who started in the fifties and is still a songwriter, producer, pianist, and vocalist is **Allen Toussaint,** one of the creators of New Orleans rhythm and blues. The R&B scene flourishes today with fifties' stars still in great form, like **Irma Thomas, Frankie Ford,** and **Clarence "Frogman" Henry.**

The Grammy-winning Neville brothers blend Louisiana pop tradition and Rock energy. The Neville brothers and **Dr. John** (Mac Rebennack) have taken New Orleans R&B into the nineties and out to the world. Other R&B artists are Johnny Adams, Walter "Wolfman" Washington, and

Snooks Eaglin. Some R&B nightclubs are **Tipitina's,** the **Maple Leaf,** and **Muddy Waters.**

Rock and Roll is alive and well, played by the Radiators, Dash Rip Rock, and the House Levelers at places like Jimmy's, The Carrollton Station, and Mid-City Bowling Lanes.

Cajun music and zydeco, its African-American Creole counterpart, are unique to the local scene. This music can be heard at restaurants like **Mulate's** and **Michael's.**

The Latin music scene still thrives in the music of Ruben "Mr. Salsa" Gonzales, Hector Gallardo, and the Iguanos.

NIGHT LIFE

New Orleans is a fun-loving city, and the party never ends. Until the wee hours of the morning, the taverns of Bourbon Street are alive with the laughter of merrymakers, the sounds of jazz, and the drumbeats that accompany the exotic dancers. People fill the streets, some of which are now pedestrian malls. They strut to the beat of the music as they window shop. **Pat O'Brien's,** a night spot surrounding a courtyard, entertains its

Figure 59. New Orleans' own Pete Fountain, one of the nation's greatest jazz artists.

207

patrons nightly at the twin piano-bar, serving the "Hurricane," a world-famous drink. The beverage, served in a 29-ounce handblown crested glass, is an item much coveted as a souvenir of New Orleans.

Spectacular views of the city can be seen from the top of the **World Trade Center** at #2 Canal Place, the **Top of the Dome of the Hyatt Regency,** the **River View of the Marriott,** and from many eating places in the **Jackson Brewery** and the **Millhouse.**

Al Hirt, Pete Fountain, and **Ronnie Kole,** are New Orleans' best known jazz artists. **Pete Fountain's Club** at the Hilton Hotel is a "must" for any visitor. A unique establishment for the jazz purist is **Preservation Hall** at 726 St. Peter Street, where one can enjoy the music for a minimal fee without the usual club-type atmosphere and the cost of food and drinks.

NEW ORLEANS, A STUDY IN CONTRASTS

New Orleans, approaching the 21st Century, is a study in contrasts. The Old Quarter, the Garden District, the University Area, Carrollton, the revitalized CBD with some old buildings still remaining next to the Superdome, skyscrapers, and high-rise hotels, Uptown, Downtown, Back-o'-Town, Riverside, Lakeside, New Orleans East and New Orleans West, growing; New Orleans North embraced by the lake, New Orleans South hugged by the river.

Built on a site where no city should ever have been built, it went about its business of commerce, defying floods, hurricanes and epidemics, and it survived. New Orleans has drained half of its living area to make it habitable, has preserved its treasured heritage, and has achieved the rank of biggest port in the United States. Considering the problems it has solved in the past, those of today do not seem insurmountable.

Population is as diverse as ever, as the city continues to draw people of all cultures and races. The city has all the problems of an urban center but all the charms of an aging metropolis, spiced with a European and Mediterranean flavor.

Volumes could be written about New Orleans as the Queen of the Mississippi and at the rate she's progressing, no one will ever write them all. She's romantic, aristocratic, decorative, scandalous, and old-fashioned, all at the same time—all the best reasons we know for calling a city She. One fact is indisputable. Once you lose your heart to her, it's lost forever.

REFERENCE SECTIONS

Selected Bibliography

Basso, Etolia S., *The World from Jackson Square,* Farrar, Straus & Co., (New York, 1948).

Capers, Gerald Mortimer, *Occupied City, New Orleans under the Federals, 1862–65,* University of Kentucky, (Lexington, 1965).

Chase, Deutsch, Dufour, Huber, *Citoyens, Progrès, et Politique de la Nouvelle Orléans,* E. S. Upton Printing Co., (New Orleans, 1964).

Cooke, John, *Perspectives on Ethnicity in New Orleans,* (New Orleans, 1979).

Davis, Edwin Adams, *Louisiana, A Narrative History,* Claitor's Publishing Division, (Baton Rouge, 1971).

DuPratz, LePage, *The Early French Histories of Louisiana* (re-print) (Baton Rouge, Louisiana 1975).

Freiberg, Edna, *Bayou St. John in Colonial Louisiana (1699–1803),* Harvey Press, (New Orleans, 1980).

Huber, Leonard V. and Wilson, Samuel, Jr. *Baroness Pontalba's Buildings,* Laborde Printing Co., (New Orleans, 1964).

Kmen, Henry A., *Music in New Orleans, the Formative Years— 1791– 1841,* LSU Press, (Baton Rouge, 1966).

LeGardeur, Rene J., Jr., *The First New Orleans Theatre—1792–1803,* Leeward Books, (New Orleans, 1963).

Lewis, Pierce F., *New Orleans: The Making of an Urban Landscape,* Bellinger Publishing Co., (Cambridge, 1976).

New Orleans City Guide, compiled and edited by Federal Writers' Project of Louisiana of the WPA, Riverside Press, (Cambridge, 1938).

Rightor, Henry, *Standard History of New Orleans,* (New Orleans, 1900).

Samuel, Martha Ann Brett, and Samuel, Ray, *The Great Days of the Garden District,* Louise McGehee School, (New Orleans, 1974).

Saxon, Lyle; Tallant, Edward; and Dwyer, Robert, *Gumbo Ya-Ya,* Bonanza Books, (New York, 1945).

Tallant, Robert, *Voodoo in New Orleans,* Collier Books, (New York, 1946).

Texada, David Ker, *Alejandro O'Reilly and the New Orleans Rebels,* University of Southern Louisiana, (Lafayette, 1970).

Glossary

Allée: A double row of trees leading from the road or river to a plantation home. (Fr. *allée,* an alley)

Armoire: A cabinet closing with one or two doors, having rows of shelves, and used for keeping clothes.

Arpent: A former land measure. A linear arpent = 191.835 feet; a square arpent is approximately 85% of an English acre.

Banquette: A sidewalk so called because the early wooden sidewalks were elevated, or banked up, above the muddy streets. (Fr. *banquette,* a low bench)

Batture: The land built up by the silting action of a river. (Fr. *battre,* to beat)

Bayou: A distributary coming out of a river or lake, not contributing to it. (Indian, *bayuk,* meaning creek or river)

Blanchisseuse: A washerwoman. (Fr. *blanchir,* to whiten, to clean)

Bouillabaisse: A stew of red snapper and redfish, with various kinds of vegetables, seasonings and spices. (Prov. *bouis-baisso,* boiled down)

Boussilage: Mud and moss mixture.

Briqueté entre poteaux: A method of construction in vogue in the 18th century in which bricks were filled in between the spaces of a framework of cypress timbers. (Fr. bricked between posts)

Café au lait: Black coffee with milk, slang expression indicating presence of Negro heritage.

Café noir: Black coffee.

Cajan: French immigrant from Acadie, (now Nova Scotia) or descendant of one who came to live in Bayou country of Louisiana. (Corruption of Acadian)

Charivari: A serenade of 'rough music' with kettles, pans and the like, originally given in derision of unpopular marriage. Often spelled *chivari.* (Med. Lat. *carivarium*)

Chef Menteur: Big Liar, Chief (among) liars. River so called because currents deceptive, ran both ways; Gov. Kerlerec so called by Indians for obvious reasons.

Code Noir: Code of behavior governing conduct of slaves and masters.

Congo: A very black Negro; a Negro from the Congo nation.

Courtbouillon: Redfish cooked with highly seasoned gravy.

Crawfish bisque: A rich soup made with crawfish, the heads being stuffed and served in the soup. (Fr. *bisque,* thick soup, cullis)

Creole: In New Orleans, referred to native born of French or Spanish parents. (Sp. *criollo,* native born) Also used in referring to native grown, e.g. Creole tomatoes.

Fais-dodo: A country dance; from the *fais dodo,* 'go to sleep,' of children's speech. (Fr. *dormir,* to sleep)

Faubourg: Plantation, suburb.

F.W.C. or *F.M.C.:* These initials found in the old documents stand for 'Free Woman of Color' or 'Free Man of Color.'

Gallery: A porch, balcony. (Fr. *galerie;* Lat. *galeria,* gallery)

Garçonniere: Bachelor quarters, usually separate from the principal part of the house. (Fr. *garçon,* boy, a bachelor)

Gris-gris: Amulet, talisman, or charm, worn for luck or used to conjure evil on enemies by Voodoo devotees. Presumably from African origin.

Gumbo: A soup thickened with the mucilaginous pods of the okra plant, and containing shrimp, crabs, and often chicken, oysters, etc. (Negro-French *gumbo,* from Angolan *kingombo*)

Gumbo-filé: A condiment made by powdering leaves of the Red Bay, powdered sassafras root often being added. Used in place of okra for thickening gumbo.

Gumbo-des-herbes: Gumbo made of herbs (greens: spinach, mustard green, etc.) instead of okra. (Fr. *herbe,* herb)

Jalousie: In Louisiana, the common two-battened outdoor blind. (Fr. *jalousie,* Venetian blind)

Jambalaya: A Spanish-Creole dish made with rice and some other important ingredient, such as shrimp, crabs, cowpeas, oysters, sausage, etc. (No origin can be found)

Lagniappe: A trifling gift presented to a customer by a merchant. (Fr. *la nappe,* the cloth, referring to grains of rice left on the cloth; Sp. *la napa,* a small gift)

Levee: An embankment on the Mississippi or smaller streams to prevent floods. (Fr. *lever,* to raise)

Make ménage: To clean house. A typical local translation of French *faire le ménage,* to clean house.

Mamaloi: The Voodoo priestess. (Probably from Fr. *maman,* mama, and *roi,* king)

Mardi Gras: Shrove Tuesday, the last day of Carnival. (Fr. lit., Fat Tuesday)

Marraine: A godmother. (Fr. *marraine,* godmother)

Mulatto: The offspring of a Negro and a Caucasian. (Sp. *mulato,* a young mule; hence, one of mixed race)

Nainaine: Creole diminutive of *marraine,* godmother.

Octoroon: The child of a quadroon and a Caucasian. (Lat *octo,* eight; suffix *oon* as in quadroon)

Papillotes: Curl papers. (Fr. *papillote,* curl paper, from *papillon,* butterfly)

Papillotes: Buttered or oiled paper in which fish, especially pompano, is broiled to retain the flavor.

Parish: In Louisiana, the equivalent of *county.* Parishes here were originally ecclesiastical, not civil divisions.

Parrain: Godfather. (Fr. *parrain*)

Perique: A unique kind of tobacco grown only in the Parish of St. James, said to have been the nickname of Pierre Chenet, an Acadian who first produced the variety of tobacco. Local term.

Picayune: Formerly the Spanish half-real, worth about 6¼ cents; now out of use, except to refer to something small and unimportant.

Pirogue: A small canoe-like boat, made by hollowing a log, used on the bayous. (Sp. *piragua*)

Pontchatoula: Hanging hair or falling hair (moss); place of moss on trees. (Indian)

Porte-cochère: The gateway allowing vehicles to drive into a courtyard. (Fr. *porte,* gate: *coche,* coach)

Praline: A bonbon made of pecans browned in sugar. (From Marechal du Plessis Praslin, whose cook is said to have invented it)

Quadroon: The child of a Mulatto and a Caucasian. A person having one-fourth Negro blood. (Sp. *cuarteron,* a quadroon)

Quartee: Half of a five-cent piece. Local term.

Soirée: An evening party. (Fr. *soir,* evening)

Sugar-house: A sugar mill or factory. Local term.

Tignon: Bandana-like headdress required for free women of color after 1786. (Fr. *tignon,* or *chignon,* the nape of the neck)

Vamoose: Get out! (Sp. *Vamos! Let's go!*)

Vieux Carre: The original walled city of New Orleans. Bounded by Canal St., North Rampart, Esplanade, and the river (Fr. lit., Old Square)

Voodoo: An African cult of witchcraft imported into America by Negro slaves. (Dahomey, *vôdu,* a diety)

Chronology

1541   Hernando DeSoto discovers the Mississippi River.

1543   *July.* Luis Moscoso and the survivors of DeSoto's expedition, descending the river on their way to Mexico, are the first white men to view the site of the future city of New Orleans.

1682   *April 9.* LaSalle claims all land drained by the Mississippi River for France, erects a cross near mouth of the Mississippi, and names the territory in honor of Louis XIV, "Louisiana."

1699   *March 2.* Iberville and his expedition stop at the present site of New Orleans, erects a cross. Same year, Bayou Mardi Gras named by Iberville; Ocean Springs settled.

1718   *Spring.* Bienville, with the assistance of Pauger and de la Tour, lays out the streets and founds *La Nouvelle Orleans* as trading colony for Company of the West.

1723   Under Governor Bienville, New Orleans becomes capital of Louisiana.

1724   *March.* Bienville promulgates the Code Noir (Black Code) regulating slavery and religious worship.

1727   *August 6.* The Ursulines arrive and establish a convent school for girls.

1728   *December.* The first company of *Filles a la Cassette* (Casket Girls) arrive in Mobile. No historical evidence that they came to New Orleans.

1729   *December.* Refugees arrive with news of Indian massacre at Fort Rosalie (Natchez), and Governor Perier begins construction of first defense works (ditch and stockade) against a possible Indian attack.

1731   Louisiana becomes a Royal colony of France again.

1743   Under Governor Vaudrieul, New Orleans becomes a gay social center.

1762   *November 3.* New Orleans transferred to Spain by Treaty of Fontainbleau.

214

| 1763 | *February 6.* Louisiana (except for New Orleans) ceded to Spain by the Treaty of Paris.
| | *July 9.* The Jesuits are expelled from Louisiana by the French authorities and their property confiscated.
| 1768 | *October.* Opposition to Spanish rule breaks into open rebellion, and Governor Ulloa departs for Havana.
| 1769 | *August 18.* General Alejandro O'Reilly arrives with an armed force and takes possession of the city. Five leaders of rebellion against Ulloa executed, seven others imprisoned. Superior Council abolished; Cabildo established.
| 1777 | Under Governor Galvez, Americans allowed to establish bases in New Orleans and send aid to revolutionary forces. After war declared between Spain and England, Galvez, in a series of campaigns, drives the English out of the country (1779–82).
| 1788 | *March 21.* Fire destroys over 800 houses and necessitates rebuilding a great part of the city.
| | *December 5.* Padre Antonio de Sedella, later known as Père Antoine, appointed Commissary of the Inquisition, sent back to Spain by Gov. Miro.
| 1792 | The Henry brothers from Paris stage the first professional theatrical performances held in New Orleans.
| 1794 | First regular newspaper, *Le Moniteur de la Louisiane,* begins publication.
| | *December 8.* A second fire destroys a great part of the city. Rebuilding begins under Spanish architects.
| 1795 | Carondelet Canal, connecting the city with Bayou St. John, is opened. Étienne Boré succeeds in refining sugar in commercial quantities. Almonester rebuilds Cathedral, Cabildo, first floor of Presbytère.
| 1803 | *November 30.* France takes formal possession of the colony from Spain in the *Place d'Armes.* French Commissioner de Laussat arrives.
| | *December 20.* William C. C. Claiborne and General James Wilkinson take possession of the city in the name of the United States.
| 1805 | *February 22.* The city of New Orleans is incorporated and the first municipal officials arrive shortly afterward.
| 1812 | *January 10.* The *New Orleans,* the first steamboat to descend the Mississippi, arrives from Pittsburg.
| | *April 30.* Louisiana is admitted to the Union and New Orleans becomes the capital of the State.
| 1815 | *January 8.* The American forces, under General Andrew Jackson, defeat the British in the final decisive action of the Battle of New Orleans.

1816	Crevasse at McCarty's plantation, part of the city flooded.
1823	*May 8.* James H. Caldwell opens the first American Theater on Camp Street, introducing the use of illuminating gas.
1825	*April 10.* Lafayette arrives in New Orleans for a five-day visit.
1827–1860	All Catholic funerals held in Mortuary Chapel (Our Lady of Guadalupe Church).
1830	Esplanade Avenue called Promenade Publique.
1831	*April.* The Pontchartrain Railroad, first railroad west of the Alleghenies, offers freight and passenger service to Milneburg.
1833	J. H. Caldwell granted exclusive privilege for street illumination by gas. Incorporation of the City of Lafayette.
1834	The first house in Carrollton is built.
1834	The Medical College of Louisiana which eventually develops into the University of Louisiana (1847) and Tulane University (1884), is established. U.S. Mint built at Esplanade and the river (operated as a mint 1838–1862 and 1879–1910).
1836	*March 8.* New charter divides city into three municipalities, each with its own board of aldermen.
1837	*January 25. The Picayune,* now the *Times-Picayune States-Item,* begins publication. *Shrove Tuesday.* First Mardi Gras parade held.
1838	The first house in the Garden District and the first on Esplanade Avenue are built.
1838	New Basin Canal opened for traffic.
1850	*October 26.* New Orleans public school system greatly enlarged from funds left to the city by John McDonogh.
1853	Ten thousand inhabitants perish in the most severe yellow fever epidemic in the history of New Orleans. *May 10.* The City Hall (now Gallier Hall) designed and built by James Gallier, Sr. is dedicated.
1859	*December 1.* The French Opera House opens its doors with the productions of *Guillaume Tell.*
1861	*January 26.* Louisiana adopts the Ordinance of Secession.
1862	*April 30.* The city surrenders to David E. Farragut and his Federal forces. *May 1.* General Benjamin Butler assumes command of the city.
1864	*May 11.* Constitution of Louisiana amended, abolishing slavery.
1866	*July 30.* Riot occurs in Mechanics Institute in which large numbers of Negroes and whites are killed and wounded.
1869	Dillard University opens its door.
1872	Rex parades for Grand Duke Alexis of Russia.
1874	The St. Louis Hotel is purchased by the State of Louisiana to serve as the state capital until the capital is moved from New Orleans to Baton Rouge in 1882.

1874	*September 14*. The White League forces defeat the Metropolitan Police in a pitched battle at the head of Canal Street.
1880	*August*. Captain James B. Eads completes the jetties at South Pass, deepening the channels and saving the port.
1884	Tulane University, endowed by Paul Tulane, takes over the buildings and equipment of the University of Louisiana. *December 16*. The Cotton Exposition opens in Audubon Park.
1886	*October 11*. Newcomb College founded.
1890	Board of Commissioners of Orleans Lakefront (the Levee Board) organized and put in charge of 129 miles of levee, 27 miles on the river, and 94 miles of inner-city levees.
1891	*March 14*. Eleven Italian prisoners, alleged assassins of Police Chief Hennessy, killed in parish prison by outraged mob of citizens, two dragged outside and hung.
1892	*September 7*. James J. Corbett defeats John L. Sullivan in a 21-round knockout victory in New Orleans.
1894	Leprosarium at Carville, Louisiana established.
1896	Board of Commissioners of the Port of New Orleans (the Dock Board) created, to have authority over all water frontage in Orleans Parish and considerable portions of river and canal frontage in adjacent parishes.
1898–1917	Storyville thrives (See text).
1905	Last of Yellow Fever epidemics occurs.
1910	Last coins minted in New Orleans.
1911	Loyola, founded by the Jesuits, becomes a college.
1912	*July 10*. Loyola becomes a university.
1912	*August 12*. The Commission form of city government adopted.
1915	*September 29*. Severe tropical hurricane inflicts serious property damage throughout the city. Xavier College established at Washington and Pine Streets.
1921	Vieux Carre Commission established.
1921	The federal government takes over the Leprosarium at Carville, and it becomes the only public health leprosarium on the North American continent.
1923	Industrial Canal connected to river by locks; Notre Dame Seminary built.
1925	Xavier becomes full-fledged university. Orleans Club founded.
1927	Last major flood.
1928	U.S. Engineers take over responsibility for flood control.
1930	Municipal Auditorium built to the rear of Old Congo Square facing Rampart Street.
1934	Industrial Canal becomes link in newly fashioned Intracoastal Waterway, which now leads from Rio Grande River in Texas to the Florida coast.

1935	*September 8*. Huey P. Long assassinated in State Capital Building in Baton Rouge by Dr. Carl A. Weiss, who was then shot by Long's bodyguards.
	December 13. Bonnet Carre Spillway is dedicated.
	December 16. Huey P. Long Bridge across the Mississippi completed and dedicated.
1936	Vieux Carre Commission authorized by State legislature to regulate architecture in V.C. through building permits.
1945	International House opens.
1947	*May 6*. International Free Trade Zone established.
	September 16–19. Hurricane kills hundreds in Louisiana, Mississippi, and Florida.
1957	First causeway, 24 miles long, built across Lake Pontchartrain.
1958	*April 15*. First span of the Greater New Orleans Mississippi River Bridge completed.
1958	*September*. UNO, originally LSUNO, opens on Lakefront as the State's first racially-integrated public college.
1963	Mississippi River Gulf Outlet officially opened, cutting 40 miles off the distance to the Gulf.
1965	*September 9*. Hurricane Betsy hits New Orleans.
1967	Second Lake Pontchartrain Causeway built, creating twin spans.
1969	*August 17*. Hurricane Camille hits New Orleans. Only Category Five hurricane to hit near New Orleans.
1973	Disastrous fire at Howard Johnson's Motor Hotel.
1973	Theater of the Performing Arts completed in what would later be Armstrong Park.
1975	Superdome opens in August with a football game. Cost: $161 million.
1980	Armstrong Park opens. Cost: $30 million. Space: ten acres at the site of the old Congo Square.
1982	*July 9*. Pan-Am Jet 759 crashes moments after take-off from New Orleans International Airport, killing 153. Second worst airplane disaster in American history.
1984	*May 4–November 11*. Louisiana World Exposition in New Orleans.
1984–94	MART—Mississippi Aerial River Transit (Gondola from World's Fair) is part of New Orleans skyline.
1987	*September 12*. Pope John Paul II visits New Orleans, saying Mass on the UNO Arena grounds at the lakefront.
1987	Fall. The New Orleans Saints are in the NFL playoffs for the first time in their 20-year existence. (Tom Benson, owner; Jim Mora, coach).
1988	*May 11*. Seven-alarm fire on third floor of the Cabildo.
1988	*August*. Republican National Convention held in New Orleans.

1988	*September 30*. Second span of GNOMR Bridge opens. Both spans called the Crescent City Connection.
1990	Aquarium of the Americas opens.
1994	*December 17*. Fair Grounds Race Track burns down.

Noted Personalities

ALMONESTER Y ROXAS, DON ANDRÉS (1725–98). Spanish grandee who provided funds for rebuilding St. Louis Cathedral after the great fire of 1788 and who built the Cabildo; father of Baroness Pontalba.

ARMSTRONG, LOUIS (SATCHMO) (1900–1971). One of the most famous personalities in the history of jazz. Over 1,500 recordings, several movies, TV performances; "good-will" ambassador for the United States.

AUDUBON, JEAN JACQUES FOUGÈRE (178?–1851). Ornithologist and artist whose *Birds of America* and *Ornithological Biography* are still highly regarded.

BARELLI, I.T. Planner of the tomb of the Italian Mutual Benefit Society in St. Louis Cemetery #1.He and the builder were the first two to be buried therein. It was afterwards known as the "Hex Tomb."

BEAUREGARD, PIERRE GUSTAVE TOUTANT (1818–93). Creole Confederate general at whose command the first shot of the Civil War was fired (at Fort Sumter, April 12, 1862).

BENJAMIN, JUDAH P. (1811–80). Confederate Secretary of War and State, who, after having been exiled, lived in England and gained international fame as a lawyer.

BIENVILLE, JEAN BAPTISTE LE MOYNE, *Sieur de* (1680–1768). French-Canadian explorer; three times governor of Louisiana under French domination; founder of New Orleans, promulgator in Louisiana of celebrated *Black Code*.

BOGGS, CORINNE C. (LINDY). Congresswoman from Louisiana since 1973, after the disappearance of her husband, Congressman Hale Boggs in a plane over Alaska in Oct. 1973. A descendant of Louisiana's first governor, Wm. C. C. Claiborne, she is one of New Orleans' outstanding citizens and leaders.

BORÉ, JEAN ÉTIENNE DE (1741–1820). Gave impetus to sugar industry by granulating sugar on a commercial scale; first mayor of New Orleans.

CABLE, GEORGE WASHINGTON (1844–1925). Gained international recognition as a novelist and short-story writer through works based on Louisiana; his uncomplimentary characterizations aroused the bitter animosity of Louisiana Creoles.

CALVÉ, JULIE (1846–1898). Native of France, star of New Orleans French Opera production of *Les Huguenots,* married Charles Boudousquié, shown in 1882 city Directory as music teacher at Holy Angels.

CAPOTE, TRUMAN (1924–1986). Best-selling author. Wrote *In Cold Blood*. Recipient of many literary awards.

CARROLLTON, WILLIAM. General in the War of 1812, had camp on site of the McCarty Plantation.

CHASE, JOHN CHURCHILL (1905–1986). Noted cartoonist, historian, author. Designer of many logos. Noted for his book, *Frenchmen, Desire, Good Children*.

CLAIBORNE, WILLIAM CHARLES COLE (1775–1817). Led Louisiana through a hectic decade as its first American Governor.

CLARK, DANIEL (1766–1813). Irish-American merchant and landowner who assisted Thomas Jefferson in negotiations leading to the Louisiana Purchase and who later wounded Governor Claiborne in a duel brought about by charges of his implication in the Aaron Burr conspiracy.

DANNA, JOSEPH ANTHONY, DR. (1877–1954). Graduated Tulane Medical School 1901, first intern and resident at Hotel Dieu 1908; senior surgeon at Charity and Hotel Dieu; left money to Loyola for Danna Student Center, dedicated 1964; knighted by the king of Italy; appointed by the Pope to the Knights of St. Gregory.

DELGADO, ISAAC (1839–1912). Philanthropist to whom New Orleans owes its art museum and boys' trades school.

DIBERT, JOHN, MRS. Philanthropist who made gifts to Dibert Tuberculosis Hospital, residence of the Sisters of Charity, and John Dibert School, among others, in memory of her husband.

DIX, DOROTHY (MRS. ELIZABETH MERIWETHER GILMER) (1861–1951). Supporter of women's suffrage and the working woman, crime reporter, columnist specializing in "Advice to the lovelorn."

DIXON, DAVE. Conceived and originated plan to build the Superdome and organized the U.S. Football League.

DEUTSCH, HERMANN B. (1889–1970). One of the deans of New Orleans journalism, served on newspapers operated by the Times Picayune Publishing Company for 47 years.

DUFOUR, CHARLES L. "PIE" (1903–   ). Newspaperman for 40 years, known for his column "A La Mode" in States Item, one of unofficial historians of New Orleans. Author: Ten Flags in the Wind.

DUPRATZ, ANTOINE SIMON LEPAGE (1695–1775). Born in Holland, came to Dauphin Island in 1718. His 3-volume work, *Histoire de la Louisiane*, tells of plantation life on Bayou St. John and in Natchez.

FITZMORRIS, JAMES EDWARD (1921–   ). Lt. Gov. of La. 1972–1980; Assistant for Economic Development to Governor Treen.

FORTIER, ALCEE (1856–1914). Teacher-historian noted for his Creole studies and historical works.

FRANCIS, NORMAN C. (1931–   ). First layman and Black to be president of Xavier University, 1968 to the present.

GAINES, MYRA CLARK (1805–85). Principal and ultimate victor of a sensational 50-year lawsuit against the city of New Orleans for the estate of her wealthy father, Daniel Clark.

GALLIER, JAMES, SR. (1798–1866). Architect who designed the City Hall and many Garden District homes in New Orleans; exponent of Greek Revival style of architecture.

GALLIER, JAMES, JR. (1827–68). Continued his father's architectural work in New Orleans; designer of French Opera House.

GALVEZ, BERNARDO DE (1746–86). As Spanish Governor of Louisiana he distinguished himself by wresting East and West Florida from the British (1780–83); later became Viceroy of Mexico.

GANDOLFO, HENRI A. (1897–1990). Author of *Metairie Cemetery: An Historical Memoir,* connected with Metairie Cemetery for 65 years, a student of memorial architecture, a repository of history and lore on the statesmen and rogues buried there.

GAYARRÉ, CHARLES ÉTIENNE (1805–95). Dabbled in politics while writing several histories of Louisiana and two novels; led Creoles in bitter controversy with George Washington Cable.

GOTTSCHALK, LOUIS MOREAU (1829–69). Considered leading pianist-composer of his day; gave concerts throughout the world; *La Morte* and *Tremole Étude* are his best known works.

GRAU, SHIRLEY ANN (MRS. JAMES KERN FEIBLEMAN) (1929–   ). Author, Pulitzer Prize winner for *The Keepers of the House* in 1965.

HANNAN, PHILIP MATTHEW, ARCHBISHOP (1913–   ). Born in Washington, D.C. Held administrative offices in many national organizations, Chaplain USAAF 1942–46 (known as the "Parachute Priest"); presided at the funeral of President John F. Kennedy at St. Matthew Cathedral, Washington. Archbishop of New Orleans—1965–1989.

HELLMAN, LILLIAN (1907–1984). Scenario writer, editor, award-winning and best selling author. Outstanding works, *The Little Foxes, Watch on the Rhine*. Political activist.

HERMAN, PETE (PETER GULOTTA) (1896–1973). Held Bantam-weight Title 1917–1920; regained it 1921—retired 1922. Career wins-71; Elected to Boxing Hall of Fame 1960.

HUBER, LEONARD V. (1903–1984). Civic worker, collector, travel-ler, lecturer and writer. Works include *New Orleans: A Pictorial History* and *Louisiana: A Pictorial History.*

JACKSON, ANDREW (1767–1845). "Savior of New Orleans" during Battle of New Orleans in the War of 1812. Popular Louisiana hero.

JACKSON, MAHALIA (1911–1972). Queen of Gospel singers, Civil Rights spokeswoman, recording star.

KANE, HARNETT T. (1910–1984). Reporter, best selling author, lec-turer, historian. Author of *Louisiana Hayride.*

KENNER, DUNCAN FARRAR (1813–87). Active in behalf of Con-federate cause and afterward instrumental in ridding the state of "car-petbaggers" and "scalawags."

KEYES, FRANCES PARKERSON (MRS. HENRY WILDER KEYES) (1885–1970). Author of numerous novels and short stories, many laid in New Orleans, world traveled owner and restorer of the Beauregard House, 1113 Chartres Street (birthplace of Paul Morphy, and home of P.G.T. Beauregard after the Civil War).

KING, GRACE ELIZABETH (1851–1932). Student of Creole life and manners whose *New Orleans, the Place and the People* and *Creole Families of New Orleans* have enriched Louisiana literature.

LAFITTE, JEAN (1780–1825). Famous smuggler and pirate who was pardoned because of his participation in behalf of the United States at the Battle of New Orleans.

LAFON, THOMY (1810–93). Black philanthropist whose charities in New Orleans won him the distinction of having a public school named after him.

LAVEAU, MARIE (1783–1881). Mulattress "Voodoo Queen," leader of a strange sect and dealer in charms, remedies and "advice."

LIVINGSTONE, EDWARD (1764–1836). Represented both New York and Louisiana in Congress; Secretary of State under Andrew Jackson and later Minister to France.

LONG, HUEY PIERCE (1893–1935). Virtual political dictator of Louisiana and leader of "Share the Wealth" program; assumed a prominent place in national affairs as U.S. Senator and Presidential aspirant; assassinated at height of career.

LONGSTREET, JAMES (1821–1904). Brigadier general in Confederate Army who after the war became a Republican; a resident of New Orleans, he became unpopular with the people of his State for his part in the politics of the Reconstruction period; appointed Minister to Turkey by President Grant.

MAESTRI, ROBERT (1889–1974). Mayor of New Orleans 1936–46, reorganized fiscal policies of the city and improved municipal facilities.

MATAS, RUDOLPH, DR. (1860–1957). Pioneer in the field of vascular surgery, recipient of medical decorations from many European and Latin American countries, a giant of medicine.

MAYO, SARA T., DR. (1869–1930). Founded a hospital for women which bears her name.

McDONOGH, JOHN (1779–1850). Wealthy merchant whose bequest formed the foundation for the New Orleans public school system.

McMAIN, ELEANOR E. Worked for Child Labor legislation, leader in the establishment of the School of Social Work; high school named in her honor.

MORIAL, ERNEST "DUTCH" (1929–1989). First black mayor of New Orleans, elected in 1977. In earlier political life, first black assistant in U.S. Attorney's office, first black member of the legislature since Reconstruction, first black juvenile court judge, and first black Circuit Court of Appeals judge. Also, first mayor to live on historic Bayou St. John during his administration.

MORPHY, PAUL CHARLES (1837–84). Considered one of the greatest chess players of all times. Born in the house his grandfather built, later called the Beauregard House, because of the general's term of residence there.

MORRISON, deLESSEPS S. (1912–1964). Mayor of New Orleans 1946–1961, when he resigned to take the post of ambassador to the Organization of American States, to which he was appointed by President Kennedy. Morrison and his son were killed in a plane crash en route to Mexico, May, 1964.

MORTON, FERDINAND LA MENTHE "JELLY ROLL" (1885–1941). Reputed "inventor of jazz," one of the jazz immortals, played piano in Storyville for $1 a night plus tips. His life is documented more than that of any other musician in jazz history. "Jelly Roll's Red Hot Peppers" always considered the peak of jazz band excellence.

NEWCOMB, JOSEPHINE LOUISE LE MONNIER (1816–1901). Founded Sophie Newcomb College as a memorial to her daughter. For this purpose, she provided contributions totalling $2,800,000.

OCHSNER, ALTON (1896–1981). Professor at Tulane 1927–1961. Served on staff of several hospitals. Founded Ochsner Foundation Hospital. Spearheaded drive against smoking as cause of lung cancer. Author.

PAUGER, ADRIEN DE (1670?–1726). Aided in plotting the city of New Orleans (laying out streets). Suggested construction of jetties to deepen channel at mouth of Mississippi River.

PINCHBACK, PINKEY BENTON STUART (1837–1921). Mulatto politician who became Lieutenant Governor of Louisiana during Reconstruction, and acting Governor (1872–1873). Only Negro ever to serve as Governor of Louisiana.

PLIMSOLL, SAMUEL. In 1867, became the leading advocate for safe loading conditions for ship operations. The Plimsoll Mark, which he originated, is a series of lines to be placed on both sides of ships, signifying the Load Line allowed for Tropical Water, Fresh Water, in Tropical Zones, and in Summer, Winter, and Winter North Atlantic.

POLLOCK, OLIVER (1737–1823). Irish-born New Orleans merchant who rendered material assistance to the American cause during the Revolution. Later, became a U.S. Commercial agent with diplomatic standing.

POYDRAS, JULIAN (1740–1824). Trader-philanthropist-poet; charitable works included establishment of dowry fund for impoverished Pointe Coupée and West Baton Rouge Parish maidens.

PRIMA, LOUIS (1911–1978). Nationally known band leader, singer, trumpet player, composer, recording, television and movie performer.

RIPLEY, ELIZA MOORE (1832–1912). Wrote entertainingly of life in New Orleans in the 1840s and '50s.

RIVERS, PEARL (MRS. GEORGE NICHOLSON) (1849–1896). First woman in New Orleans to earn her living on a newspaper, *The Picayune,* first woman publisher of an important newspaper in the United States, founded the organization that grew into the S.P.C.A.

RUMMEL, JOSEPH FRANCIS, ARCHBISHOP (1876–1964). Born in Baden, Germany, he first served as Papal Chamberlain; in 1935, appointed Archbishop of New Orleans. Buried in a crypt of St. Louis Cathedral.

SAXON, LYLE (1891–1946). About 1926, started writing short stories, then books, about New Orleans beginning with *Father Mississippi.*

Born in Baton Rouge, Saxon was a bon vivant, typical plantation gentleman, conversationalist, an artist with a jigger of vermouth, a writer without an enemy.

SEDELLA, ANTONIO DE (1748–1829). Expelled from colony of Louisiana for attempting to set up office of the Spanish Inquisition here, he later returned as a loving pastor to endear himself as "Père Antoine."

SCHULTE, FRANCIS BIBLE, ARCHBISHOP (1927–   ). Born in Philadelphia, appointed member of President Bush's Education Policy Advisory Committee 1989; appointed member of Vatican Congregation for Catholic Education 1989; appointed 12th archbishop of New Orleans 1988.

SLIDELL, JOHN (1793–1871). Prominent in State and National affairs in 1850s. Minister to France under the Confederacy.

SOULÉ, GEORGE (1834–1926). Mathematician and educator; established first commercial college in New Orleans.

STERN, EDGAR B. (1886–1959). Member of the Board of Charity Hospital, the State Welfare Board, and the Louisiana Development Commission. From 1944 until his death, he was on the Board of Administrators of Tulane University and a founder of the Bureau of Governmental Research.

STERN, EDITH ROSENWALD (MRS. EDGAR B.) (1895–1980). In 1977, *Centennial of States-Item* newspaper, she and Mr. Stern named outstanding philanthropists in New Orleans for first century of paper's existence. Since her death in 1980, Longue Vue, her home, has been operated as a museum of the Decorative Arts & Horticulture.

TALLANT, ROBERT (1909–1957). Author who wrote on subjects concerning New Orleans and Louisiana, including Gumbo Ya-Ya; won the Literary Award of the Louisiana Library Association in 1952 for *The Pirate Lafitte and the Battle of New Orleans*. Revised New Orleans City Guide.

TAYLOR, ZACHARY (1784–1850). Migrated from Kentucky to Louisiana, achieved fame in the Mexican War, and became 12th President of the United States.

TOOLE, JOHN KENNEDY (1937–1969). Pulitzer-prize winning novelist, for his *Confederacy of Dunces,* published 10 years after his suicide, believed to have been brought on by his failure to obtain literary recognition.

TOURO, JUDAH (1775–1854). Gave liberally to numerous charities during his lifetime (Touro-Shakspeare Home, Touro Infirmary, and Touro Synagogue, New Orleans).

226

TREIGLE, NORMAN (1927–1975). Leading male star of the New York City Opera, with over 50 roles to his credit; considered to be one of the great actors in opera. Frequent co-star with Beverly Sills.

TULANE, PAUL (1801–1887). Donated over a million dollars to the University of Louisiana (now Tulane University, New Orleans).

VACCARO, JOSEPH and his brothers established the Standard Fruit Company, whose ships sail in the Gulf and Caribbean between New Orleans and Central America.

VAUDRIEUL, PIERRE FRANCOIS DE RIGAUD, *Marquis de* (1698–1765). Made New Orleans a center of culture and gaiety while French Governor of Louisiana. Referred to as the Grand Marquis.

WARMOTH, HENRY CLAY (1842–1931). Dominated "Carpetbag" regime as Reconstruction Governor; author of *War, Politics, and Reconstruction*.

WHITE, EDWARD DOUGLAS (1845–1921). Entered Confederate Army at 18; became associate justice of the Louisiana Supreme Court at 33; later, U.S. senator, and finally, Chief Justice of the Supreme Court.

WILSON, SAMUEL, JR. (1911–1993). Architectural historian, co-author of *New Orleans Architecture, Volumes I and IV; Louisiana Purchase; The St. Louis Cemeteries of New Orleans;* and other publications.

WOOD, ALBERT BALDWIN. Electrical engineer, in 1914 invented 12-foot screw pumps capable of draining ten million cubic feet of water out of below-sea-level New Orleans every year. Underground pipes and pumping stations drained the swamps of New Orleans, making it habitable.

WRIGHT, SOPHIE BELL (1866–1912). Teacher-humanitarian responsible for night schools and many social-service agencies in New Orleans. First woman to win Picayune Loving Cup.

YOU, DOMINIQUE (1775–1830). As a member of Lafitte's "hellish banditti," he distinguished himself in the Battle of New Orleans, and settled down to become a law-abiding citizen.

Governors of Louisiana

The Governors of Louisiana as a French Colony

1699	Pierre LeMoyne, Sieur d'Iberville (founder)
1699–1701	Ensign Sauvole
1701–1713	Jean Baptiste LeMoyne, Sieur de Bienville
1713–1716	Antoine de la Mothe Cadillac
1716–1717	Jean Baptiste LeMoyne, Sieur de Bienville (acting)
1717–1718	Jean Michiele, Sieur de Lepinay
1718–1725	Jean Baptiste LeMoyne, Sieur de Bienville
1725–1726	Pierre Dugue, Sieur de Boisbriant (acting)
1726–1733	Etienne de Périer
1733–1743	Jean Baptiste LeMoyne, Sieur de Bienville
1743–1753	Pierre Rigaud, Marquis de Vaudreuil
1753–1763	Louis Billouart de Kerlérec
1763–1765	Jean Jacques-Blaise D'Abbadie
1765–1769	Charles-Phillipe Aubry (acting)

The Governors of Louisiana as a Spanish Colony

1766–1768	Antonio de Ulloa (did not assume full power)
1769	Alexander O'Reilly (military commander sent by Spain)
1769–1777	Luis de Unzaga
1777–1785	Bernardo de Galvez
1785–1791	Estevan Miro
1792–1797	Francisco Luis Hector, Baron de Carondelet
1797–1799	Manuel Luis Gayoso de Lemos
1799	Francisco Bouligny (acting)
1799–1801	Sebastian de la Puesta y O'Farrill Marques de Casa Calvo
1801–1803	Juan Manuel de Salcedo

The Governor of Louisiana before the Louisiana Purchase

1803 — Pierre Clement de Laussat (November 30– December 20)

The Governor of Louisiana as a Territory

1803–1812 — William Charles Cole Claiborne

Governors of Louisiana as a State

1812–1816	William Charles Cole Claiborne
1816–1820	Jacques Philippe Villere
1820–1824	Thomas Bolling Robertson (resigned)
1824	Henry Schuyler Thibodeaux (as president of the Senate succeeded Robertson)
1824–1828	Henry S. Johnson
1828–1829	Pierre Derbigny (died in office)
1829–1830	Armand Beauvais (as president of the Senate, succeeded Derbigny)
1830–1831	Jacques Dupres (as president of the Senate succeeded Beauvais)
1831–1835	Andre Bienvenu Roman
1835–1839	Edward Douglass White
1839–1843	Andre Bienvenu Roman
1843–1846	Alexandre Mouton
1846–1850	Isaac Johnson
1850–1853	Joseph Marshall Walker
1853–1856	Paul Octave Hébert
1856–1860	Robert Charles Wickliffe
1860–1864	Thomas Overton Moore
1862–1864	George F. Shepley (military governor within Union lines)
1864–1865	Henry Watkins Allen (elected governor within Confederate lines)
1864–1865	Michael Hahn (elected governor within Union lines, resigned)
1865–1867	James Madison Wells (as lieutenant governor succeeded Hahn)
1867–1868	Benjamin F. Flanders (military governor)
1868	Joshua Baker (military governor)
1868–1872	Henry Clay Warmoth (impeached)
1872–1873	P.B.S. Pinchback (acting)
1873	John McEnery (elected, but counted out)
1873–1877	William Pitt Kellogg (de facto governor)
1877	Stephen B. Packard (de facto governor, ousted)

1877–1880	Francis Tillou Nicholls
1880–1881	Louis Alfred Wiltz (died in office)
1881–1884	Samuel Douglas McEnery (as lieutenant governor succeeded Wiltz)
1884–1888	Samuel Douglas McEnery
1888–1892	Francis Tillou Nicholls
1892–1900	Murphy J. Foster
1900–1904	William Wright Heard
1904–1908	Newton Crain Blanchard
1908–1912	Jared Young Sanders
1912–1916	Luther E. Hall
1916–1920	Ruffin G. Pleasant
1920–1924	John M. Parker
1925–1926	Henry L. Fuqua (died in office)
1926–1928	Oramel H. Simpson (as lieutenant governor succeeded Fuqua)
1928–1932	Huey P. Long (resigned to take seat in U.S. Senate)
1932	Alvin O. King (as president of the State Senate suceeded Long)
1932–1936	Oscar K. Allen (died in office)
1936	James A. Noe (as lieutenant governor succeeded Allen)
1936–1939	Richard Webster Leche (resigned)
1939–1940	Earl K. Long (as lieutenant governor succeeded Leche)
1940–1944	Sam Houston Jones
1944–1948	Jimmie H. Davis
1948–1952	Earl K. Long
1952–1956	Robert F. Kennon
1956–1960	Earl K. Long
1960–1964	Jimmie H. Davis
1964–1972	John J. McKeithen
1972–1980	Edwin W. Edwards
1980–1984	David C. Treen
1984–1988	Edwin W. Edwards
1988–1992	Charles Elson "Buddy" Roemer III
1992–	Edwin W. Edwards

Mayors of New Orleans

United States Military Mayors

1862 (Nov)	–1864 James F. Miller
1864 (July)	–1865 Stephen Hoyt
1865 (May)	S.M. Quincy
1865 (Nov)	–1866 H. Kennedy
1866 (Apr)	John T. Monroe
1866 (Dec)	–1867 Edward Heath, Acting Military Mayor
1867–1868	Edward Heath (became Mayor)
1868–1870	John R. Conway
1870–1872	Benjamin Franklin Flanders
1872–1874	Louis A. Wiltz

End of Military Mayors in New Orleans

1874–1876	Charles J. Leeds
1876–1878	Edward Pilsbury
1878–1880	Isaac W. Patton
1880–1882	Joseph Ansbetequi Shakspeare
1882–1884	William J. Behan
1884–1888	Joseph Valsin Guillotte
1888–1892	Joseph A. Shakspeare
1892–1896	John Fitzpatrick
1896–1899	Walter C. Flower
1900–1904	Paul Capdeville
1904–1920	Martin Behrman
1920–1925	Andrew J. McShane
1925	Martin Behrman (died in office)
1926–1929	Arthur J. O'Keefe
1929–1930	T. Semmes Walmsley (Acting Mayor)
1931–1936	T. Semmes Walmsley (resigned)
1936–1946	Robert S. Maestri
1946–1961	deLesseps Story Morrison (resigned to become Ambassador to the OAS)

New City Hall Dedicated 1957

1961–1962	Victor Hugo Schiro (appointed Acting Mayor)
1962–1970	Victor Hugo Schiro (elected)
1970–1978	Maurice "Moon" Landrieu
1978–1986	Ernest N. Morial
1986–1994	Sidney J. Barthelemy
1994–	Marc Marial

Compiled by Coralie Davis
Library, University of New Orleans
1982. revised 1994

Directions in New Orleans

Where y'at? A very familiar query in New Orleans, uniquely expressed, is also uniquely answered. To explain to a visitor his location in the Crescent City invites a longer association than the inquirer anticipates.

First, you must explain where the city is before you can identify where you are *in* the city. A city, located between a serpentine river and a shallow lake, surrounded by marshes, cut up into small segments by canals and bayous, defies location because most of its boundaries are liquid. It's hard to imagine, when arriving by plane, how the landing will be accomplished without pontoons. Once the city location has been established and the visitor understands we are not on the Gulf of Mexico, as most maps seem to indicate, we can get to the job at hand.

In New Orleans, a compass is a useless instrument, since the four points needed for reference are not north, south, east or west, but Uptown (upriver), Downtown (downriver), Lakeside and Riverside. It isn't that we don't use north, south, east, and west directives; it's just that we use them in a different way.

It's a bit disconcerting to the visitor to watch the sunrise on what we call the "West" Bank. It is even more confusing to find yourself at the intersection of *South* Carrollton and *South* Claiborne. Are these Southerners still so hostile to the Yankees that they won't even use the word "North" as a direction? No, they're just following Old Man river as he winds around the city.

The river is the force that brought the city to life, and it is the central location from which all other directions are given.

JOAN GARVEY

Statues and Monuments in New Orleans

STATUES:

Louis Armstrong,
Father of New Orleans Jazz

Battle of New Orleans,
Monument 100′ high

Gen. P.G.T. Beauregard
Fired first shot at Fort Sumpter, S. Carolina,
starting Civil War

Bienville Monument,
Bienville, priest, and Indian

St. Francis Xavier Cabrini,
First American saint

Celtic Cross commemorating the Irish who
died of Yellow Fever (1832–3) building the
New Basin Canal

Churchill Circle

Henry Clay, American Statesman

Confederate heroes: Col. Dreux, first Con-
federate soldier from La. killed in Civil
War, July 5, 1861; Gen. Albert Pike,
Episcopal Bishop, Confederate soldier;
Father A.J. Ryan, poet chaplain of the
South

LOCATION:

Armstrong Park, Rampart
Street

Chalmette National Park

City Park entrance, end of
Esplanade Ave.

Union Station: Howard and
Loyola

Harrison Ave. and Canal
Blvd.

New Basin Canal Park,
between West End Blvd.
and Canal Blvd.

Hilton Hotel

Lafayette Square, 1806;
originally stood at Canal
and St. Charles, placed in
Lafayette Square in 1901

Jefferson Davis Parkway at
Canal, monument to Gen.
Pike, 1957

STATUES:	LOCATION:
Jefferson Davis, President of the Confederacy	Jefferson Davis Parkway at Canal, 1911
Benjamin Franklin	Lafayette Square, 1956
Bernardo de Galvez, Spanish governor of Louisiana, gift from Spain to New Orleans, 1977, commemorating our bicentennial	Spanish Plaza
Margaret Gaffney Haughery, benefactor of orphans, white marble statue engraved "Margaret"	Camp, Prytania, and Clio Sts., 1884
Italian Piazza, reminder of contributions of Italians to our heritage	Poydras Street
Andrew Jackson on horse, hero of Battle of New Orleans; Clark Mills, sculptor	Jackson Square, 1856
St. Joan of Arc, Maid of Orleans, gift of France to New Orleans	Rivergate, 1972
Rev. Martin Luther King, Jr., Civil Rights leader	Martin Luther King Blvd. and S. Claiborne
Krewe of Poydras, 20-foot welded steel structure by Ida Kohlmeyer painted in enamel	New 1515 Poydras St. Bldg., 1982
Latin American heroes: Simon Bolivar, liberator of S. America, gift from Venezuela, 1957; Benito Juarez, hero of Mexico, separated church and state in Mexico, gift from Mexico, 1965; General Francisco Morazon, Central American idol, gift from Honduras, 1966	Basin Street
Robert E. Lee, 16.5' figure, facing north atop 60' Doric column	Lee Circle, 1884
Liberty Monument, granite shaft erected by Crescent White League to commemorate battle against carpetbag Metropolitan Police	Woldenberg Park

STATUES:	LOCATION:
Molly Marine, monument inscribed, "Free a Marine to Fight"	Elks' Place and Canal Street, 1943
McDonogh, John, benefactor of public schools, monument	Civic Center
deLesseps S. Morrison, Mayor of New Orleans, monument	Civic Center, 1965
"Ocean Song," 16-foot kinetic steel sculpture by John Scott	Woldenberg Riverfront Park, 1989
Mother Elizabeth Seton, first native American saint	Tulane Avenue
Spanish-American War Veteran honoring Louisiana armed forces—1898–1902	Poydras and Loyola
Spring, Summer, Winter, Fall	At Four Corners, Jackson Square
Monument to the Tile Makers to show terracota tile; dedicated to the historian Charles Gayarre. First shown at 1884 Cotton Exposition	Bayou Road Esplanade Tonti
Monument to Vietnamese and American Veterans of Vietnam War	Basin and Iberville Sts., 1988
Vietnam War Memorial	The Superdome at Poydras, 1987
Wading pool sculptures by Enrique Alferez	City Park
Bust of George Washington dressed as a mason, given to city by Free Masons	Civic Center, 1960

236

STATUES:	LOCATION:
Edward Douglas White, Chief Justice of the Supreme Court, from Louisiana	Supreme Court Building
Sophie B. Wright, sculpted by Enrique Alferez	Sophie B. Wright Place and Magazine St., 1988

Index

MARY LOU SCHULTIS WIDMER is a novelist-historian whose first book, *Night Jasmine,* set in New Orleans in 1906, was published by Dell Publishing Company in 1980. Her second, *Lace Curtain,* set in New Orleans in 1832, was released by Berkley in 1985. It was awarded the Irish Cultural Society's Caomhnoir Award, presented annually to one who is a "keeper" of Irish traditions in America.

Between these two novels came a long research for the book *Beautiful Crescent, a History of New Orleans,* which she and her partner, Joan Garvey, co-authored and co-published in 1982.

Since her last novel, Mary Lou has written four illustrated nostalgia books, published by Pelican Publishing Company, one each year beginning in 1989, entitled *New Orleans in the Twenties, New Orleans in the Thirties, New Orleans in the Forties,* and *New Orleans in the Fifties.*

Born in New Orleans, Mary Lou graduated from Loyola University. After teaching for sixteen years, she retired to devote herself fulltime to writing. She is married to Albert F. Widmer, Sr., and has two children and four grandchildren. She is past president of Romance Writers of America's South Louisiana Chapter, and a member of the U.S. Daughters of 1812 and Louisiana Colonials, having certified her descent from ancestors living in Louisiana before 1803.

JOAN BOUDOUSQUIÉ GARVEY is the facilitator for curriculum and instruction for the gifted and talented program of the New Orleans Public Schools, and since 1978 has been an instructor in New Orleans History and Tour Guiding in the University of New Orleans' Metro College. She is a study guide and lecturer for Smithsonian Institute Southern Tours. She has given lectures on New Orleans and Louisiana history in training sessions for the Louisiana Tourist Promotion Association, Friends of the Cabildo, and parish school systems throughout the state.

Joan received the UNO Pi Delta Kappa Researcher of the Year award in 1985–86 for her research for *Beautiful Crescent*.

Born in New Orleans, she received her education in New Orleans schools, receiving an MA from the University of New Orleans. She and her husband designed and operated The Little Toy Shoppe in the French Market and Sugar and Spice, a sweet shop on Jackson Square. Joan is married to Walter Garvey. They have seven children and nine grandchildren.

The study of New Orleans history came out of a love for the city carried over from her ancestors, Gus and Francis Williams, maternal uncles, who were active participants in New Orleans politics in the '30s; a paternal ancestor, Antoine Boudousquié, printer to the Spanish king in 1795; and Charles Boudousquié, a paternal great-grandfather, the impresario of the French Opera before the Civil War.

GARMER PRESS, INC.
981 Navarre Ave.
New Orleans, LA. 70124

Send me _____ copies of *BEAUTIFUL CRESCENT, A History of New Orleans,* at $13 a copy, plus $2 for postage and handling.

Enclosed is my check or money order for $ _____.

NAME _____

STREET _____

CITY, STATE, ZIP _____

Make checks payable to **GARMER PRESS, INC.**

GARMER PRESS, INC.
981 Navarre Ave.
New Orleans, LA. 70124

Send me _____ copies of *BEAUTIFUL CRESCENT, A History of New Orleans,* at $13 a copy, plus $2 for postage and handling.

Enclosed is my check or money order for $ _____.

NAME _____

STREET _____

CITY, STATE, ZIP _____

Make checks payable to **GARMER PRESS, INC.**